RULER OF
THE NATIONS

Other books by Gary DeMar

God and Government:
    A Biblical and Historical Study, 1982

God and Government:
    Issues in Biblical Perspective, 1984

God and Government:
    The Restoration of the Republic, 1986

RULER OF THE NATIONS

Biblical Blueprints for Government

Gary DeMar

Dominion Press
Ft. Worth, Texas

Published by Dominion Press, Ft. Worth, Texas.

Printed in the United States of America

Unless otherwise noted, all Scripture quotations are from the New American Standard Version.

Library of Congress Catalog Card Number 86-050792

ISBN 0-930462-19-8

To my children
David and James

TABLE OF CONTENTS

The question of freedom is first of all a question of sovereignty and of responsibility. Who is sovereign, and to whom is man responsible? This source of sovereignty is also the source of freedom. If sovereignty resides in God and is only held ministerially by men, then the basic responsibility of ruler and ruled is to God, who is also the source of freedom. But if sovereignty resides in the state, whether a monarchy or democracy, man has no appeal beyond the law of the state, and no source of ethics apart from it. He is totally responsible to that order and has only those rights which the state chooses to confer upon him. The word *comprehend* means both "to contain" and "to understand." That which *contains* man is also the source of our *understanding* of man. If man is a creature of the state, then he is to be understood in terms of the state. Aristotle's man, a social animal, can never transcend his political order. Christian man, however, created in the image of God, cannot be contained in anything short of God's eternal decree and order, nor understood except in terms of God Himself. Man therefore is not understandable in terms of man but in terms of God. Absolute monarchy and democracy, statism in other words, came into existence as revivals of paganism and as anti-Christian movements, whatever their ostensible claims otherwise.

R. J. Rushdoony*

---

*Rushdoony, *This Independent Republic* (Fairfax, VA: Thoburn Press [1964] 1978), p. 15.

EDITOR'S INTRODUCTION
by Gary North

Thus saith the LORD God; Remove the diadem and take off the crown: this shall not be the same: exalt him that is low, and abase him that is high. I will overturn, overturn, overturn it: and it shall be no more, until he come whose right it is, and I shall give it to him (Ezekiel 21:26-27; King James Version).

God rules the nations. He sets up rulers and removes them (Daniel 2:21). He alone is the true Sovereign of the world. All other sovereign rulers are merely *delegated* sovereigns, whether or not they admit this fact to themselves or to their followers.

It is each man's job to restructure his thoughts, words, and deeds to conform to God's standards of righteous rule. If each person would do this perfectly (an impossibility, given the effects of sin), every human institution would be restructured to conform to God's standards for it. God's inescapable rule would then be made manifest by every institution.

We must not be misled: God rules, whether or not men acknowledge this. God has standards for the proper administration of every person (and therefore all institutions), whether or not anyone admits this. The proper historical question regarding God's rule is this: To what extent does the operation of any given human institution conform to God's standards at any point in history? To answer this, we first need to know what the standards are that God has established for all of the institutions of government.

God and Government

Gary DeMar is best known for his three-volume set *God and Government*. This little book is a digest of those large workbooks. What he does is to take the reader through some of the fundamental aspects of God's designated units of government: self-government, family government, church government, and civil government. He makes it clear that the Bible designates all four as governments, and that it is one of the major errors of the modern world to treat civil government as *the* government.

The modern humanist believes that civil government (the State) is the primary agency of government. This should not be surprising. As DeMar shows in this book, there is an intellectual war going on, a war between two rival views of God, man, law, and society. On one side is Christianity, with its doctrine of plural governments, plural institutional sovereignties, checks and balances, and the Bible as the Word of God. On the other side are the anti-Christians. They hold a completely different view of the world. They believe that man, not God, is the sovereign agent of lawful authority, or at least man's institutions are: the State, the Party, Science, etc. Man rules. If we want to invent a word for this, we might call this a *homocracy* (*homo* = man, *kratos* = rule).

Homocracy

Under the political theory of homocracy, mankind as a whole is regarded as sovereign. Mankind is in control. "Man has got to take control of man," the slogan goes. This means, as C. S. Lewis has pointed out, that *some* men have to take control over all the others. Mankind does not actually speak out and say what it wants. So it needs representatives to speak for it, to act in its name. There's the rub. There are a lot of individuals and groups that claim to represent silent humanity. Anyone who challenges this claim can in some cases get himself killed.

Those who want to exercise control in the name of humanity need a chain of command. The chain of command allows them to speak their sovereign word, and their will be done. Unlike God, who literally spoke the universe into existence (Genesis 1), men cannot do this. Their *fiat* (spoken) word is not powerful. They need tools to enforce their words—levers, if you will. They need *leverage*.

How do they get it? By gaining the cooperation of others. How do they gain it? By many means, but they all boil down to two: the carrot and the stick. They buy cooperation, or they compel it. In a free market society, the accent is on buying it; in a socialist (command) society, the emphasis is placed on forced cooperation.

Mankind lives on, but men die. So how does a system of government survive the founders? How do people on top remain on top, and how do their successors remain on top? Who chooses their successors? How do those on the bottom get on top?

These are the basic questions of all organizations, and all governments. They are asked over and over in the history of man. The answers vary in details, but there are not many different kinds of answers.

The Covenant Structure

To get the right answers, we need first to ask the right questions. For a long, long time, Christians and Jews have had the right questions right under their noses, but no one paid any attention. The questions concerning lawful government are organized in the Bible around a single theme: *the covenant*.

Most Christians and Jews have heard the word "covenant." They regard themselves (and occasionally even each other) as covenant people. They are taught from their youth about God's covenant with Israel, and how this covenant extends (or doesn't) to the Christian church. Everyone talks about the covenant, but until late 1985, nobody did anything about it.

Not in 3,400 years of Bible commentaries.

Is this too strong a statement? It may be. But the fact remains, if you go to a Christian or a Jew and ask him to outline the basic features of the Biblical covenant, he will not be able to do it rapidly or perhaps even believably. Ask two Jews or two Christians who talk about the covenant, and compare the answers. The answers will not fit very well.

For over four centuries, Calvinists have talked about the covenant. They are known as *covenant theologians*. The Puritans wrote seemingly endless numbers of books about it. The problem is, nobody has ever been able to come up with "the" covenant model in the writings of Calvin, let alone all his followers. The Calvinists have hung their theological hats on the covenant, yet they have never put down on paper precisely what it is, what it involves, and how it works—in the Bible or in church history.

Then, in late 1985, Pastor Ray Sutton made an astounding discovery. He was thinking about Biblical symbols, and he raised the question of two New Testament covenant symbols, baptism and communion. This raised the question of the Old Testament's covenant symbols, circumcision and passover. What did they have in common? Obviously, the covenant. But what, precisely, is the covenant? Is it the same in both Testaments (Covenants)?

He began rereading some books by Calvinist theologian Meredith G. Kline. In several books (collections of essays), Kline mentioned the structure of the Book of Deuteronomy. He argued that the book's structure in fact parallels the ancient pagan world's special documents that are known as the suzerain (king-vassal) treaties.

That triggered something in Sutton's mind. Kline discusses the outline of these treaties in several places. In some places, he says they have five sections; in other places, he indicates that they may have had six or even seven. It is all somewhat vague. So Sutton sat down with Deuteronomy to see what the structure is. He found five parts.

Then he looked at other books of the Bible that are known to be divided into five parts: Psalms and Matthew. He believes that he found the same structure. Then he went to other books, including some Pauline epistles. He found it there, too. When he discussed his findings in a Wednesday evening Bible study, David Chilton instantly recognized the same structure in the Book of Revelation. He had been working on this manuscript for well over a year, and he had it divided into four parts. Immediately he went back to his computer and shifted around the manuscript's sections electronically. The results of his restructuring can be read in his marvelous commentary on the Book of Revelation, *The Days of Vengeance* (Dominion Press, 1987).

Here, then, is the five-point structure of the Biblical covenant, as developed by Sutton in his excellent book, *That You May Prosper: Dominion by Covenant* (Institute for Christian Economics, 1987).

1. The transcendence and immanence of God
2. Authority/hierarchy of God's covenant
3. Biblical law/ethics/dominion
4. Judgment/oath: blessings and cursings
5. Continuity/inheritance

Simple, isn't it? Yet it has implications beyond your wildest imagination. Here is the key that unlocks the structure of human government. Here is the structure that Christians can use to analyze church, State, family, and numerous other non-covenantal but contractual institutions.

It can be used to unlock the long-debated structure of the Ten Commandments: 1-5, with a parallel 6-10. I spotted this almost as soon as Sutton described his discovery, just as I was finishing my economic commentary on the Ten Commandments, *The Sinai Strategy* (Institute for Christian Economics, 1986), which I outlined in its Preface. It can also be used to make sense out of some of the basic concepts of economics, as I show in my book in the Biblical Blueprints Series, *Inherit the Earth* (1987). In fact, once you begin to work with this model, it becomes difficult not to see it everywhere you look. This means that Sutton's model is either very powerful or very hypnotizing.

Where the intellectual pay-off really gets high is in the field of government. Gary DeMar did not deliberately structure the first draft of this manuscript around Deuteronomy's five-point covenant model. Nevertheless, as I read it, I recognized the five points. I simply moved his chapters around. He had already covered the basic topics of government that the five-point model reveals: in two sets of five chapters. Once again, we see the power of this covenant model. Without deliberately imitating it, DeMar asked the questions raised by the covenant model. He just didn't originally ask them in the covenant model's order.

Let us consider the five simple questions that this model raises for those studying the various institutions of government.

1. Who's in charge here?
2. To whom do I report?
3. What are the rules?
4. What happens to me if I obey (disobey)?
5. Does this outfit have a future?

If every textbook in political theory, or the history of political theory, were written around these five questions, students would have a lot less trouble sorting out the subject matter of political theory. If I had understood it back in those long-gone years of the Eisenhower Administration, when I first struggled with these problems, I might have figured out why political participation was so important to my deeply religious humanist instructor. I might also have recognized more clearly the nature of his religion.

You have a great advantage over most other Christians, not to mention political theorists. You now know something about this covenant structure. If you intend to do anything about the crises we are in, or will be in shortly, you will find it most useful.

Humanist Theocracy vs. Biblical Theocracy

If you believe that God truly rules every area of life, then you are a defender of Biblical theocracy. You say in confidence that God rules. The Greek word for God is *theos*. The Greek word for rule is *kratos*. From these two words we derive the English word *theocracy*. This does *not* mean the rule of the institutional church. That system would be an *ecclesiocracy* (church = *ekklesia*.) The Bible is opposed to ecclesiocracy.

A theocracy is what God has *already* set up: He already rules in the affairs of men. To the extent that any God-established institution of lawful government — self-government, family government, church government, or civil government—conforms itself progressively to God's standards, it steadily reflects *this already existing theocracy*.

Thus, to use the term theocracy to describe a civil government that is run by the institutional church is a deliberate falsifying of the Biblical meaning of theocracy. It is the humanists' favorite and most successful verbal trap. They have defined theocracy to mean what *they* want it to mean, and then they have scared Christians into political retreat by yelling "Theocracy! Theocracy!" at them whenever they raise the question of God's permanent standards for every area of life. Most humanists define all of life in terms of politics, or see politics as the primary way to make life better. Then they redefine theocracy to mean the church's rule over politics, for politics is the heart and soul of humanism. (On this point, see the book by George Grant in the Biblical Blueprints Series, *The Changing of the Guard*.)

Humanists usually think of "government" as a top-down bureaucracy that controls almost everything in society. The Bible teaches that government is actually a general term for self-government, family government, church government, and civil government. The Bible rejects the whole idea of government as a top-down bureaucracy. The Bible teaches that government is a bottom-up appeals court structure. Thus, when humanists paint a picture of theocracy as tyrannical, they are using a false model—indeed, an ancient humanist model—to guide their painting.

What the Bible says is that *every area of life is to be ruled by God's permanent principles*. This is the Biblical meaning of theocracy: an earthly reflection of what the Bible says has always existed, namely, the rule of God in *every* area of life, not just civil government.

Gary DeMar's book has made the meaning of theocracy clear. From this time on, Christians who read it should be able to handle the misleading (and highly effective) challenge of the humanists against the rule of God.

Yet despite DeMar's clarity, it will take an act of will on the part of each Christian reader to say to himself mentally: "God rules. God rules *everything*. He is the only Creator and the final

Judge. It is His desire that everything men build should reflect His perfection. Therefore, theocracy means that all governments — self-government, family government, church government, and civil government — are *theocratic governments* (plural). God rules them all. He rules in terms of His revealed law. Biblical theocracy therefore does not mean tyranny. *Humanist theocracy* means tyranny: the rule of self-proclaimed sovereign man."

The humanists have brainwashed Christians when it comes to the Biblical meaning of theocracy. Christians should recognize from the very beginning that *humanists have already brainwashed them*. It is time to get "*un*brainwashed." We must begin this intellectual "de-programming" process by reading carefully and by thinking about what we are reading. It takes real effort to pay attention to the meaning of words. Christians must not allow themselves to slip back into using the false definition of theocracy that humanists have provided for us in order to destroy us.

Training People for Self-Government

Each of the three institutional governments in the Bible is designed to lead people into self-government under God. Spiritual slaves resent this process of liberation, as do the earthly masters of spiritual slaves. We see this clearly in the account of the exodus. The Hebrew slaves were angry at Moses for his having angered the Pharaoh (Exodus 5:20-21). They were not angry at the Pharaoh, the tyrant. Slaves need tyrants in much the same way that tyrants need slaves: a condition of mutual dependence that is not based on self-government under God.

The need of governments to train subjects to exercise independent judgment is obvious in the case of family government. Parents who keep their children under their thumbs for life will die in old age in poverty, or at least insecurity, for their children will be unreliable supporters. Patriarchy in the Bible was always based on the idea that the father would leave the sons their share of the family's property before he died. He would give his sons their appropriate blessings (assets) when they reached maturity. Abraham gave Sarah's tent to Isaac when Isaac married Rebekah

(Genesis 24:67); then he married Keturah and moved east (Genesis 25:1-7). Abraham dropped out of covenant history as a major figure at that point, although he fathered more children, including Midian, who in turn fathered the Midianites (25:2). Isaac received his portion, and covenant history developed through him.

We recognize that patriarchs who try to maintain direct control over their sons and sons-in-law are implicitly petty tyrants. In the United States, immigrant groups that have had a tradition of patriarchy abandon that tradition within a single generation. The children will no longer put up with such nonsense. Only in a tyranny like the Mafia—an imitation family—can such paternalism be sustained, and only through violence and the promise of great financial gain. Few people see the Mafia as a valid family model. The freedom that the West has provided has revealed lifetime patriarchy as a pagan anachronism. It destroys the initiative of the heirs. Paternalism is a curse, creating dependence and an incentive for rebellion at the same time.

The same criticisms are equally applicable to the paternalism of either church or State. God judges such systems. Any tightly-knit, top-down hierarchy of bureaucracy eventually breaks down. It splinters churches and States. It produces followers who show no initiative. The paternalistic institution becomes stagnant. Its followers expect the leaders to work to build the organization, while the leaders expect the followers to carry them on their shoulders economically.

The proper goal of Biblical theocracy—in family, church, and State—is personal independence and self-responsibility. This is why Biblical theocracy is hated by modern humanist theocrats who want to make the State into god, and then rule other men through a system of top-down political power. Biblical theocracy kills humanist theocracy, for it destroys the economic, legal, and psychological dependence of the masses of people on their elite rulers. Besides, all humanistic theocracies eventually die anyway, for they cannot stand the competition that they receive from newer, hungrier, more energetic institutions. This is the fate of every human empire in history.

Summary

Only the innovation and flexibility of self-governed people under the rule of God's law can sustain the growth of God's kingdom over time. Men will be ruled by God, or else they will be ruled by men who imitate God. There is no escape from the rule of other men; the question is: By what standard will rulers rule, and also be governed? Everyone is under another person's authority in most areas of his life. Everyone answers for his actions. The doctrine of "divine rights" applies only to God: *God alone answers to no one else.* There is no divine right of kings, priests, parents, or voters. There is no divine right of anyone on earth. Everyone is accountable to other people. But this accountability is *judicial:* an appeals court system. *Initiative remains with the individual.* In the immortal words of Grace Hopper, a developer of the computer language Cobol, and who in her late seventies in the early 1980s was the oldest officer still on active duty in the U.S. Armed Forces (Navy): "It's easier to say you're sorry later than to ask permission." This outlook is the essence of self-government under God. Ask God; then say you are sorry to men later on, if necessary.

FOREWORD

by John Whitehead

In our present society, the issue of authority has provoked great strife between Christians and the state. When, for example, is the state performing a proper function and when is it encroaching upon the rights and responsibilities that God has entrusted to the family or the church? The severity of the conflict is evident in many court cases that have arisen because people who chose to live by their religious convictions stumbled head-first into state resistance.

Gary DeMar's book, *Ruler of the Nations*, presents a clear and well-substantiated description of the three types of government established by God—the family, the church, and the civil government—each given its own specific and *limited* jurisdiction. These three governments were intended to work cooperatively with one another under the ultimate authority of God.

Unfortunately, that relationship of cooperation has been replaced by one of competition and contention. The state—having severed itself from all accountability to God—has increasingly seized control of areas that rightfully belong to the family or the church. But equally damaging is the way in which the church and family have *voluntarily* relinquished many of their responsibilities to the government bureaucracy.

But the trend is not irreversible. DeMar recommends several effective actions for the family and the church to take to wean themselves from false dependency on the state (particularly in the area of social services) and reassert their claim to their rightful obligations. Christians should read this section with a mind toward application.

The creeping statism of our society will never be stopped until Christians are ready to obey God's mandate and take responsibility for the duties He has assigned. This book could prod many in the right direction.

Part I
BLUEPRINTS

AUTHOR'S INTRODUCTION

Any kingdom divided against itself is laid waste; and any city or house divided against itself shall not stand. And if Satan casts out Satan, he is divided against himself; how then shall his kingdom stand? (Matthew 12:25-26).

Jesus was here contrasting His kingdom with Satan's. Christ's is a unified kingdom. God is sovereign over His kingdom, yet men are responsible agents. God runs it from the top with perfect justice and perfect knowledge, a kingdom based on law. But men choose whom they will serve. They are either covenant-keepers or covenant-breakers. God's kingdom is unified, and it serves as leaven, steadily replacing the divided kingdoms of the devil.

This book is about God's kingdom. God's kingdom begins in heaven, but it extends to earth. Christ announced after His death and resurrection: "All authority has been given to Me in heaven and on earth. Go therefore and make disciples of all the nations, baptizing them in the name of the Father and the Son and the Holy Spirit, teaching them to observe all that I have commanded you; and lo, I am with you always, even to the end of the age" (Matthew 28:18-20). With these words, Matthew ends his gospel.

There are five crucial concepts found in these words. These concepts pattern the ten commandments found in Exodus 20. The first table of five commandments deals with what man owes to God while the second table shows what man owes to his fellow man. Without the first five the second five will not work. The sanctity of life, respect for the marriage relationship, and the rights of private property are dependent upon a transcendant God who gives mandates in an unchanging law for individuals and

3

governments. The structure of Jesus' command to His disciples is
the very structure of the ten commandments:

1. Christ is sovereign over heaven and earth, yet present
with His people. He is both transcendent (high above) and immanent (present) with us.

2. He is the Supreme Commander over a hierarchy, so His
followers are to bring the nations under Christ's authority
through baptism.

3. His kingdom is a kingdom of law, meaning ethics, for
Christians are commanded to teach men to observe (obey) all
that He commands.

4. He judges the nations, for baptism is a covenant sign, a
form of oath taken before God; violating the terms of the Biblical
covenant always brings cursings (Deuteronomy 28:15-68), while
obedience brings blessings (Deuteronomy 28:1-14).

5. There is continuity over the generations of man, for He
promises to be with His people always, to the end of the age.

What Jesus was saying is that His kingdom will stand, but
Satan's will fall. Nation by nation, Satan's inherently divided
kingdom will fall to Christ, through the preaching of the gospel
and the disciplining of the nations under Christ's law. Like a long
row of dominoes, Satan's nations will inevitably fall in history.
Christ promised: "I will build My church; and the gates of Hades
[hell] shall not overpower it" (Matthew 16:18).

Empires and Dominoes

Today's world is divided into two rival camps, with everyone
else doing his best to stay out of the way of the giants. The Cold
War is a reality. It has been going on ever since the Russian Revolution of 1917, and it has escalated since the end of World War II.
But another cold war has been going on since the garden of Eden.
It is a war between good and evil, between God and Satan. The
stakes for this competition are very high: eternal life or eternal
judgment.

In the Vietnam war, it was common to hear the argument that

South Vietnam was a domino. If it fell to the Communists, then all of Southeast Asia would fall, country by country. Then the Far East would fall. We had to defend South Vietnam, or else experience the domino effect. Well, South Vietnam fell, and now Vietnam is in a war against the Communists in Laos and also against the Communists in Cambodia. (In other words, Laotians hate Cambodians, Cambodians hate Vietnamese.) The Red Chinese and the Soviets have "their" client states. (Everyone hates the Chinese and the Russians, especially each other.) Hardly any American knows what is going on there, or which Southeast Asian nation is allied with which Communist giant, but 55,000 American troops didn't return alive.

Meanwhile, the tiny city-state of Singapore is getting ever richer, the Malaysians are getting richer, and Thailand is still outside the Communist sphere of influence. If the domino effect was really true in 1970, it has not yet been proven.

We are also seeing the Soviet Union fighting desperately in the African nations of Angola and Mozambique to destroy anti-Communist freedom movements. Their empire is threatened. So far, no client state of the Soviet Union has yet to fall to a national anti-Communist revolution, but the Soviet Union's leaders are spending billions annually to keep it from happening. They fear the domino effect, as do all empires. Lose one, they believe, and you may lose them all. They also believe that they face the domino effect.

Why? Because empires are top-heavy. They are held together by force and money. If either force or money wane, "emperors" ask themselves, what will hold the hostile national groups together? What will bind the many to the one? How will the tyrannical laws of a distant elite be maintained in the lives of other men who obey today only out of fear? If men's hearts and minds are not at peace in the kingdom, how will it survive when power wanes?

That is the problem facing the top-down empires of today. It is a question that has faced every empire in history. So far, no empire has found a solution. No empire ever will (Daniel 2:36-43).

The kingdom of God will conquer them all: ". . . the God of
heaven will set up a kingdom which will never be destroyed, and
that kingdom will not be left for another people; it will crush and
put an end to all these kingdoms, but it will endure forever" (Daniel 2:44). God's kingdom is a kingdom of the heart, not a top-
down centralized power that crushes the lawful desires of men,
thereby creating rebels.

If a house is divided against itself, it cannot stand. Man's political houses are divided against themselves. They shall not stand.

A Different Kind of Domino Effect

There is a governmental domino effect that also seems to be
facing nations. *Government* too often has been defined solely in *political* terms. The Bible's definition of government is comprehensive. It includes self-government, family, government, church
government, and civil governments at all jurisdictional levels.
There are those, however, who want to narrow the definition, and
thus create a *domino effect*: the denial of God's sovereign rule over
all of life, and the denial of all earthly governments established by
God—parents and children in family government, elders and
members in church government, and rulers and citizens in civil
government. In effect, the State,[1] civil government, is the last
domino to fall. All governmental distinctions are eliminated in
favor of the State. The State is everything. For Hegel, "The State
incarnates the Divine Idea upon earth." In effect, the State is god.
Benito Mussolini declared, "Everything for the State; nothing
outside the State; nothing against the State."

Adolf Hitler, one of the greatest tyrants who ever lived, understood the domino effect. It begins with the elimination of the individual will for the benefit of the State:

---

1. State with an uppercase S will refer to the federal or national civil government of any nation or a single political entity. For example, since the Soviet
Union cannot be described in constitutional terms, the term State will refer to the
oppressive political system of that regime. The use of state with a lowercase s
refers to one of the fifty states.

It is thus necessary that the individual should finally come to realize that his own ego is of no importance in comparison with the existence of his nation; that the position of the individual ego is conditioned solely by the interests of the nation as a whole . . . that above all the unity of a nation's spirit and will are worth far more than the freedom of the spirit and will of an individual. . . .[2]

When the First Domino Falls

When the first domino of *self-government* falls, we can expect the fall of all the governmental dominoes. Why? Self-government, or submission to God and faithfully obeying Him in all things, undergirds all *institutional* governments like the family, church, and State. Self-government is exclusively moral, because it does not align itself with any earthly throne. God, through His Word, directs the self-governed Christian. Self-government, therefore, deals with what is right and wrong in terms of what God prescribes. Without self-government, all institutional governments will be corrupt, reflecting the corruption of the individual. In 1682, William Penn wrote: "Let men be good, and the government cannot be bad; if it be ill, they will cure it. But, if men be bad, let the government be never so good, they will endeavor to warp and spoil it to their turn." This is why the apostle Paul puts such an emphasis on the "fruit of the Spirit," especially self-control (self-government): "love, joy, peace, patience, kindness, goodness, faithfulness, gentleness, [and] self-control" (Galatians 5:22-23).

He contrasts the self-governed individual with those who follow "after their own lusts," those who are not self-governed under God's absolute government (Jude 18). The vices of those who lack self-government are: "immorality, impurity, sensuality, idolatry, sorcery, enmities, strife, jealousy, outbursts of anger, disputes, dissensions, factions, envyings, drunkenness, carousings, and things like these . . ." (Galatians 5:19-21).

---

2. Adolf Hitler at Buckenburg, October 7, 1933; *The Speeches of Adolf Hitler,* 1929-39, ed. N.H. Baynes (2 vols., Oxford, 1942), I:871-72. Quoted by Leonard Peikoff, *The Ominous Parallels* (New York: Stein and Day, 1982), p. 3.

If we see these characteristics in civil government, we can most assuredly conclude that they first manifested themselves in self-government. The all-embracing State feeds on poor self-government. Statists are assured that those who lack self-government will elect leaders who will promise them relief from their own sin. Of course, relief never comes, only tyranny.

Moral Criteria for Leadership

Those who cannot govern themselves cannot be expected to govern others. There is a direct relationship between poor self-government and family and church governments. For example, a ruler in the church

> must be above reproach, the husband of one wife, temperate, prudent, respectable, hospitable, able to teach, not addicted to wine or pugnacious, but gentle, uncontentious, free from the love of money. He must be one who manages his own household well, keeping his children under control with all dignity (but if a man does not know how to manage his own household, how will he take care of the church of God?); and not a new convert, lest he become conceited and fall into the condemnation incurred by the devil. And he must have a good reputation with those outside the church, so that he may not fall into reproach and the snare of the devil (vv. 2-7).

When moral self-government under God's law is not operating because the sovereign government of God is denied, and His law is repudiated, we can expect the family and church to suffer the inevitable wicked effects. The one human government that seems always to be ready to pick up the pieces is *civil government*, meaning the State. Once all the dominoes fall against that last domino of civil government, those in power scoop up all the dominoes and go home, obliterating the multiple governments under God and denying the individual and the God-ordained governments of the family and the church. The limited, *delegated sovereignty* given to them by God is denied. The new rulers assume that there is no need for self-government undergirding the family, church, and State. In fact, even God's sovereign rule is denied. The State rules and overrules.

If Christians are to change things at the higher levels of civil government, *things must first change at the bottom*, first in the hearts of men, second in the realm of self-government, third in church government, fourth in family government, fifth in local civil government, and only then in distant central government. *Christian reconstruction is an inside-out process, a bottom-up process.* Nevertheless, this process can take place nearly simultaneously during a major revival, as it did in Nineveh under the preaching of Jonah. Changes eventually must occur at both ends of the domino spectrum. Those who rule at the highest levels of civil government must cease to see themselves as independent of God's government over them. At the same time, the citizenry must stop looking to the State for salvation and get their own households in order. The government at the top (civil government or the State) is a reflection of the government at the bottom (the type of self-government supporting the family and church). In effect, you get what you vote for.

Israel's Example

Israel's history is the scene for the Biblical "domino effect." The apostle Paul wrote:

> For I do not want you to be unaware, brethren, that our fathers were all under the cloud, and all passed through the sea; and all were baptized into Moses in the cloud and in the sea; and all ate the same spiritual food; and all drank the same spiritual drink, for they were drinking from a spiritual rock which followed them; and the rock was Christ. Nevertheless, with most of them God was not well-pleased; for they were laid low in the wilderness. *Now these things happened as examples for us, that we should not crave evil things, as they also craved.* And do not be idolaters, as some of them were; as it is written, "The people sat down to eat and drink, and stood up to play." Nor let us act immorally, as some of them did, and twenty-three thousand fell in one day. Nor let us try the Lord, as some of them did, and were destroyed by the serpents. Nor grumble, as some of them did, and were destroyed by the destroyer. *Now these things happened to them as an example, and they were written for our instruction, upon whom the ends of the ages have come* (1 Corinthians 10:1-11).

God was rejected as their sovereign redeemer. Instead of "craving" God, they "craved evil things." Instead of worshipping God, they became "idolaters." Their rejection of God started the dominoes falling. Forty years were wasted in the wilderness as the people ignored God's sovereign government and endured His judgment (Numbers 13-14). An entire generation died in the wilderness. A new generation entered the land and again were warned by God: "This book of the law shall not depart from your mouth, but you shall meditate on it day and night, so that you may be careful to do according to all that is written in it; for then you will make your way prosperous, and then you will have success" (Joshua 1:8).

After the conquest, when a new generation was about to take over the reins of dominion, Joshua repeated the earlier admonition: "Now, therefore, fear the LORD and serve Him in sincerity and truth; and put away the gods which your fathers served beyond the River in Egypt, and serve the LORD. And if it is disagreeable in your sight to serve the LORD, choose for yourselves today whom you will serve: whether the gods which your fathers served which were beyond the River, or the gods of the Amorites in whose land you are living; but as for me and my house, we will serve the LORD" (Joshua 24:14, 15).

Summary

In our day, we have imitated the Israelites in their sin, not their faithfulness. We are facing similar problems. At all levels, governments (plural) are experiencing crises: crises in authority, standards, financing, and stability. Until men turn to the Biblical standards for righteous government, beginning with self-government under God's law, there will be no long-term solutions. The conflicts between man's empires will continue. The dominoes will continue to fall, threatening whole civilizations.

But Christians have forgotten their Biblical heritage. They stand silent, yet they have the Bible in their hands. They must turn to it again for guidance, and ask themselves: *What does it mean to disciple the nations for Christ?* It means that we must announce that Jesus Christ is *ruler of the nations*.

1

GOD IS SOVEREIGN, NOT MAN

For the LORD is our judge, the LORD is our lawgiver, the LORD is our king: He will save us (Isaiah 33:22).

"The voice of a god and not of a man!" (Acts 12:22). Herod believed the words of his subjects. He fell for the grand delusion: the belief that those who rule are self-styled gods, independent of God's government over them. God did not take long to remind King Herod and the people that He rules in heaven *and* earth, and all rulers are subject to His sovereignty and law. For his denial of God's sovereignty over him, Herod became a diet for worms: "And immediately an angel of the Lord struck him because he did not give God the glory, and he was eaten by worms and died" (Acts 12:23).

Today, the United States finds herself in the midst of making a similar choice. It's true that our coins have "In God We Trust" stamped on them. But it's probably equally true that our nation puts more trust in the money where the acknowledgment appears than in the God who supplies all wealth. This nation is being warned, just as Israel was warned. God is reminding the United States that her prosperity and security do not come by way of the State. As Christians, we must heed God's warning that a forgetful nation is a doomed nation. Have we come to the place where we now believe that "My power and the strength of my hand made me this wealth" (Deuteronomy 8:17)? God's assessment of such presumption is not easy to take for an unrepentant nation:

But you shall remember the LORD your God, for it is He who is giving you power to make wealth, that He may confirm His covenant which He swore to your fathers, as it is this day. And it shall come about if you ever forget the LORD your God, and go after other gods and serve them and worship them, I testify against you today that you shall surely perish. Like the nations that the LORD makes to perish before you, so you shall perish; because you would not listen to the voice of the LORD your God (Deuteronomy 8:18-20).

Herod saw himself as a god. But what is even more frightening, is that the people accepted him as a god. It is no less true today that people reject the God of the Bible and His faithful provisions of life, liberty, and property and turn to the State for sustenance and security. Where we are told to pray, "Our Father who art in heaven. . . . Give us this day our daily bread" (Matthew 6:9, 11), we too often turn to the State for our daily bread. Where the Bible tells us that God is our Father, more often than not the people make the State their father, because the State can provide them all the financial aid they need. (See Chapter Five for more details.)

This is why the first commandment must be our starting point for the proper ordering of ourselves, our families, our churches, and our nation. We must never put any of man's laws before the first commandment: "I am the LORD your God . . . you shall have no other gods before Me" (Exodus 20:2, 3). Adherence to the first commandment protects us from those who would rewrite it to read "I, the State, am your God. You shall have no other gods before me." This is the first point in the Biblical covenant structure: *the absolute sovereignty of a transcendent God who is always present (immanent) with His people.* He sets up a hierarchy (point two), lays down the law (point three), judges men continually and also at the end of time (point four), and preserves His kingdom (point five).

When a ruler decrees either by words or deeds that he is independent of God's government, or that justice is defined according to his self-made laws, or that man looks to the State for salvation, then God responds with judgment. A nation might not see God's judgment in the same way Herod did, but time brings all things to light. Choosing man as the sovereign ruler, independent of God, will lead a nation to slavery and eventual destruction.

For the despot, power is all that matters. Words and what they mean, what they *can* mean, are used to change opinions. When man makes up his own meaning on the basis of his own power, chaos results. Then a power struggle takes place among all those people who want their word to rule. For humanism, power determines meaning.

God Speaks or Newspeak

What if a *change in meaning* results in the erosion of legitimate power and authority *from* individuals, families, churches, business establishments, and city, county, and state governments? What if "government of the people, by the people, and for the people" becomes "government over the people in the name of the people"? What if this change in definition works for the creation of a single political entity that sees itself as "God walking on earth"? What if the denial of God's many governments means that the State, a centralized civil government, becomes the all-embracing power that orders society through power, all in the name of security, peace, and prosperity?

In George Orwell's terrifying novel *1984*, "Newspeak" was the official language of "Oceania," a futuristic place where Big Brother reigned. "The purpose of Newspeak," Orwell writes, "was not only to provide a medium of expression for the world-view and mental habits proper to the devotees of Ingsoc [Newspeak for *English Socialism*], *but to make all other modes of thought impossible*."[1]

The purpose in a shift in definition is to have the people think one-dimensionally, to think in terms of the accepted (meaning *imposed*) definition and no other. A shift in meaning has taken place with the word "government." Today, when the word government is used, *civil* government at the state or national level is what most

---

1. George Orwell, *Nineteen Eighty-Four* (New York: Harcourt, Brace and Company, 1949), p. 303.

people have in mind, obliterating by definition the legitimate governments of family, church, and the various local civil governments like the city, county, and the many states.

Noah Webster

Let's briefly look at some older definitions of the word to see
that government meant more than the State, that is, civil government at the national level. The dictionary is always a good place
to begin. Noah Webster's *An American Dictionary of the English Language* (first published in 1828) defines government this way:

> GOVERNMENT, *n.* Direction; regulation. "These precepts will
> serve for the *government* of our conduct."
>
> 2. Control; restraint. "Men are apt to neglect the *government* of
> their temper and passions."
>
> 3. The exercise of authority; direction and restraint exercised
> over the actions of men in communities, societies or states; the
> administration of public affairs, according to the established con-
> stitution, laws and usages, or by arbitrary edict. "Prussia rose to
> importance under the *government* of Frederick II."
>
> 4. The exercise of authority by a parent or householder. "Chil-
> dren are often ruined by a neglect of *government* in parents. Let
> family *government* be like that of our heavenly Father, mild, gentle
> and affectionate."

Did you notice the emphasis here? All human government
begins with the *individual*. We've been calling this self-government
or self-control (Galatians 6:23; Acts 24:25). Self-government undergirds all institutional governments, including the mothers and
fathers in family government, *elders* in church government, and *civil*
servants at all jurisdictional levels in civil government. Webster
does not define government as the State and only the State.

Where did these early definers of government get these fundamental ideas? From the Bible. When the Bible speaks of "government" in the singular, it refers to *the* government of Jesus Christ
that encompasses all other governments:

> For a child will be born to us, a son will be given to us; and *the*
> government will rest on His shoulders; and His name will be

called Wonderful Counselor, Mighty God, Eternal Father, Prince of Peace. There *will be no end to the increase of His government or of peace*, on the throne of David and over His kingdom, to establish it and to uphold it with justice and righteousness from then on and forevermore. The zeal of the LORD of hosts will accomplish this (Isaiah 9:6, 7).

His government is as comprehensive as His creation. He created all things; He rules over all things.

The One Government of God

The word "government" has a comprehensive definition that includes self-government, family government, church government, and civil government. The operation of these plural governments (families, churches, and civil government at the local, county, state, and federal levels) is dependent upon the one government of God as expressed in Isaiah 9:6, 7 and other passages. Jesus "upholds all things by the word of His power" (Hebrews 1:3) and "for by Him all things were created, both in the heavens and on earth, visible and invisible, whether thrones or dominions or rulers or authorities — all things have been created by Him and for Him. And He is before all things, and in Him all things hold together" (Colossians 1:16, 17).

God then is the *model* for all types of governments. The created order *images* God. The study of the law given to individuals, families, churches, and nations will show that these divine directives reflect God's attributes. For example, the individual is to be holy as God is holy; the love that Jesus expressed in giving His life for the church is to be copied by husbands in their love for their wives (Ephesians 5:22-34); the discipline that fathers give their children is a model of God's discipline of His children (Hebrews 12:1-13); the State is God's "minister . . . an avenger who brings wrath upon the one who practices evil" (Romans 13:4; cf. 12:19).

How does the principle of the "many" governments work itself out in family, church, and State? Children are commanded to obey their parents in the Lord (Ephesians 6:1). There is real authority here and parents have jurisdiction within their own family structure.

Church members are part of a jurisdictional government called "ecclesiastical government." The church is given the "keys of the kingdom of heaven" and with these keys the leadership can "bind" and "loose" within the church (Matthew 16:19). The church, that is, those who are in authority, have the authority to excommunicate unrepentant members (Matthew 18:15-18). The church is even given power to handle legal matters that many would see as the exclusive power of the State (1 Corinthians 6:1-11). In the book of Hebrews, we are told to "Obey your leaders, and submit to them; for they keep watch over your souls, as those who will give an account" (Hebrews 13:17). Ultimately, God will demand an accounting from men regarding their obedience to the authorities, but this includes *all* authorities, not just civil authorities.

The State has the power of the sword: "[I]t does not bear the sword for nothing" (Romans 13:4). Because the State has legitimate authority, Peter can write: "Submit yourselves for the Lord's sake to every human institution, whether to a king as the one in authority, or to governors as sent by him for the punishment of evildoers and the praise of those who do right" (1 Peter 2:13, 14).

The One and the Many

God has established numerous authorities for the proper ordering of society. Mothers and fathers have authority over their children (Proverbs 6:20, 21; 15:5; 30:17; Ephesians 6:1-3; Colossians 3:20). Church leaders, elders and deacons, hold authority in the church (Matthew 16:19; 18:15-20; 1 Thessalonians 5:12, 13; 1 Timothy 5:17, 18; Hebrews 13:17; 1 Peter 5:1-3). Civil rulers exercise political authority by God's decree (Matthew 22:21; Romans 13:1-7; 1 Peter 2:13, 14).

In other relationships, contracts can bind individuals and groups subject to the stipulations of a contract. The employer-employee relationship is contractual and carries with it legitimate authority (Leviticus 19:13; Deuteronomy 25:4; 1 Timothy 5:18; cf. Matthew 10:10; Luke 10:7). The courts, the judicial arm of civil authority, enforce the obligations of contracts by punishing the contract-breaker and seeing to it that restitution is paid to the contract-keeper. A contract is based upon God's covenantal design. God sets forth obligations, benefits for obeying the covenant, and reprisals for breaking covenant stipulations. Organizations can lawfully enforce contracts like God enforces His covenants.

The concept of multiple delegated authorities is patterned after the Divine One and Many—the Trinity. There is one God (Unity) and there are three Persons (Diversity) in the Godhead, each of whom is God. Each member of the Trinity, Father, Son, and Holy Spirit has authority (unity of purpose in the exercise of authority), yet each performs a different task in history (diversity of function in the use of authority to accomplish the one purpose).

The Triune God has impressed His creation with this divine pattern. Thus, He has ordained the family, the church, and civil governments as institutions, lesser authority structures, under His jurisdiction: *many* institutions, but *united* by *one* purpose and duty—obedience to God for His glory.

What, then, should be ultimate in society? The one or the many? Unity or diversity? The individual or the group? Should we have one monolithic authority or should every individual be an authority unto himself?

The creation reflects the Creator. We find that it reflects God's unity and His diversity. In the creation, and in mankind's institutions, unity is not to swallow up diversity, and diversity is not to blow apart unity. Thus, we should expect to find that debates over the proper form of civil government always return to this theme: Which is primary, unity or diversity? And the Biblical answer is simple in principle (though difficult to achieve in practice): *neither!*

What kinds of political structures do anti-Christian civilizations recommend? They insist that God is *not* a Trinity. He is *not* simultaneously One and Many. He is *not* "three Persons, yet also One Person." They deny that there is *equal ultimacy* of the One and the Many, meaning that the unity of God is not ultimate over the plurality of the Persons of the Trinity, each of Whom is God. They insist that God is either one or many, either unified or totally diverse. A nation's view of government reflects its view of God and God's legal relationships with mankind. So, govern-

ments recommended by anti-Christians tend either toward
statism or anarchy, rule by the one or the many.

Anarchy

One proposed solution to the problem of how power and authority ought to function in society is to place sovereignty totally
with the individual. (Whenever we see the word "total" or "totally"
with respect to man and his institutions, beware: tyranny is lurk-
ing in the shadows.) Anarchy is the ultimate implication of this
philosophy: every man his own judge and jury. The Bible tells us
that God is man's ultimate Judge and Jury. God lays down the
law. He places man and the creation under the restraining factor
of His law. Furthermore, the Fall of man into sin made even more
external restraint necessary.

The anarchist believes that external restraints, perpetuated by
civil governments, are the culprits for all of our ills. The individual must work to remove the shackles of external restraint and
open the floodgates of unbridled freedom for all people. For the
anarchist, civil government is the enemy of society, simply
because it rules over the individual. The word anarchy is made up
of two Greek words, *a* which means "no" and *arche* which means
"rule" or "power." An anarchist despises any power greater than
himself and he will work in a violent way to overthrow any authority that works to curtail any of his individual freedoms, no
matter how deviant or dangerous to the broader society.

Modern-day terrorism is a manifestation of anarchy under the
guise of "freedom." The counter culture of the '60s fostered anarchy as a way of reversing the order of society. Much of the rock
music fanned the flames of the '60s radicalism.

The revolutionary anarchist believes in the inherent goodness
of *some* men, and that with an overthrow of the existing order and
the death of the remaining evil men, a new society will emerge
from the rubble. The pacifist anarchist (such as the Russian
writer Tolstoy) believes in the innate evil of man's coercive institutions, and so withdraws from power, leaving those who believe in
salvation by power in greater control. Either way—escape or .

power—anarchy is nothing more than a short cut to tyranny. Marxism uses the disenchantment of some people to create so much chaos that the only solution to a nation's problems is totalitarian rule. Under communism, anarchy is the first ideology eliminated after the revolution succeeds.

Many Christians, who have grown frustrated at the slow progress the people of God seem to be making in society, have turned to anarchy as the only solution to a creeping tyranny. Consider David's response to murderous King Saul. Did David murder Saul when Saul persecuted him? David was forced to flee Israel and pretend to be crazy in the presence of the Philistines—and not just the Philistines, but the king of Gath, the city of Goliath (1 Samuel 21:10-15). David was God's anointed, yet he did not challenge Saul. He did not surrender, either. He wrote: "I shall not die, but live, and declare the works of the Lord" (Psalm 118:17).

Anarchy is the way of historical losers and short-sighted thinkers. It is not surprising to learn that when Lenin began to consolidate his power in Russia after the Russian Revolution, he deported the anarchists or had them shot. Yet they had supported revolutionary violence in the name of abolishing all political and State blueprints. There will always be State blueprints. The question is: Whose? God's or some petty dictator? The Bible's or some humanist planning elite?

Autocracy

Another way to solve the dilemma of political power is to consolidate it in one man, to create a messianic figure. An autocrat is someone who is an independent ruler. His power (*kratos*) is self-derived (*auto*). He continues in power by his own decree and is backed by military might. In the book of Judges we find the Israelites harassed by the Midianites: "And the power of Midian prevailed against Israel. Because of Midian the sons of Israel made for themselves the dens which were in the mountains and the caves and the strongholds" (Judges 6:2).

Israel's "predicament" was the result of disobedience: "Then the sons of Israel did what was evil in the sight of the LORD; and the LORD gave them into the hands of Midian seven years" (Judges 6:1). Instead of turning to God in repentance, the people looked for a *political* solution to their "problems." The people were trusting in their man-made "tower" (Judges 8:9). Instead of putting their trust in God as their "Mighty Fortress" (Psalm 46), they chose the supposed power of man and man's puny fortresses. Gideon promised to "tear down this fortress," this idol of security and salvation (Judges 8:9; cf. v. 17).

After Gideon defeated the enemies of Israel, the people were ready to set up a centralized political regime: "The men said, 'Rule over us, both you and your son, also your son's son, for you have delivered us from the hand of Midian'" (Judges 8:22). The problem the Israelites had with the Midianites happened because they had rejected God as their King. Now that God had delivered them, they still failed to acknowledge that "The LORD should rule over them" (Judges 8:23). Instead, they opted for a centralized, humanistic, and perpetual social order with Gideon and his family as permanent rulers. To them, Gideon was more than a judge, a localized civil ruler, he was to be their king who would sit on a throne and make them secure. A centralized social order is better for man than putting one's trust for safety and security in the Lord!

With forty years of peace behind them, the people had forgotten who brought them peace (cf. Deuteronomy 8). The people began to "play the harlot with the Baals, and made Baal-berith their god" (Judges 8:33). Once again, the rejection of God as their King led them to look to man and some sort of centralized social order. One of Gideon's sons, Abimelech attempted to centralize power and authority and place all sovereignty in himself. Abimelech took advantage of the weakened commitment of the people to the Lord. If they were ready to worship a synthetic god (Baal-berith means "Baal of the Covenant"— a mixture of Baalism and the promises of the Covenant), then they might have been ready to rally around him for security, a synthetic king. (Abimelech's father was an Israelite, while his mother was a Canaanite.) To ensure his scheme to power, Abimelech killed off all his political competition: "He went to his father's house at Ophrah, and killed his brothers the sons of Jerubbaal, seventy men, on one stone" (Judges 9:5).

Jotham escaped the bloodbath at Ophrah and went to Mount Gerizim to warn the Israelites not to rally around a king who promised security and at the same time demanded unconditional loyalty. The result of such an alliance would be their destruction. He told them, "If in truth you are anointing me [Abimelech] as king over you, come and take refuge in my shade [the promise of security]; but if not, may fire come out from the bramble and consume the cedars of Lebanon [the reality of tyranny]" (Judges 9:15).

As with all centralized political regimes, judgment and ruin are inevitable. This centralized administration of Abimelech was made up of "worthless and reckless fellows" from Shechem (Judges 9:4). It was not long before the administration of this new dynastic ruler fell into ruin, and those who followed him to visions of power became disenchanted:

> God sent an evil spirit between Abimelech and the men of Shechem; and the men of Shechem dealt treacherously with Abimelech, in order that the violence done to the seventy sons of Jerubbaal might come, and their blood might be laid on Abimelech their brother, who killed them, and on the men of Shechem, who strengthened his hands to kill his brothers. And the men of Shechem set men in ambush against him on the tops of the mountains, and they robbed all who might pass by them along the road; and it was told to Abimelech (vv. 23-25).

An autocratic government is inherently unstable. Assassination and political coups are always present when there are other ambitious men seeking the same power. The people are rarely safe. Each successive ruler often changes the rules and regulations at his own whim. The people have little if any input into the workings of the government. There is no check on the king's power. Samuel Rutherford (1600-1661), in an attempt to counter the "divine right of kings" position, which was nothing more than autocratic government, wrote *Lex Rex: or The Law and the Prince* in 1644. Rutherford's position put even the king under God's Law.

As would be expected, *Lex Rex* was outlawed in England and Scotland. Rutherford's view so jeopardized the "divine right of kings" mandate that he was condemned to death for his views. He died before he could be executed as a rebel of the autocratic State.

Oligarchy

The word "oligarchy" is derived from a Greek word meaning "rule (*archein*) by the few (*oligos*)." In our day, the Supreme Court acts as an oligarchy. The justices on the Court are considered the final court of appeal. The law is what they say it is. The Court is a closed system. Nothing outside the Court, nothing higher than the Court, rules. While Congress can overrule the Supreme Court and even impeach justices who consistently rule contrary to the Constitution, it rarely, if ever, happens. These justices are then an oligarchy by default.

What restrains the Court from overstepping its constitutional authority? In the words of Justice Stone's famous remark of 1939, "the only check upon our exercise of power is our own sense of self-restraint." But the very purpose of government is to check the inability of man to monitor his self-restraint. To give absolute control of government to a small group of men and women flies in the face of the Biblical doctrine of total depravity.

Power in the hands of men whose only check is their own "sense" of what they believe is right or wrong puts a nation at risk. "Power corrupts," said Lord Acton, "and absolute power corrupts absolutely." What happens if the philosophy chosen by the court is assumed to be just and right and yet results in the tyranny of the masses? What happens when a small group of men pronounce that an unborn child is not protected by the Constitution, that he has no rights, that his "mother" has the constitutional right to kill him at will? Nine men, an oligarchy, sentenced 20 million unborn babies to death.

Democracy

Most Americans are under the impression that our nation is a democracy. To be sure, there are certainly democratic elements in our constitutional system. The First Amendment to the Constitution states that "The people" have the right "to petition the Government for a redress of grievances." The petition of the people is only as good as the character of the people. Keeping in mind the Biblical doctrine of the depravity of man, our constitutional framers steered clear of a democracy. Constitutional attorney John W. Whitehead writes: "It must be remembered that the term *democratic* appears neither in the Declaration of Independence nor in the Constitution. Actually, when the Constitution is analyzed in its original form, the document is found to be a serious attempt to establish a government mixed with democratic, aristocratic, and monarchical elements — a government of checks and balances."[2]

A democracy places all power in the people. It's a government of the masses. (The word "of" is tricky. It can mean "by" or it can mean "over." The bloody tyrannies of our day have been imposed over the people in the name of the people.) Democratic law is based on the will of the majority. If the whims and fancies of the people change, the law changes. In the *Federalist Papers*, which were popular newspaper articles written in defense of the ratification of the Constitution in 1787 and 1788 by Alexander Hamilton, James Madison, and John Jay, democracies were described as "spectacles of turbulence and contention." Democracies are "incompatible with personal security or the rights of property. . . . In general [they] have been as short in their lives as they have been violent in their deaths."

Democracies degenerate into exploitation because some voters discover that they can vote themselves political and financial favors out of the public treasury. Those seeking power through majority rule always vote for the candidate promising the most benefits. The results are certain: democracies collapse because the public treasury is milked dry because of greater voter demand. A dictatorship normally follows.

---

2. John Whitehead, *The Separation Illusion* (Milford, Michigan: Mott Media, 1977), p. 47.

Socialism

Socialism, along with its illegitimate son Communism, is advancing around the world. Socialism appeals to man's desire to get something for nothing through the agency of an omnipotent State government. Under Socialism, the means of production is owned by the State. The State interferes in the everyday affairs of all the people, even in the transactions they make. The State determines what will be produced, how much of an item will be produced, how it will be produced, where it will be produced, by whom it will be produced, what it will sell for, how people will get the product, and how it will be used.

Under Socialism, the individual is given little incentive to invent, produce a better product, or to be more efficient so a product can be sold at a lower price and thus benefit all of society. The State determines everything. Socialism is rarely democratic; that is, the people have little to say about who gets elected to office to set socialistic policies. Like a democracy, socialists stay in power by the "promise." The voting public is always "promised" a share of the State's monies. From this, the rulers are able to purchase the votes they need to stay in power. When the people are dissatisfied with one Socialist leader, they will vote him out for another who promises to make his promises good. The bottom line is that the rulers prostitute themselves in order to maintain power.

Those who submit to Socialism are rewarded. "Those who do not submit, as the English Fabian socialist George Bernard Shaw (1856-1950) so urbanely quipped, will 'be mercifully put out of the way.' "[3] All Socialism begins with "interventionism," the gradual manipulation of the economy through governmental decree. Again, it's always with the promise that things will be better if the State steps in to "fix" things.

---

3. Tom Rose, *Economics: The American Economy from a Christian Perspective* (Mercer, Pennsylvania: American Enterprise Publications, 1985), p. 121.

Summary

The first principle of Biblical government—church, State, family, and self-government—is that God is in charge. Government must begin with *self-government under God*. This is as true of civil government as for all other forms of government.

Humanism's denial of God's government means in practice that the individual's will is absorbed and denied by the will of the State. Public policy overrules any contradictory policy held by an individual, a church, a business, or a civil jurisdiction at the state, county, or city level. When tyranny finally happens, when the State's will becomes the people's will, the citizenry looks at the prevailing conditions and asks how it could have happened. Fingers are pointed all around, when in fact, the finger-pointing ought to begin with each of us.

A nation that denies God's government over the individual, the family, the church, and the State will find itself enslaved to those who want to be master. The sad thing is that many of us are willing to let it happen. More than this, we wanted it to happen. There is always the promise of security, the giving up of a little more self-determination, the handing over of a bit more jurisdiction to those who want to make us so secure.

The doors of tyranny are closing. Are we motivated to follow God through the opening, or will we forever find ourselves locked in the grip of willing power merchants who will use us for their evil ends? The choice is ours.

The term 'government' has many meanings today. Most people define it in solely political terms. Older dictionaries, especially Noah Webster's *American Dictionary of the English Language* (1828), define 'government' with a multiplicity of meanings and referring to numerous jurisdictions. Older textbooks see government as beginning in the home, what we would call "family government."

Government in the singular belongs to God alone. The church is a legitimate government with authority and power. God has established multiple governing authorities, one of which is *civil* government. These many authorities were not designed to compete

but to cooperate. Multiple created authorities are patterned after
the Divine One and Many, the Triune God. The One is not to be
exalted over the Many. The Many are not to be exalted over the
One. The many governments established by God are each placed
over a domain designated by God in Scripture. Civil government
is a God-ordained government that has a very limited jurisdiction
that is designed to punish evil doers and promote the good.

In summary:

1. Rulers speak in the name of the god of the society.

2. Societies are therefore ruled either by the words of God or
by the words of men.

3. A nation that forgets God is doomed in history.

4. God is the ultimate source of peace and prosperity.

5. To say that any human institution provides us with peace
and prosperity is to make a god of that institution.

6. God judges institutions that rule in the name of any other
god.

7. The words of man can be manipulated by men.

8. One source of political power in history has been the ability of rulers to redefine words.

9. A shift in meaning has taken place in the word "government": government as only the State.

10. Noah Webster's 1828 dictionary defined all government as
beginning with self-government.

11. The Bible teaches that human governments are plural.

12. In the Bible, "the" government (singular) refers only to the
rule of Christ.

13. God is the model for all governments.

14. God is a Trinity: both One and Many.

15. Anti-Christian views of government destroy either the
unity or diversity of society.

2

A BOTTOM-UP HIERARCHY

Now listen to me: I shall give you counsel, and God be with you. You will be the people's representative before God, and you bring the disputes [of the people] to God, then teach them the statutes and the laws, and make known to them the way in which they are to walk, and the work they are to do. Furthermore, you shall select out of all the people able men who fear God, men of truth, those who hate dishonest gain; and you shall place these over them, as leaders of thousands, of hundreds, of fifties and of tens. And let them judge the people at all times; and let it be that every major dispute they will bring to you, but every minor dispute they themselves will judge. So it will be easier for you, and they will bear the burden with you (Exodus 18:19-23).

Moses faced a problem. Everyone seemed to be suing everyone else, and they had only been out of Egypt a month. Slaves do not govern themselves well. These recent slaves could not settle their disputes. So they lined up in front of Moses' tent daily, to get judgment.

Jethro, Moses' father-in-law, saw what was happening. He suggested a solution. First, serve as God's representative, an intermediary between God and the people. Second, teach them God's law, so they will know what to do. They will learn to govern themselves. Third, establish an appeals court system, with righteous men serving as judges. Let them take the easier cases, saving the hard ones for you to take before God.

What was Jethro really saying? "You are not God; you need help. Acknowledge your weaknesses and limitations, share in the authority of being a judge, and you will not wear out these people, nor will they wear you out. In short, don't imitate Pharaoh, who thought of himself as a god. That is the way of destruction. Don't treat these people as slaves, even if they want to be slaves. Slavery is the way of destruction. God has delivered you out of Egypt; don't go back to Egypt governmentally."

Jethro recognized a basic fact of institutional life: the second point in the Biblical covenant, that is, the necessity of *hierarchy*. There has to be a system of policy-making, and also a system of appeals. To what extent are policies set at the top and at the bottom? Where does primary institutional sovereignty lie, at the top or the bottom? The question facing Moses was this: Which kind of human hierarchical authority structure is required by God, top-down or bottom-up?

Egypt's Bureaucratic Theocracy

The Great Pyramid of Cheops or Khufu, at Gizeh near Cairo, is the only surviving edifice of the Seven Wonders of the World. The Great Pyramid is a solid mass of limestone blocks, covering 13 acres. It contains about 2.3 million blocks that weigh on average two tons and a half each. If laid end to end, they would stretch two-thirds of the way around the earth at the equator. In its original state it was 768 ft. square and 482 ft. high.

The Great Pyramid and the smaller pyramids are a lasting testimony to the building prowess of the Egyptians. They are also evidence of the religion and political theory of Egypt. The very shape of the pyramids tells us something about Egypt's political philosophy. Egypt was a top-down system of total control. The Pharaohs believed in political centralization. All of life was controlled through the Pharaoh's decree. Who built the pyramids for the Pharaohs? Why, the people. Voluntarily? Certainly not. The pyramids were the classic public works program of all time: very expensive, but without any long-term benefits, except for rulers trying to make a name for themselves.

The Pharaohs were not incorporating a new idea in the development of their political philosophy. All those who reject the true

God want to be "like God" (Genesis 3:5). God is the controller of all things. Rebels against God want to control, to manipulate, and eventually to enslave. This is the dream of all empire-builders. Given enough power and authority, these power merchants believe that all of life can be controlled by man and for man.

Pyramid Power

The Tower of Babel, the first Tower of Power, is a good place to start in our understanding of the nature of political power. These early empire-builders wanted to make a name for themselves (Genesis 11:4), to supplant the government of God and replace it with a centralized, bureaucratic government where all of life would be controlled from Babel. Making a name for themselves, like naming in general, was an act of *sovereignty* and *power*; it was to declare and claim *authority over* the thing that is named (See Genesis 2:20, 23; Daniel 1:6, 7).

In Genesis 11 we find the purposed overthrow of God's order and the elimination of God's name. Those involved in this conspiracy (see Psalm 2) were humanistic, man-centered kingdom-builders who wanted to consolidate their efforts and establish Babel as the center of power and authority. The individual and the diverse makeup of society would be eliminated. The State would dominate society.

The symbol of their centralized power was the tower — a representation of Satan's theology: "I will ascend to heaven; I will raise my throne above the stars of God, and I will sit on the mount of the assembly in the recesses of the north. I will ascend above the heights of the clouds; I will make myself like the Most High" (Isaiah 14:13-14). God's government is the only centralized government. He is the Planner. The builders of the tower wanted to be what God is. The tower represented the seat of power — God's throne. Those who built the tower wanted to rise above "the stars of God." In Scripture, stars often represent rulers and/or kingdoms (Judges 5:20; Daniel 8:10; Matthew 24:29; Mark 13:25). According to Babylonian "theology," the gods made their throne and counseled together in the far north. In effect, the dictators in

Babel wanted to rule the world. Their centralized kingdom would be located in the "land of Shinar." Man, through the agency of statist power, would become God as he ascended the Tower of Power, grabbing for himself more and more control over God's created order, centralizing his domain and subjugating the people to do his bidding.

Decentralization

In contrast to the pyramid system, God's system of political power is *decentralized*. No single institution has been established by God to bring about social order. Freedom and order are realized when men throughout a society strive to follow the blueprint God has given for the reconstruction of all family, ecclesiastical, social, and political institutions. For example, Genesis 10 is a list of *many* families that represent a decentralized social order. The builders of Babel wanted to eliminate the *many* governments and consolidate family, ecclesiastical, and political power in the *one* State. God would have none of it. God "scattered them abroad from there over the face of the whole earth; and they stopped building the city" (Genesis 11:8).

This language is very similar to what God says of anyone who works to substitute God's blueprint for an orderly society with man's blueprint for tyranny and oppression: "Nevertheless you will be thrust down to Sheol, to the recesses of the pit" (Isaiah 14:15). All the kingdoms in Nebuchadnezzar's dream, a reflection of the Tower of Power, "were crushed all at the same time, and became like chaff from the summer threshing floors; and the wind carried them away so that not a trace of them was found" (Daniel 2:35). Man's Towers of Power will be "thrust down," "crushed," and "scattered." God's kingdom—God's government—will become "a great mountain" that will fill "the whole earth . . . and will itself endure forever" (Daniel 2:35). While centralized political regimes will be "scattered," the government of Jesus Christ will have "no end" (Isaiah 9:7).

Bearing in mind that God ordains authority, what should a Biblical political structure look like? Should the pyramid and the tower be our example? Should each individual be sovereign, every man doing what he believes is right in his own eyes (Judges 17:6)? Solving the problem of who ought to rule and how much power they ought to have is a difficult one.

Government Under God

God has the ultimate authority to govern (Jeremiah 27:5; Proverbs 8:15; 21:1; Matthew 28:18). If we were to make a diagram, it would be a hierarchy that looks something like this:

GOD
Independent and Unlimited Governing Authority
(Isaiah 9:6, 7)

MAN AND HUMAN INSTITUTIONS
Dependent and Limited Governing Authority
(Exodus 18 and Romans 13:1-4)

Family	Church	Civil (all levels)
(Self-governing individuals under God)	(Self-governing individuals under God)	(Self-governing individuals under God)

Parents exercise authority over their children, employers over employees, teachers over students, elders or bishops over the church members, and civil servants over citizens. In all these cases authority is backed up by penalties: a parent may spank a child, an employer may fire an employee, a teacher may fail a student, the church may excommunicate a member, and civil representatives may force a law-breaker to pay restitution for a crime.

The Biblical pattern of authority establishes that God is our ultimate authority, and He alone establishes earthly governments.

In Romans 13:1 we are instructed to subject ourselves "to the governing *authorities*," each of which is "established by God." Notice that there are *multiple* authorities. We owe no single earthly authority our total allegiance.

Those hostile to the Christian faith despise such Biblically mandated governmental pluralism: a system that maintains there is one Law and one Lawgiver, but a plurality of jurisdictions or authorities to which we must all submit. Such a system of government cannot be easily controlled. No one jurisdiction can claim the right to rule over all other established authorities. All are ultimately responsible to God for legitimacy. No authority can claim independency from the Triune God.

God's design in establishing multiple authorities means that no one government should cancel the authority of any other government. Ideally, all legitimate governments cooperate. They exist in the world by God's design. Each exercises real power in its limited sphere of operation. The breakdown of authority comes when any authority abdicates legitimacy and responsibility and turns rulership over to a greater human authority hoping for security. In Old Testament Israel, family, church, and State were meant to operate under the jurisdiction of the One True King. As sin prevailed and judgment came, the people turned to the State for security. They abandoned personal, family, and ecclesiastical authority and responsibility and looked to the State for salvation. They rejected God as King over them and chose a king to judge them "like all the nations" (1 Samuel 8:5).

The people were looking for salvation. They were looking for someone to guarantee them their inheritance. God was rejected. The State became the god of the people.

Jurisdictional Diversity

When talking about authority and power as they relate to government, two extremes need to be avoided. The first extreme to be avoided is the belief that the individual is a law unto himself, responsible only to himself. This extreme attempts to counter its opposite, that the *many* are ultimate. If the many were ultimate, anarchy would result. Many individuals could claim authority on their own terms.

Second, no one institution, group, nation, or society is ultimate. This opposes the idea that the *one* should be ultimate. If the one becomes ultimate, an institution, group, church, nation, or society can claim to be the final arbiter of truth and power, putting all diversity under its rule. Only God is ultimate; the one and the many are governed by God's Law in all things. Thus, the one and the many in society are balanced under the one authority of the Triune God.

Many delegated governments decentralize the centers of power. Corruption and tyranny are heightened when authority structures, from the individual to civil governments at the local, county, and state levels, break down, and all authority then rests in one institution, usually the State.

Reclamation of multiple authorities comes about when the individual assumes his responsibilities under God and thoroughly transforms his family, and working with other like-minded individuals, transforms his school, church, vocation, local community, state, and national civil government. We cannot expect diverse authority structures to arise on their own, however. Regeneration, the basis of all godly authority, begins with God working in the individual, and it extends to every facet of life.

Looking for Relief

A word of caution is needed here. Too often Christians turn to the State for relief because of the failure of individuals, families, businesses, schools, churches, and civil governments at the local, county, and state levels. The State has limited jurisdiction and competence, and is not man's answer for sin, except in temporal punishment for criminal acts. In fact, as recent history so well proves, the State frequently compounds the ills of society—the economy, education, welfare, the courts—when it acts outside of the area of its proper authority and jurisdiction.

It has been established that all authority belongs to God and that all earthly authority, whether family, church or State, is delegated and limited. The delegation of authority is purposely multiplied. This hampers the sinful tendency toward tyranny of any one governmental institution. For example, the authority of the State is not the same as that of a father who exercises authority as head of his household.

While each government should follow guidelines laid down in Scripture for its particular area of jurisdiction, not all Biblical laws apply to each in the same way. For example, the symbol of family authority is the rod (Proverbs 13:24), while the symbol of church authority is the keys (Matthew 16:19), and for the State, the sword (Romans 13:4).

Laws found in Scripture give parents the authority to exercise discipline over a child with a rod, but not over an erring brother in Christ. This authority belongs to the church. The church can discipline a member, but cannot use the rod or wield the sword as punishment. The church has the power of the "keys" to bar unrepentant members from the Lord's table and finally to excommunicate them if they remain unrepentant (Matthew 18:15-20).

The State has authority to wield the sword as punishment for capital offenses, but it cannot use its authority to influence the inner workings of the family or church. These "institutions" are outside its jurisdiction. If, however, a family member commits a crime, the State may have jurisdiction unless voluntary restitution is made.

These various institutions must often defer judgment to the more legitimate area of jurisdiction. Jesus' words in Luke 20:22-25 establish the authority of the State and also set the boundaries for its civil jurisdiction. Men asked Him, " 'Is it lawful for us to pay taxes to Caesar, or not?' But He detected their trickery and said to them, 'Show me a denarius. Whose head and inscription does it have?' And they said, 'Caesar's.' And He said to them, 'Then render to Caesar the things that are Caesar's, and to God the things that are God's.' "

When the church disciplines a local church member over an ecclesiastical matter, the State cannot rightly be approached to use its authority to override what the disciplined member might consider an unfair decision. Even the jurisdictional boundaries of ecclesiastical bodies must be respected, though this is difficult in a multi-denominational context. When one church disciplines a member and excommunicates that member, it is the duty of other ecclesiastical bodies to grant at least initial respect to the jurisdiction of the disciplining ecclesiastical court.

Jurisdictional authority can only be understood when the Biblical "chain of authority" is considered. This follows under the theology of "headship." Paul writes, "But I want you to understand that Christ is the head of every man, and the man is the head of a woman, and God is the head of Christ" (1 Corinthians 11:3). In Ephesians 5:23 Jesus is said to be the "head of the church." In the book of Revelation Jesus is designated "the ruler of the kings of the earth" (Revelation 1:5; Psalm 72). In all these cases we find everyone responsible to someone else, and ultimately all are responsible to God. Even Jesus in His humanity, as the Son of God, is under the headship of His Father (Luke 22:42).

The Biblical Answer: A Constitutional Republic

We find in Exodus 18 a description of what a godly civil government should look like. Moses, as God's unique representative, appointed righteous judges over the people in a hierarchy. But this hierarchy was not a top-down pyramid. Rather, it was a bottom-up *appeals court*. God had given them His law (as He has given to us), and the people were to take their disputes to God-fearing men, who would render honest judgment. If a case was too hard for them, then the judges would refer it to the next level upward.

This leaves individuals free to work out their own salvation with fear and trembling (Philippians 2:12). Each person is to be self-governed under God. In ancient Israel, God required His law to be read to the whole nation every seventh year (Deuteronomy 31:10-13), which revealed the terms of civil righteousness to everyone. Each person was therefore made responsible for his actions. This is God's system of self-government. Only when people disagree about the legal boundaries between them do they call in the judges. Thus, there is liberty at the individual level, but there is also a court system for achieving peaceful settlements of disputes. This is the same sort of appeals system that Christ established for the settling of disputes in the church (Matthew 18:15-20).

God therefore provided a hierarchy for them, but a bottom-up hierarchy. He gave them His law (Exodus 18:20). He made righteousness the fundamental principle of holding office: "Moreover you shall select from all the people able men, such as fear God, men of truth, hating covetousness; and place such over them as to be rulers of thousands, rulers of hundreds, rulers of fifties, and rulers of tens" (v. 21).

The principle of Biblical representative government stems from this Old Testament innovation. The primary issue is ethics — righteousness. Secondary to this is competence, but always secondary: Paul said that it is better to be judged by the least competent person in the church than by an anti-Christian civil judge (1 Corinthians 6:4).

The representative is under God and sworn to uphold God's law. He represents men before God and God before men. He speaks in God's name. This is the meaning of all government. Someone on earth must speak in God's name. The Biblical test of the speaker's authority is his lawful ordination; the test of his continuing right to ordination is his faithfulness to God's Word. If he fails this test, he is to be removed from office by the people he serves and judges.

All authority is God-given. God grants original authority to the ruled to choose who will rule over them. He therefore also grants authority to the rulers. Ultimately, if people refuse to obey rulers, they can topple any system of government. The people are sovereign, but they are not *originally* sovereign. Only God possesses original sovereignty. A constitutional republic best reflects this dual grant of civil authority: from God to men in general and to specific rulers.

Summary

The second basic principle in the Biblical blueprint for government is that God has established a hierarchical yet decentralized political order where neither the individual nor the group is ultimately sovereign. There are checks and balances in order to preserve liberty, authority, and stability. No single human institution or branch of civil government is absolutely sovereign. Only God is absolutely sovereign.

Authority and power to govern are *delegated by God*; thus, those who govern are obligated to govern according to God's law, for they are *ministers* of God (Romans 13:1-7). There really is no other option. When men cease to believe in God, they do not end up believing in nothing, but what is worse, they believe in anything, however absurd or sinister. They substitute another god to fill the vacuum. Some political system will prevail, and it will be directed by some god.

Throughout history, as a nation moves away from God as Governor of all of life, the State claims for itself more and more power. All competing governments are removed — usually by force, always by intimidation. In time, the people suffer under the weight of unbridled oppression. What was once a promise of security by those centralizing authority and power, becomes a choking tyranny. The oppression continues and turns the people either into slaves or rebels. The solution to the plight of tyranny is not to place authority and power in the hands of the individual. Nor is the solution found in the ruling abilities of a self-appointed elite.

Centralization was the prevailing political structure in the history of the world. Egypt used the people to construct a society, using the energies of the masses to implement the goals of the State, governed by the Pharaohs. The pyramid, the tower, and Nebuchdnezzar's colossus are visible manifestations of centralized political planning. God works to disestablish centralized political regimes. His blueprint for life is decentralization, with the individual working and having freedom in the family, church, business, and civil government. No one man or institution is to rule over all other aspects of society. The way to a just order is not found in anarchy where man is a law unto himself, in socialism where the State owns the means of production, in an oligarchy where a planning elite rules and overrules, or in a democracy where the people can change the direction of a nation by whim and fancy. God has established a decentralized society best described as a Constitutional Republic where the best are elected to office and yet are still responsible to the vote of the people.

In summary:

1. Slaves do not govern themselves well.

2. The civil government is an intermediary between God and man.

3. The civil government is to announce the laws of God.

4. The ruler is to appoint righteous judges to handle the less difficult cases.

5. This means that God wants men to establish governmental hierarchies (point two of the Biblical covenant).

6. Egypt's hierarchy was bureaucratic: top down.

7. This was reflected in the design of the pyramids.

8. The Tower of Babel was another pyramid of power.

9. Only God centralizes power.

10. Decentralization is what God requires for man's governments.

11. God scattered those who built the Tower of Babel.

12. Man's governments (plural) are always hierarchical.

13. The Bible teaches pluralism: plural governments under God's unified law.

14. Governments possess multiple jurisdictions.

15. Too often Christians turn to the State for answers.

16. The Biblical solution for civil government is a constitutional republic.

17. This involves representative government.

18. Rulers are supposed to represent men to God and God to men.

19. Such authority is delegated originally to specific men from God, and secondarily from the ruled (who also possess God-given authority) to the rulers.

3

PLURAL LAW SYSTEMS, PLURAL GODS

> To the law and to the testimony! If they do not speak according to this word, it is because there is no light in them (Isaiah 8:20).

Justice! What a long quest it has been for mankind. In every society, men seek justice, and they never seem to find it. Why not? Because they do not seek the God of the Bible, in whom alone there is perfect justice. Why not? Because He dispenses perfect justice, and imperfect men know what this means: "For all have sinned and fall short of the glory of God" (Romans 3:23).

What men say they are seeking is honest judgment. But honest judgment implies a standard: honest law. Honest judgment is not based on the wishes of the few or the will of the mighty. It is based on the wishes of the Mighty One. Honest judgment can only be secured when we turn to a law that rests outside the partisan interests of fallen men. *Honest judgment must rest on objective norms of law and justice.* But modern man does not want to admit that such objective standards exist. They tell us to search elsewhere. Should we appeal to the latest polling statistics? Is the United States Supreme Court the final court of appeal for Americans?

What the Bible says is that *the final court of appeal is the judgment seat of God.* There is unquestionably a Supreme Court, but it is not some national Supreme Court; it is a heavenly court. No earthly court of appeals should be given absolute and final jurisdiction.

Biblical Laws or Anti-Biblical Laws

The study of any subject must be placed within the limits of a Biblical worldview. The third principle of the Biblical covenant is that God lays down the law to man. Man is supposed to exercise dominion by means of Biblical law. To speak of justice, or anything else for that matter, which is isolated from a Biblical covenantal structure, is to lead us into a sea of ethical subjectivity. A recent example of such a quest for Bible-less law is the revival in some Christian and conservative political circles of a so-called "natural law ethic" as a substitute for Biblical law. (Humanist legal scholars do not take this revival seriously; they fully understand that Darwinian evolutionary thought destroyed any concept of humanistic natural law. Man makes his own rules in the post-Darwin world.)[1]

We must understand that there is no neutrality in making laws. A law says one thing is right or wrong. This inevitably infringes on someone's money, lifestyle, or dreams. Who wins, who loses? If humanist man has his way, God will lose, and all those who stand with God. When autonomous (self-law) man's law prevails, we can expect God's law to be invalidated (Mark 7:8, 13).

Satan attacked God on the basis of His law: "Indeed, has God said, 'You shall not eat from any tree of the garden?'" (Genesis 3:1). He appealed to Adam and Eve to be a law unto themselves — to "be like God" (v. 5). Even the devil knew there was no neutrality. (Of course, the devil is an expert in all of God's ways. He's also an expert in disobeying all of them.) His law and God's law could not coexist.

But ours is a day of "pluralism." The God of Scripture has spoken, but so has the god of convenience, and the god of tolerance, and the god of expediency, and the god of majority opinion, and the god of experience, and the god of any other ethical system that seeks to be a part of America's legal mainstream.

---

1. Gary North, *The Dominion Covenant: Genesis* (Tyler, Texas: Institute for Christian Economics, 1982), Appendix A: "From Cosmic Purposelessness to Humanistic Sovereignty."

Supposedly all religions are of equal worth and validity. If so, then rival laws of these rival gods are of equal worth and validity. "Yes" and "no" are of equal validity. True and false are of equal validity. Life and death are of equal validity, especially death, especially of unborn infants. ("All unborn infants are equal, but some are more equal than others . . . those allowed to live.") This pluralism of faiths has led to civil laws that are often inconsistent. They reflect the values of the many gods. Our courts are thus schizophrenic. There is no consistency because there is no single standard that must be followed.

One Lawgiver, One Law

In Biblical terms, there is but one law and one Lawgiver. God thought enough of His law to send His Son to keep it in every detail. If the Son of God was required to keep the law, should anything less be expected of the sons of God? Jesus was tempted at every point with respect to obeying the commands of God, yet He remained sinless throughout His life (Hebrews 4:15). He kept the law perfectly. There was no need for Jesus to offer up sacrifices for His own sins because He committed no sins (Hebrews 7:26-28). Instead He offered Himself up as a lamb without blemish as the law required, in order to cleanse us of our sins (Hebrews 9:14).

The entire human race has been found "guilty" on the basis of God's law. While the law ceases to condemn the Christian (Galatians 3:13) because of Jesus' perfect obedience and His substitutionary atonement, all people are held accountable to keep the law as a standard of right and wrong (Romans 3:31). Individuals, families, schools, churches, business establishments, and civil governments must choose the law of God as the standard for decision-making. Since the individual is not free to break the law, the courts are not free to judge on any other basis of law-order than that set forth in the Bible.

When a dispute arose among the people, Moses directed them to the law of God: "When they have a dispute, it comes to me, and I judge between a man and his neighbor, and make known the statutes of God and His laws" (Exodus 18:16). The judges appointed by Moses to share in the task of settling disputes also were required to judge according to the law of God (vv. 19-20). The people as a whole must be careful not to add to the law of God or take away from it (Deuteronomy 4:2). This indicates that God's law must be used as it is and not mixed with the changing laws of men. Men often are tempted to adapt God's commandments to fit the times. Thus the judgment of man is deemed superior to that of God, and the commandments of God often are nullified (cf. Mark 7:13).

The Levitical priests as well as the judges of Israel were bound to follow the law. The people of Israel also were instructed to heed the judges' verdict because the decision was based upon the unchanging law of God and not upon the decision of men: "According to the terms of the law which they teach you, and according to the verdict which they tell you, you shall do; you shall not turn aside from the word which they declare to you, to the right or the left" (Deuteronomy 17:11).

Reforming Society

When Jehoshaphat initiated reforms, one of the first areas of reformation was the judicial system: "And he appointed judges in the land in all the fortified cities of Judah, city by city. And he said to the judges, 'Consider what you are doing, for you do not judge for man but for the LORD who is with you when you render judgment. Now then let the fear of the LORD be upon you; be very careful what you do, for the LORD our God will have no part in unrighteousness, or partiality, or the taking of a bribe'" (2 Chronicles 19:5-7). Reformation came from the top and bottom. Judges' decisions must not issue from political or economic pressures or calculations, or any merely human purposes, but from obedience to the Lord of heaven, earth, and history, and to the righteous laws He has revealed to us in Scripture.

The prophets of Israel continued to warn the nation that only the law of God serves as a legal system's foundation: "To the law and to the testimony! If they do not speak according to this word, it is because they have no dawn" (Isaiah 8:20). Any attempt to repudiate the law of God as a standard for righteousness establishes man as judge, lawgiver, king, and savior; it leaves man under the rule of darkness. The Bible clearly shows that law originates in the character of God, and definitions for justice and righteousness find their meaning in Him and not in the finite, fallible, and fallen nature of the creature: "For the LORD is our judge, the LORD is our lawgiver, the LORD is our king; He will save us" (Isaiah 33:22).

The Bible presents law as abiding forever because it reflects God's own immutable character:

> The works of His hands are truth and justice; all His precepts are sure. They are upheld forever and ever; they are performed in truth and righteousness (Psalm 111:7, 8).

> Thy testimonies are fully confirmed; holiness befits Thy house, O LORD, forevermore (Psalm 93:5).

> All commandments are truth. Of old I have known from Thy testimonies, that Thou has founded them forever (Psalm 119:151b-152).

> The sum of Thy word is truth, and every one of Thy righteous ordinances is everlasting (v. 160).

> The word of our God stands forever (Isaiah 40:8).

The word of man is feeble because his nature is finite and fallen:

> All flesh is grass, and all its loveliness is like the flower of the field. The grass withers, the flower fades, when the breath of the LORD blows upon it; surely the people are grass. The grass withers, the flower fades, but the word of our God stands forever (Isaiah 40:6-8).

A Law Unto Themselves

The modern use of law makes it arbitrary, based in one case on a judge, in another, on the word of a Führer like Adolf Hitler. Thus man becomes the lawmaker, and the word of human authority becomes the new law. The courts, therefore, no longer are bound by any law. They have in effect become a law unto them-

selves. Satan's lie is alive and destroying our nation: "And you will
be like God, knowing good and evil" (Genesis 3:5).

As soon as Adam and Eve sinned, the accusations began. God
cross-examined Adam and Eve, beginning with the responsible
agent in the family, Adam. Adam blamed his wife, and ultimately
God: "The woman whom Thou gavest to be with me, she gave me
from the tree, and I ate" (v. 11). God then cross-examined Eve.
Eve blamed the serpent: "The serpent deceived me, and I ate"
(Genesis 3:13). In other words, both of them blamed their environment. Both of them implicitly blamed the One who made their
environment, God. But God was not responsible; neither was
their environment. Adam sinned wilfully, and was fully responsible. Eve sinned because she had been deceived (1 Timothy 2:14),
but she was also fully responsible. God punished both of them for
their sin (Genesis 3:16-19). He also punished the serpent (Genesis
3:14)—a punishment that promised ultimate victory to the seed of
the woman over the forces of evil (3:15).

Murder (Genesis 4:8, 23) and other acts of violence (6:2) then
became part of the cursed created order. God therefore im-
plemented laws to deal with the violence that resulted from man's
sinful desires: "Whoever sheds man's blood, by man his blood
shall be shed, for in the image of God He made man" (9:6). Laws
protecting life (Exodus 20:15), property (v. 13), and personal/
neighbor relationships (vv. 12, 14, 16) were made part of the system of laws that Israel was bound to follow. Justice, therefore, was
defined in terms of the law, God's law.

The Power of the Sword

While the church is given the authority of the "keys" (Matthew
16:19), the State has the power of the "sword" (Romans 13:4). The
"sword" means the power to inflict violence. There are certain
crimes that necessitate the use of the sword (e.g., capital crimes)
where the church has no jurisdiction. Church and State are separate, God-ordained monopolies in their respective realms.

Israel's governmental systems were decentralized. Judges and
their officers, and the elders of the people were appointed to a

variety of cities on the local level. They were responsible to administer justice in the locale where they were installed to power: "If a slain person is found lying in the open country in the land which the LORD your God gives you to possess, and it is not known who has struck him, then your elders and your judges shall go out and measure the distance to the cities which are around the slain one" (Deuteronomy 21:1-2). Atonement had to be made for the death of a person found in an open field outside the boundaries of any particular city. The city closest to the slain body was responsible to make atonement. The city was represented by elders (representing civil affairs) and judges (representing judicial matters). While cities had numerous elders and judges, the law of God bound them to follow the same legal procedures. The law of God insured that people were being judged by "righteous judgment," no matter which judge kept court.

When a foundation of law is denied, those who rule in our nation's courts establish themselves and their own ethical "ideals" as the standards for righteousness. Often an individual who dislikes the verdict handed down in one court appeals to a higher court to find a judge who operates with a different set of judicial principles based upon a different law. Judicial decisions from state to state often differ because of the absence of any standard of righteousness.

In many courts throughout our land there is a decided bias *against* the Christian religion. Law has become sociological, pragmatic, and utilitarian. Law becomes a shifting foundation, determined by minorities that can whip up majorities, or control the courts. Law loses its reliability. People then lose faith in the court system. The result is lawlessness, rebellion, and even greater efforts to centralize civil power.

Judicial Safeguards

The standard for justice already has been established—the Word of God. Judges are unable to judge rightly unless the standard of righteousness comes from the law of God. To operate contrary to justice is to deny the Word of God:

First, the status of a person involved in or accused of a crime would not be taken into account when he is judged. Fallen man tends to favor the rich because they hold greater influence in the community where the judge resides. The poor are easily disadvantaged because their meager living does not afford the options often available to the affluent. On the other hand, the poor often are pitied when they commit a crime, and thus are able to use their economic condition to arouse pity and to overrule requirements of the law. God's law makes no provision for favoring the rich or pitying the poor when a crime is committed: "You shall do no injustice in judgment; you shall not be partial to the poor nor defer to the great, but you are to judge your neighbor fairly" (Leviticus 19:15).

Second, Paul says the "love of money is a root of all sorts of evil" (1 Timothy 6:10). The Bible warns the judge not to be influenced by bribes. Moreover, in choosing men for the office of judge, one requirement is that they "hate dishonest gain" (Exodus 18:21). Instead of seeing the law as the standard of judgment, money too often becomes the dispenser of justice. This is why the Bible again and again prohibits the taking of bribes by judges or governors.

Third, the law of God is not one law among many to be chosen at will to fit only certain circumstances. The Asherah was a female deity of the Canaanites (Baal was the male counterpart) usually represented by a wooden pole or a luxuriant tree that was considered to be sacred. When the Israelites entered the land they were commanded to destroy the foreign sanctuaries so the pagan religion of the Canaanites would be rejected in the minds of the people. Any attempt to mix the prevailing religion of the day with the purity of the faith delivered to Israel was prohibited.

The religion of the creature and true faith delivered by the Creator have no common ground. Given enough time, the religion of man perverts the Christian faith. For example, Jesus commends the church of Ephesus because they "cannot endure evil men" and "put to the test those who call themselves apostles" (Revelation 2:2). Moreover, they "hate the deeds of the Nicolaitans" (Revelation 2:6). On the other hand, Jesus rebukes the church of Thyatira because they "tolerate the woman Jezebel, who calls herself a prophetess, and she teaches and leads My bond-servants astray, so that they commit acts of immorality and eat things sacrificed to idols" (Revelation 2:20). Tolerating an admixture of pagan influence eventually leads to outright apostasy.

When a nation's judicial system seeks to institute a law system that mixes the law of God with the laws of men, over a period of time God's law will be repudiated. The shift from a legal system based upon the law of God to a legal system based upon the wavering laws of men takes time, however. The shift is often imperceptible. *When man's laws, based upon the independent reasoning of the creature, are made equal with revelation, we can be assured that the new law system is in place.* Christians must know that there can be no so-called neutral system of law. When the law of God is replaced by any other system of law, that pagan system of law is an Asherah next to the altar of God.

The Reformation of the 16th century attacked the idea that there was a foundation for law outside the Bible. Man's intellect, the church, and the State were bound by the absolute authority of the Bible. This Reformation thinking was carried to the various colonies by the Pilgrims and Puritans during the seventeenth century. Many of the state constitutions of the eighteenth century reflect the *Biblical* basis for law. The will of the people or the decree of the State did not serve as the foundation for justice.

Natural Law: A Wolf in Sheep's Clothing

There were many in the latter part of the 18th century, however, who attempted to overthrow the Christian foundation of law by establishing the people's "collective conscience" (the so-called Social Contract) as the standard for law. Liberal John Locke and radical Jean Jacques Rousseau are the two most famous 18th-century social contract theorists. Natural law theory led to the establishment of an elite lawmaking group that determined the nature and direction the courts would take.

Darwinian evolutionism served as the death knell to the concept of absolute law. Law no longer was rooted in the Creator, but found its meaning in experience or in the evolving "natural order" of things. Autonomous reason has been erected in the courts of our day. Law, rooted in the mind or will of man, has replaced the law of God. The will of some earthly court is final. While the judicial system of the United States was originally established to *interpret* the Constitution in light of Biblical law, along the lines laid down by Blackstone, the court system now has set itself *above* the law where it *makes* law independent of any fixed authority.

It is unfortunate that in our day, when the world is crying for reliable and absolute standards to help in decision-making, many Christian scholars and leaders still appeal to a natural law solution, even though they know full well that its origins are pagan. According to Connaught Marshner, here is what passes for a "good system of ethics":

> Natural law ethics are adequate to the task. The philosophy of natural law has been time honored since the *ancient Greeks*. Though intellectual fashions change, the objective moral order, *knowable* by man and within the reach of mankind, can be *reasonably* seen as the most stable basis of personal, national and international order and happiness.[2]

Mrs. Marshner admits that natural law theory comes from ancient Greece, where the philosophies of homosexuals like Plato and Aristotle placed man at the center of the universe. She goes on to say that they are "knowable by man" and "can be reasonably seen." Why then is there so much disagreement around the world as to what constitutes a just society if reason is the only problem? "Right Reason" certainly does not work in the minds of the Soviet leadership or in the mind of a pro-abortionist. The murder of nearly 60 million people by Joseph Stalin (1879-1953), and the death of nearly two million unborn babies every year in the United States since 1973 is the result of the repudiation of Biblical law in favor of natural law. Natural law is rooted in nature, and nature is evolving to bring about the inevitable. What ever is, is right. So we are told.

---

2. Connaught Marshner, "Right and Wrong and America's Survival," *Future 21: Decisions for America in the 21st Century* (Greenwich, Connecticut: Devin-Adair, 1984), p. 129. Emphasis added.

Those who advocate natural law see it as equal to Biblical law. We are told that we need "both" standards. Mrs. Marshner continues:

> If order is to be restored to society, and the underpinnings·of freedom preserved, America must return to non-consequential ethics. What would be the basis for such ethics? Some say the sole possible basis is revealed religion. *This is a mistake. First of all, the Bible and other revealed documents do not answer explicitly all the ethical questions that arise. . . .*[3]

If revealed religion (the Bible) is not the "sole possible basis" for decision-making, then what is? The Bible says "no one can serve two masters" (Matthew 6:24). The apostle Paul writes that Christians are not to be unequally yoked with unbelievers (2 Corinthians 6:14). How then can Christians be unequally yoked with unbelieving ethical systems? "For what partnership have righteousness and lawlessness, or what fellowship has light with darkness? Or what harmony has Christ with Belial, or what has a believer in common with an unbeliever?" (vv. 14, 15)

The premise of these natural law advocates is that the Bible cannot be used as an ethical handbook to deal with issues like "genetic screening, nuclear weapons systems, or *in vitro* fertilization" because "the scriptures speak only by interpretation."[4] But can't the same thing be said about every ethical system? There's always interpretation. At least with the Bible, we know that our starting point is reliable.

Natural law is flawed from its inception because it assumes that "nature" (creation) is not fallen, that man's reasoning abilities are not distorted due to the Fall, and that ethics is based on "philosophy" and not "religious precepts." Again, Mrs. Marshner has little use for the Bible: "Citizens must defend their rights, and they must defend them intellectually, by employing and invoking an objective system of right and wrong. This new traditional system of ethics is based on *philosophical precepts, not on religious precepts,*

---

3. *Ibid.*, p. 128. Emphasis added.
4. *Ibid.*, p. 128.

and can be understood and accepted by anyone willing to master the intellectual rigors of it."[5] Who will determine what an "objective system of right and wrong" will be? What if the precepts of the Bible are rejected by those "willing to master the intellectual rigors" of these "philosophical precepts"? If history is any indicator, the Bible will be rejected in favor of self-serving, humanistic natural law. Religion is an enemy to natural law. Stalin's words should silence all who appeal to the supposed inherent reasonableness of natural law: "We guarantee the right of every citizen to combat by argument, propaganda and agitation, any and all religion. The Communist Party cannot be neutral toward religion. It stands for science, and all religion is opposed to science."[6] So much for objectivity, "non-consequential ethics," and "philosophical precepts."

One last nail needs to be driven into the coffin of natural law. If natural law is adequate as a basis for ethical standards, why were the Israelites required to hear the *revealed* law read at least once every seven years? Gary North writes:

> Human reason, unaided by God's revelation — untwisted by God's grace — cannot be expected to devise a universal law code based on any presumed universal human logic. What mankind's universal reason *can* be expected to do is to *rebel* against God and His law. Ethical rebels are not logically faithful to God.
>
> Biblical law had to be read to everyone in Israel at least once every seven years (Deut. 31:10-13). God presumed that men would not understand His law unless they heard it (Deut. 31:13). Every resident of the land had to listen to this law. If the whole of biblical law had been ingrained into the consciences of all men from the beginning of time, or if the terms of the law, including the law's explicit penalties, were always available to all men through the exercise of man's universal reason, then the law would not have required the priests to read the Mosaic law before the congregation of Israel every seventh year.[7]

---

5. *Ibid.*, p. 132. Emphasis added.

6. "Declaration to American Labor Delegation," Moscow, September 7, 1927.

7. *Moses and Pharaoh: Dominion Religion Versus Power Religion* (Tyler, Texas: Institute for Christian Economics, 1985), p. 236.

"The heart is deceitful above all things, and desperately wicked; Who can know it?" That question of the prophet Jeremiah (17:9) rings just as true today. The heart that says it can interpret neutral, universal, reasonable natural law is deceitful and desperately wicked. Who therefore can know natural law?

What is needed is an interpreter. The Bible is that interpreter. Many people may interpret the Bible differently, but over time, God rewards those who interpret it correctly and also apply it faithfully. God blesses those who are covenantally faithful. Thus, history progressively reveals true law from false law, though not without historical defeats for the faithful in periods of general apostasy (principle five of the covenant: continuity).

Summary

The third basic principle in the Biblical blueprint for civil government is that *God's law as revealed in the Bible is the standard for personal righteousness and national obedience.*

The world is looking for answers to life's most basic ethical problems. The promise of freedom under the lie of moral relativism has lead our nation down the path of destruction and hopelessness. In our attempt to play god, we have turned into the worst kind of devils. We have fooled ourselves into believing that life without law is the closest thing to utopia. The definition of utopia, "no place," is the direction we're headed if we do not get back on the path God has set before us. It is only in His light that we see light.

To what will we return? Will Christians lead the way with an objective, transcendent, and revealed law, or will we compromise with some brand of "natural law"? Now is the time for Christians to set forth the sure and clear Word of God to a world literally dying in a sea of moral subjectivism.

This is not the time for compromise. The saving work of Jesus Christ to redeem sinners dead in trespasses and sins and His law as a system of personal and societal righteousness are the only hope. If we opt for some morally neutral ethical system, then we will confront a world without Christ. Only the law of God is a tutor that will lead people to Christ. No other law system can do the job that God's law was designed to do.

A nation's judicial system rests on law — the law of God or the law of man. Both church and State are bound to follow the law of God as revealed in Scripture. The modern understanding of law makes it arbitrary, and man becomes the standard for all ethical decision-making.

The State has the power of the sword to punish law breakers as defined by the Bible. Without God's law as the standard, the State is free to establish its own law. Public policy prevails. Politics is king. The individual must bow in submission to the will of the State.

The status of an individual involved in or accused of a crime is not to be taken into account when a judge hears his case. The Bible warns judges not to be influenced by money.

The Law of God is not just one law among many. The acceptance of God's law is not an option for us as individuals or as a nation.

Natural law is inadequate as a standard for righteousness. Natural law is determined by man and man alone. The survival of the fittest is "natural." Should we codify such behavior? In effect, we have. The right of a woman to abort her defenseless unborn baby is the net result of a consistent natural law ethic.

In summary:

1. Men have always sought justice.
2. God is the source of justice that is truly just.
3. Honest judgment always rests on objective law.
4. The Bible tells men what a just legal system looks like.
5. Dominion is always exercised in terms of a specific view of the world.
6. To search for justice apart from the Bible is to pursue ethical subjectivism: many opinions, many voices, many laws.
7. Natural law is one such fruitless, self-defeating search.
8. Legal pluralism is the reign of subjectivism and relativism.
9. There is only one law-giver, and therefore only one true law.

10. All people are held accountable before God to obey Biblical law.

11. Jesus Christ met this legal standard perfectly.

12. Biblical reformation comes from both the top and the bottom: from rulers and ruled.

13. Modern law is arbitrary.

14. God judged Adam and Eve in terms of His law, not theirs.

15. The State possesses the power of the sword: violence.

16. Law is never neutral.

17. Modern laws are increasingly anti-Christian.

18. God has established safeguards for His law.

19. These safeguards are reduced when men mix rival views of law with Biblical law.

20. Natural law is one such rival law system.

21. Who will establish which law is truly "natural"?

22. In the Old Testament, Biblical law had to be read to the people every seventh year; "natural law" was not sufficient.

23. God blesses covenantally faithful societies over time.

24. True law is thereby distinguished from rival laws.

4

GOD JUDGES THE NATIONS

> And the LORD said, "The outcry of Sodom and Gomorrah is indeed great, and their sin is exceedingly grave. I will go down now, and see if they have done entirely according to its outcry, which has come to Me; and if not, I will know" (Genesis 18:20-21).

The day of doom was about to arrive for Sodom and Gomorrah. They had been the most blessed cities of the land of Canaan. It was to Sodom that Lot turned, when offered any place in the land by Abraham. "And Lot lifted up his eyes and saw all the valley of the Jordan, that it was well watered everywhere — this was before the LORD destroyed Sodom and Gomorrah — like the garden of the LORD, like the land of Egypt as you go to Zoar" (Genesis 13:10). But their hour was about to come.

God is the Judge of the nations. Judgment is the fourth point of the Biblical covenant structure. He created the earth. He also brought the judgment of the great flood. After the flood, God created the nations in an act of His sovereign judgment (Genesis 10). After they attempted to create a one-world State (meaning a one-State world), He divided mankind linguistically at the Tower of Babel (Genesis 11:1-9). The pyramid of power that mankind was about to build at Babel was destroyed by God.

He then scattered mankind across the face of the earth. This was a curse on mankind, yet it was also a blessing, for it withdrew men from the jurisdiction of a one-world bureaucratic State. It divided mankind into independent, sovereign, language-based nations, thereby destroying forever the possibility of fulfilling covenant-breaking man's dream of man becoming a unified god. It

54

decentralized political power, leaving men free to work out their cultural gifts and skills in their own way.

God went to Sodom and Gomorrah as a Judge. He went to see whether the sinful outcry of these cities was as bad as it sounded. Like Abel's blood crying to God from the ground (Genesis 4:10), sin cries up to God, and God hears. But as a Judge, He first conducts a trial, like the one He conducted in the garden, when He cross-examined Adam and Eve before bringing judgment, or just as He cross-examined Cain after Cain had murdered Abel (Genesis 4). He gathers evidence. Then He judges it in the light of His law. Then He announces His judgment and brings either blessings or cursings.

Collective Responsibility

Abraham bargained with God to spare Sodom (and therefore Lot) as soon as he was told that God was about to judge Sodom. "Wilt Thou indeed sweep away the righteous with the wicked?" Abraham asked (Genesis 18:23). Are righteous men who happen to be dwelling among the unrighteous also to be destroyed, just because of the sins of the immoral majority?

God's answer was clear: *Yes.* Abraham knew this. But he haggled with God over the "price." Will you spare the city for fifty righteous people? Yet Abraham's language is highly significant: "Far be it from Thee to do such a thing, to slay the righteous with the wicked, so that the righteous and the wicked are treated alike. Far be it from Thee! Shall not *the Judge of all the earth* deal justly?" (18:25). God is the Judge of "all the earth" and not just of some people at certain times in history. All nations are subject to His rule. His law is for *all the nations*.

God, knowing full well that there was but one righteous man in the city, was willing to promise Abraham that He would indeed spare the city for the sake of fifty righteous people. So Abraham tried to get a better deal. What about forty-five righteous people? God agreed: He would spare it for forty-five (18:28). And so it went, until Abraham got God to agree to spare the city for as few as ten righteous people (18:32).

Then God sent two angels to Sodom in order to warn Lot to get out. He in turn warned his daughters and their prospective (betrothed) husbands, but the two men scoffed (Genesis 19:14). So only Lot, his wife, and his two daughters left the city, and God then sent fire and brimstone down on Sodom and Gomorrah.

Fire and brimstone: These words have become synonymous in the English language with preaching that emphasizes hell and final judgment. This is quite proper; this is exactly what God's destruction of Sodom and Gomorrah is supposed to remind us of. But what Christians fail to recognize is the context of those fearful words. God was not raining fire and brimstone down on the heads of people as individuals; He was raining fire and brimstone down on a pair of cities. Individuals perished, of course, but they perished as members of cities whose sins had cried out to God for *collective judgment.* Abraham in his negotiating with God, had described God well: the Judge of all the earth.

God would have spared the two cities for the sake of as few as ten righteous people. But this was easy for God to agree to: There were not that many righteous people in those cities. The principle is clear, however: God is sometimes willing to spare a large number of evil people for the sake of a few righteous ones. It was so bad in Jeremiah's day, that God challenged him to locate a single righteous person: "Roam to and fro through the streets of Jerusalem, And look now, and take note. And seek in her open squares, If you can find a man, If there is one who does justice, who seeks truth, Then I will pardon her" (Jeremiah 5:1). God knew that Jeremiah would not find that person.

In Elijah's day, over a century earlier than Jeremiah, God promised the destruction of Israel, the northern kingdom. They would be destroyed by the sword, and carried into captivity. God promised to preserve seven thousand righteous people who would not bow the knee to Baal (1 Kings 19:18). In this case, there were not enough people in the land to save Israel from God's historic judgment. Still, this did not mean that every righteous person would die. He would keep a handful of them alive—not many, but a few. In this case, He judged the collective, but kept a remnant alive in the midst of the judgment. This, too, is God's way of dealing with men in history. Israel was judged for the sin of one man, Achan. Thirty-six men died because of one man's sin (Joshua 7:5). David's sin of "numbering the people" brought judgment to the nation and the death of "seventy thousand men of the people" (2 Samuel 24:15).

What God does is to look at those in authority. Are they righteous men? If so, he is willing to delay His judgment for a season, for the sake of the righteous leader, or even a few righteous residents. God delivered Judah out of the hands of the army of Assyria, and the city did not fall to the Babylonians until righteous King Hezekiah had died. Hezekiah had prayed the prayer that God always honored in the Old Testament era. He prayed that the army of the enemy would not capture the city, so "that all the kingdoms of the earth may know that Thou alone, O LORD, art God" (2 Kings 19:19b). For this prayer, and also for the sake of the memory of King David (v. 34), God spared His collective people from external judgment. But His mercy lasted only for a few more years. Then the prophet Jeremiah and other righteous people went into captivity in Babylon. "For out of Jerusalem shall go forth a remnant, and out of Mt. Zion survivors. The zeal of the LORD shall perform this" (v. 31). The judgment came: blessings (the survival of a remnant) and cursings (captivity for all). There would be continuity (the survival of a remnant and Judah's eventual return to the land) within discontinuity (the enslavement of the people to Babylon and then to Medo-Persia).

The writings of the prophets are filled with judgments against the nations. Isaiah warns the following nations of the judgment to come after He is finished judging Israel: Assyria (Isaiah 14:25-27), Philistia (14:29-31), Moab (15, 16), Damascus (17), Egypt (19), Tyre and Tarshish (23). Indeed, the whole earth will be judged:

> Behold, the LORD lays the earth waste, devastates it, distorts its surface, and scatters its inhabitants. And the people will be like the priest, the servant like his master, the maid like her mistress, the buyer like the seller, the lender like the borrower, the creditor like the debtor. The earth will be completely laid waste

and completely despoiled, for the LORD has spoken this word. The earth mourns and withers, the world fades and withers, the exalted of the people of the earth fade away. The earth is also polluted by its inhabitants, for *they transgressed laws, violated statutes, broke the everlasting covenant.* Therefore, a curse devours the earth, and those who live in it are held guilty. Therefore, the inhabitants of the earth are burned, and few men are left (Isaiah 24:1-6).

The prophet Obadiah warned Edom (the heirs of Esau) of coming judgment. Nahum warned Nineveh. Zephaniah warned Ammon and Moab, the heirs of Lot's incest (2:8-11). He also warned Ethiopia (v. 12) and Nineveh (vv. 13-15). Jonah also warned Nineveh, and Nineveh's people believed and repented for a season. Jeremiah warned pagan nations, too (46-51).

Everyone is guilty in Adam. God graciously allows men to live, history to continue. But God can "call in men's debts" at any time. He has the legal right at any time to bring total judgment in history.

Collectives rise and fall as units, despite the fact that every member is personally responsible before God. The church is also a collective before God, (1 Corinthians 12), yet each member is fully responsible before God. The blessings and cursings of God fall on collectives, as Deuteronomy 28 spells out in detail.

Individualism: Denying the Covenant

Because so few Christians have heard or believed the message of the covenant, they have been easily led into a non-Christian outlook called individualism. They have neglected the social implications of the doctrine of the Trinity. They have in theory recognized the equal ultimacy of the One and the Many in the Godhead, but they have not recognized the equal ultimacy of the one and the many in society. This failure has led to disastrous consequences. Christians have been unable to challenge modern statist humanism (the unity of the one) without adopting the arguments of modern anarchism (the pluralism of the many).

There has been a tendency for humanists to overemphasize collective responsibility because of their commitment to collectivism, planning, and the denial of personal responsibility before God and man. On the other hand, there has been a tendency among Bible-believing Christians to overemphasize the case for individualism because of their commitment to personal salvation at the expense of social and institutional transformation and healing. They want to restrict the limits of God's salvation because they do not want the responsibility of applying God's law to society. Thus, they have denied the rule of God's law outside Christian churches and Christian families.

They have been consistent in this anti-covenantal position by also denying that God blesses and curses nations, and other collectives, with the exception (inconsistently) of churches and families. To some degree, they still recognize the covenant in churches and families, and so they recognize God's sovereignty, His institutional authority and hierarchy, His law, His judgment, and His continuity of relationships over time. But by denying that God rules over national and cultural collectives, modern Christians have denied the covenant. This has left humanists in control of politics, education, the media, and just about everything else.

There is no doubt that each person stands alone on judgment day. He is not judged by a committee (unless we mean the Trinity), nor do other human committee members stand at his side and take some of the blame. This accurate vision of final judgment has led Christians to a false conclusion: Since God judges individuals as individuals *outside of history*, He therefore judges only individuals inside history. But the testimony of the Old Testament is very different: It describes the judgments of God against nations and collectives far more often than His judgments against individuals.

New Testament Judgments

It could be argued that in the New Testament, God's relationship to men has changed. Now He judges only individuals. But then how can we make sense out of the fall of the Roman Empire? Daniel prophesied that God's kingdom would crush the fourth empire, Rome.

You, O king, were looking and behold, there was a single great statue; that statue, which was large and of extraordinary splendor, was standing in front of you, and its appearance was awesome. The head of that statue was made of fine gold, its breast and its arms of silver, its belly and thighs of bronze, its legs of iron, its feet partly of iron and partly of clay. You continued looking until a stone was cut out without hands, and it struck the statue on its feet of iron and clay, and crushed them. Then the iron, the clay, the bronze, the silver and the gold were crushed all at the same time, and became like chaff from the summer threshing floors; and the wind carried them away so that not a trace of them was found. But the stone that struck the statue became a great mountain and filled the whole earth (Daniel 2:31-35).

What was the interpretation of the king's dream? Nebuchadnezzar, king of Babylon, was the head of gold, the greatest king. There would be three kingdoms after his, ending with the fourth, which was iron, breaking all other kingdoms and consolidating them in clay and iron (vv. 40-42). "And in the days of those kings the God of heaven will set up a kingdom which will never be destroyed, and that kingdom will not be left for another people; it will crush and put to an end all these kingdoms, but it will itself endure forever" (v. 44).

Christ established His kingdom in history, as manifested by (but not encompassed by) the church. This took place during the Roman Empire. The fulfillment of this prophecy came as the Roman Empire disintegrated, rival emperors fought each other, and the church became the only institution with enough strength to pull society out of the chaos that Rome became. This happened three centuries after the cross. So God still deals with collectives as collectives in New Testament times, just as the prophecy of Daniel promised; "so the dream is true, and its interpretation is trustworthy" (v. 45b).

Antinomianism

Those who deny that God judges collectives in the midst of time are arguing implicitly that God does not place nations and groups under His laws. It is an argument in favor of God's law over the actions of individuals, but not over collectives. It is an argument against Biblical law: social (institutional), economic, cultural, and civil.

This sort of argument is not simply implicit in our day; it has become explicit. Christian intellectuals, especially in Christian colleges, repeat endlessly that the Bible offers no blueprints for society. Christians are regenerated, they say, but God has given His people no revealed standards or appropriate sanctions in the Bible. But what about the Old Testament standards and sanctions? These are no longer valid, the antinomians say.

Modern fundamentalists until very recently have argued the same way. Because of this, they long ago abdicated their role as God's representatives and ambassadors, and turned over the Christian colleges, Christian magazines, and other institutions to liberal intellectuals who have spent their academic lives defending the legal autonomy of today's covenant-breaking pagan antinomians, who are in fact tyrants. The pagans have set the terms of debate in every field, and Christian antinomians have agreed with the pagans' starting point: The God of the Bible is irrelevant to the terms of discourse. A God who does not judge in history according to His law is irrelevant to history.

Sanctification

Moral regeneration is a fact of conversion. But how is it to be understood? We know that Christ died for the sins of all mankind, because only His death satisfied God's covenantal stipulations governing man. History went forward after Adam's sin only because God looked forward in time to the cross, and then He imputed this perfection of Christ's humanity, as well as His death and resurrection, back to all mankind. He does not bring all men to saving grace, but He certainly gives all men gifts that they do not deserve on their own merits. He brings rain and sunshine on all mankind (Matthew 5:45). He does this only because His wrath has been placated by Christ's work on the cross. Thus, God is "the

Savior of all men, *especially* of believers" (1 Timothy 4:10b).[1]

So all men are sanctified—set apart—in history in the limited sense that *for a time*, they are set apart from God's perfect judgment. They are given time, what we can call a stay of execution. Christ's death and resurrection are the basis of this stay of execution for the covenant-breakers. Nothing else will suffice.

When a man is regenerated by God's grace (Ephesians 2:8-10), God *imputes* Christ's perfection to him—not Christ's divinity, but His perfect humanity. God says, in effect, "I declare you not guilty, for I will look on My Son's perfect righteousness and His sacrificial death instead of looking at you." This is a *judicial act*. God *declares* us not guilty. He does so on the basis of Christ's *objective* fulfillment of God's *objective* law. Christ's moral perfection is therefore imputed to man. We call this perfection *definitive sanctification*.

Yet Christians still sin. Paul writes about running a good race (1 Corinthians 9:24-26) and fighting the good fight (1 Timothy 6:12). Life is a struggle—a moral (ethical) struggle. We attempt in history to conform our lives progressively to the image of Christ's perfection. To deny that we are still sinners is to make liars of ourselves: "If we say that we have no sin, we are deceiving ourselves, and the truth is not in us" (1 John 1:8). So this struggle to improve our lives, so that we will measure up to Christ's perfection, never ends until we die. We call this *progressive sanctification*.

Then, at the day of judgment, God declares us righteous again, and rewards us in terms of our works (1 Corinthians 3:10-14). Of course, our ability to do these works is itself given to us by God's grace (Ephesians 2:10). So there is final moral sanctification. We call this *final sanctification*.

We preach all three kinds of personal sanctification: definitive, progressive, and final. If we did not preach definitive sanctification, we could not explain how we pass from death to life, how God makes us new creatures. If we did not preach progressive personal sanctification, we could not explain why sin does not

---

1. Gary North, *Common Grace and Dominion* (Tyler, Texas: Institute for Christian Economics, 1987).

immediately kill us. We also could not explain the rewards God gives to each of us on the day of judgment because of our individual acts of righteousness. We need a doctrine of final sanctification to enable us to escape final judgment: God declares at the end of history that His gift of salvation to us was valid.

Collective Sanctification

Collectives do not have souls to bless or curse. Nevertheless, they do have effects in history, as we have seen. God judges them in history, as we have also seen. But if He judges them, then this judgment must be in terms of their performance, for good or evil. The collective sins of Sodom cried out to God. What else can this mean but that God decided that all the sins of Sodom, taken as a cultural unit, deserved judgment in history as a warning to future societies?

Each person has gifts and weaknesses. Each person's sins and successes are in terms of his gifts and environment, including his historical opportunities for good and evil. God judges us in terms of what we know, say, and do. This is what personal history is all about.

We use the same line of argumentation concerning collectives. Each society or separated (set apart) group has its specialized gifts and weaknesses. Each society's sins and successes are in terms of the collective gifts and environment in that society, including its historical opportunities for good and evil. God judges societies in terms of what its members know, say, and do. This is what national history is all about.

We recognize that some men are morally superior to others. The civil government (a collective responsibility, such as juries) punishes convicted criminals (individuals) for their sinful actions. Other people get rewards, such as medals or public praise. History therefore has meaning. It makes a difference in history how people live. This difference is reflected in the judgments of men and God in history.

We also recognize that some societies are better than others. One civil government punishes another (evil nations) in wartime

for certain kinds of sinful actions. Other nations get rewards, such
as military spoils or special trading rights. Historians write well of
the victors. History therefore has meaning. It makes a difference
in history how collectives live. This difference is reflected in the
judgments of men and God in history.

Thus, we have to conclude that in some sense, God imputes
Christ's righteousness to collectives. He certainly does this to the
church. He presumably does this with nations. If he didn't, then
why has He judged them in history the way He judged Sodom
and Gomorrah? The blessings and cursings of Deuteronomy 28
include military victories (v. 7) or defeats (v. 25). Military events
take place to collectives. A bad general makes decisions that affect
his troops. Satan is just such a bad general, and his troops have
suffered and will suffer again. The point is, collective judgments
come in the midst of history: blessings and cursings.

Victimless Crimes

A popular argument today is that the State should not enforce
laws against pornography, prostitution, homosexuality, gambl-
ing, and even drug abuse because such acts are voluntary acts between (or among) consenting adults. So long as they do not affect
anyone who is not a party to the transaction, there should be no
laws against such acts.

What is the Biblical response? That *God judges sin*. Sexual sins
are seen in the Bible as sins of idolatry. The whole Book of Hosea
is built around this theme. There is no such thing as a victimless
crime. If society allows rampant public sin to go on without sanctions against it, it (a collective) has thereby *sanctioned these sins*. Its
members have collectively *covenantally* declared: "We are not concerned about God's righteous requirements for us as individuals;
we will continue in our sins."

The result, as venereal disease testifies throughout history, is
the judgment of God in history. In our day, AIDS threatens to become God's judgment against a society that has neglected His
laws regarding homosexuality. Because God sees and hears, and
because sins "cry out to God" in history, *there can be no such thing as a*

"victimless" crime. Crime is crime. Crime is an attack on God, a defiance of His law. Adam and Even sinned in private. They were "consenting adults." But they sinned against God. They were punished by God, and as representatives for all humanity, they brought sin and judgment into our lives.

God expects lawfully constituted civil governments to restrain public evil. God's wrath will come upon any society that allows public evil to go on without opposition from the civil government. He will bring horribly painful judgments on those who do not participate in such sins, but who are governed by evil rulers. This is what happened to the seven thousand righteous Jews who went into captivity to the Babylonians.

Ruler of the Nations

A ruler is a tool that establishes the limits of measurement. We call it a ruler because it limits us. But without the limits imposed by units of measurement, we would be blind. We could not exercise dominion. We would be "flying blind." The limits imposed by a ruler is the basis of our freedom.

Similarly, a ruling official imposes limits. He enforces the law. In the case of God, the law is imposed by the Enforcer. God is the Law-maker and the Judge. He is also the jury. He is the witness. But aren't there supposed to be at least two witnesses to convict a person? Yes, and there are: Father, Son, and Holy Spirit.

We say that God rules the nations. This must mean that He rules the nations *in history*. If so, then this means that God *judges* the nations in history. Any ruler who refuses to impose his judgment on those under his authority has abdicated. He has resigned his office. Or else he has died.

"God is dead!" a few silly but consistent pagan theologians shouted to the world for about two years, 1966-68. For a brief moment in history, intellectuals played openly with "death of God" theology. The fad faded rapidly, but in reality, modern man acts as though he really does believe that God is dead. So did pagan man. So did Adam in his sin.

Such a challenge really affirms the death of man. A person

does not challenge the God of the Bible unless he is suicidal. Man knows who God is, Paul writes in the first chapter of Romans, but man rebelliously worships the creature rather than the Creator (vv. 18-23). So when men act as though God is dead, they call God's wrath down on them. They commit suicide. On the day that Adam ate of the tree of the knowledge of good and evil, he did surely die, and killed his posterity with him.

If we do not preach to men that God judges individuals, groups, and nations *in history* then we are adopting the false doctrine that God has abdicated His office and has stepped down from His throne. He may step back to His throne on judgment day, or sometime during an earthly millennium in which Jesus physically returns to rule visibly on earth, but until then, we are saying, "There is no heavenly ruler of the nations."

This leaves the office of judge open and the throne empty. Guess who will rush to the empty throne? Man. More specifically, power-seeking elitists who want to play God.

There must always be judgment in history. The question is: Whose? God's or man's?

Summary

We have to affirm the Trinity. We have to affirm the equal ultimacy of the One and the Many. We have to affirm the reality of individuals and collectives. We therefore have to affirm the reality of God's judgments in history against individuals and collectives. This is the message of the covenant.

Sodom and Gomorrah were judged in the midst of their sins, in the midst of history. God sent no prophet to warn them. They were responsible before God for their sins, and in the midst of prosperity, the day of doom came upon them.

God judges collectives. He will sometimes spare an evil collective for the sake of a few righteous people. But eventually judgment comes in history, and the righteous minority suffers. God judges collectives as collectives.

The nations have broken God's covenant and have transgressed His law, Isaiah warned. Thus, they are always ripe for historic judgment. Their citizens may pretend that they do not recognize God's claim on them, but they cannot play pretend forever. Eventually, judgment comes.

Individualism denies the covenant. It denies that God judges collectives in the midst of time. Without covenant sanctions by God against nations, there can be no doctrine of covenant law over nations. Thus, individualism results in social antinomianism.

There must be sanctification of individuals: definitive, progressive, and final. There must also be sanctification of collectives: definitive and progressive, though not final (day of final judgment). This is the basis of all history, which includes individuals and collectives.

There is no such thing as a victimless crime. A crime is a crime against God primarily, and man secondarily. Thus, the State should enforce God's laws, even if the violators are "consenting adults."

A God who does not bring judgments against nations in history is not the ruler of the nations. If He is the ruler of the nations, then He does bring judgment against individuals and collectives. He does so in terms of His laws that govern individuals and collectives.

In summary:

1. God judged Babel, Sodom, and Gomorrah.
2. God therefore judged nations other than Israel.
3. Responsibility is collective.
4. God has promised in the past to protect a whole society for the sake of a few righteous people.
5. He spared Judah for the sake of one righteous king.
6. The prophets warned pagan nations that they should repent.
7. Individualism denies the covenant.
8. God judges only individuals on judgment day (Revelation 20:11-15).
9. He judges nations and groups within history.
10. A denial of collective judgment usually is accompanied by a denial of God's law for collectives (blueprints).

11. Sanctification (God's setting apart morally) applies to individuals and also to collectives.

12. There is no such thing as a victimless moral crime.

13. A measuring ruler is a tool of dominion; so is a government ruler. Both impose *limits*.

14. God judges nations in history for disobeying His limits.

15. God has not abdicated His office as ruler in history.

5

CALL NO MAN YOUR FATHER

> And do not call anyone on earth your father; for One is your Father, He who is in heaven. And do not be called leaders; for One is your Leader, that is Christ (Matthew 23:9, 10).

Before the Bible will be used as the blueprint for civil government, Christians will have to repudiate the promise made by politicians: "We will take care of you."

God is the source of our protection. He alone can provide true safety—from invaders, criminals, famine, pestilence, and all the other judgments that happen to men. Most important, He protects His people from the final judgment of hell. God alone is our Father in heaven. We have no father in Washington, London, Paris, Moscow, or any other national capital.

Most modern advocates of the caretaker State, meaning the paternal State, believe that the only hope for mankind is the citizen's relinquishing of personal responsibility and handing more and more authority over to the "experts" who work in the bureaucratic halls of civil government. Some have called this "womb to tomb" security. This is the false security of the prison cell. Any society that seeks to substitute the State for God will eventually find itself enslaved. There is no freedom apart from Jesus Christ and His saving grace. There is no freedom apart from God's covenant. Our long-term safety is assured by God to us if we are covenantally faithful. This is the fifth point of the Biblical covenant: continuity. Nothing else can give our work continuity. Only God shows mercy to His people for thousands of generations, *if they keep His commandments* (Exodus 20:6).

Our Father

It is no accident that God is called "Our Father." God, because He is our Father, gives us "life and breath and all things" (Acts 17:25). God is our Father by *creation*. The State has not called us into existence. (The State also cannot end our eternal existence, just our physical existence.) "Life, Liberty, and the Pursuit of Happiness" are not given to us by the State; rather, they are an "endowment," gifts from God's gracious hand to be *protected* and *secured* by the State. When the State refuses to do this, it becomes a thief, or an accomplice of thieves.

God is our Father because *He gives life and takes it away:* "Naked I came from my mother's womb, and naked I shall return there. The LORD gave and the LORD has taken away. Blessed be the name of the LORD" (Job 1:21). The State has nothing to give but that which it first takes.

God is our Father in that *His Words are our sustenance*. All the promises of provision made by the State are temporary: "Man shall not live on bread alone, but on every word that proceeds out of the mouth of God" (Matthew 4:4; cf. Deuteronomy 8:3). Jesus cited this verse when the devil asked Him to turn stones into bread as a sign of His miraculous power (Matthew 4:4). But Christianity is not based on magic; it is based on the Word of God. It is based on *ethics*, not manipulation.

If we want earthly wealth, we are to work hard and faithfully, saving for the future, thereby seeking the kingdom of God in a lawful manner. This message is repeated over and over in the Book of Proverbs. There is no legitimate substitute, especially not theft. Yet today's society is based on the politics of theft: "Thou shalt not steal, except by majority vote." Such a view of civil government is immoral. God wants us to look to Him for provision, not to the State:

> All the commandments that I am commanding you today you shall be careful to do, that you may live and multiply, and go in and possess the land which the LORD swore to give to your forefathers. And you shall remember all the way which the LORD your

God has led you in the wilderness these forty years, that He might humble you, testing you, to know what was in your heart, whether you would keep His commandments or not. And He humbled you and let you be hungry, and fed you with manna which you did not know, nor did your fathers know, that He might make you understand that man does not live by bread alone, but man lives by everything that proceeds out of the mouth of the LORD. Your clothing did not wear out on you, nor did your foot swell these forty years. *Thus you are to know in your heart that the LORD your God was disciplining you just as a man disciplines his son* (Deuteronomy 8:1-6).

Nearly every time Israel was in need of provisions, they wanted to go back to Egypt, back to the imagined security of a fatherly State. When the freed Israelite slaves were hungry, instead of turning to God their Father for provision, they turned to the supposed security of tyrannical Egypt: "Would that we had died by the LORD's hand in the land of Egypt, when we sat by the pots of meat, when we ate bread to the full; for you have brought us out into this wilderness to kill this whole assembly with hunger" (Exodus 16:3). Their god was their appetite (Philippians 3:19): "For such men are slaves not of our Lord Jesus Christ but of their own appetites" (Romans 16:19).

Finally, God is our Father in that He redeems us. In one sense, God is the Father of all. But in a very special sense, God is Father only to His adopted children. Jesus called the Pharisees children of their father the devil because they repudiated His redeeming work (John 8:31-47). We are adopted children who can now cry out, "Abba! Father!" (Romans 7:15).

God Feeds Us

God fed the Israelites in the wilderness, and yet they sought the supposed security of Egypt instead of the freedom and security they had with God as their Father. Even after God provided them the food they needed, they still grumbled. Egypt still seemed attractive. "And the rabble who were among them had greedy desires; and also the sons of Israel wept again and said, 'Who will

give us meat to eat? We remember the fish which we used to eat
free in Egypt, the cucumbers and the melons and the leeks and
the onions and the garlic, but now our appetite is gone. There is
nothing at all to look at except this manna'" (Numbers 11:4-6).
They were, in essence, saying, "You can't beat security . . . three
meals a day . . . a roof over our heads . . . steady work . . . .
'Slavery?' That's such an unpleasant word . . . . We always knew
where our next meal was coming from. . . . That's security." No,
that's a dog's life.

Did you catch what they said? They actually believed that
these things had been "free" in Egypt. Free? They had been
slaves! They had paid for these things with their own lives. A
return to Egypt meant bondage to a system where they had no
voice in the way they lived. There was no future for them in
Egypt. Their children's children would be slaves, called into service to build a civilization to the glory of Pharaoh. Marching on to
Canaan meant a promised land "flowing with milk and honey"
where they could build a civilization based on the blueprint laid
out in Scripture for the glory of God and as a beacon to the nations (cf. Deuteronomy 4).

Slaves or Servants

In both Hebrew and Greek, the word for "servant" is the same
as the word for "slave." Yet we know that it is better to be a servant
than a slave. What is the difference, Biblically speaking?

All men are servants by nature. We are creatures made in
God's image. We are made to serve God, and therefore we are
made to *rule* in the name of God (Genesis 1:26-28), under the law
of God (Deuteronomy 8), always in light of the fact that we will be
judged by God (Revelation 20:11-15). We are creatures, not the
Creator. God alone is not a servant by nature. He is the Master
by nature—His own self-existent Nature.

What about slavery? *Slavery is the demonic imitation of service to
God.* It is service to a creature, Satan, the enemy of God. He, too,
seeks servants, but service to him necessarily involves bondage to
sin. Those who reject God as loving Master will eventually seek

another lord: Beelzebub, "lord of the flies." When men rebel against God, they are rejecting God as their Lord and Master. In doing so, they fall under the mastery of sin and ultimately under mere men as their rulers.

Slaves to the State

We should not expect God's covenant people to choose being slaves to the State over freedom in Christ: "If therefore the Son shall make you free, you shall be free indeed" (John 8:36). The status that the Christian has is no longer one of abject slavery but of servant-sonship: "God has sent forth the Spirit of His Son into our hearts, crying, 'Abba! Father!' Therefore you are no longer a slave, but a son; and if a son, then an heir through God" (Galatians 4:6, 7).

When the people reject God as their King, they once again adopt the slave mentality. They look for security outside of Christ. There are always powerful men who are ready, willing, and able to accommodate this evil search, and such men find their way to the exercise of power: the State. They seek political slaves. They find them, too. Instead of turning to God in repentance, slave mentality people turn to political rulers for earthly security, even after God warns them of the consequences of their rejection of Him (1 Samuel 8:7).

A Prophet's Neglected Warning

What the Bible teaches is that *sin is the first step toward slavery.* The story of Israel is one long testimony of the truth of this cause-and-effect relationship. Israel never learned the truth of the story, and so God scattered them, again and again. Eventually, He took the kingdom from them and gave it to the hated gentiles (Christ's church), who would bring forth righteous fruits (Matthew 21:43).

During the period of the Judges, all the governing institutions of Israel had become corrupt: from the individual in self-government, where "every man did what was right in his own eyes" (Judges 17:6), to the judges in civil government who "did not walk in [Samuel's ways], but turned aside after dishonest gain and took bribes and perverted justice" (1 Samuel 8:3). Even the church, the priesthood, was corrupt: "Now the sons of Eli [who were priests] were worthless men; they did not know the LORD and the custom of the priests with the people" (1 Samuel 2:12, 13).

The corruption of the individual resulted in the corruption of family, church, and State. The nation rejected God's prescription for such wholesale corruption—repentance! Instead, they turned to Samuel and demanded a "king to judge us like all the nations" (1 Samuel 8:5). In making this demand, God told Samuel: "Listen to the voice of the people in regard to all that they say to you, for they have not rejected you, but they have rejected Me from being king over them" (1 Samuel 8:7). Their choice of security by repenting and turning to God as their Savior, Lord, and Provider was rejected. Instead, they turned to the false security offered to them by a civil government that would subject them to slavery in the name of security.

God told Samuel to warn them of the judgment they could expect. Each of the following kingly provisions is an idolatrous substitute for God's faithful provision to His people:

1. The king would raise an army for his purposes in opposition to the law (Deuteronomy 20). Samuel told the people that war would be a way of life in Israel: "He will take your sons and place them for himself in his chariots and among his horsemen and they will run before his chariots" (1 Samuel 8:11). Instead of appearing before the LORD "three times a year" as part of God's army (Exodus 23:17), the men would appear before this king "like all the nations" (1 Samuel 8:5).

2. The king would use this army for personal profit: "He will appoint for himself commanders of thousands and of fifties, and some to do his plowing and to reap his harvest and to make his weapons of war and equipment for his chariots" (1 Samuel 8:12). What was designed to benefit the nation in the organization of God's host (Exodus 18:21), would alone benefit Saul.

3. The young women of Israel would be subject to the whims and fancies of the king: "He will take your daughters for per-

fumers and cooks and bakers" (v. 13). God cares and provides for his daughters (Exodus 3:22), while Saul abuses the daughters of Israel.

4. Private property will no longer be safe. The property and labor of others will be used to pay for political favors: "He will take the best of your fields and your vineyards and your olive groves, and give them to his servants" (v. 14). What belongs to God and is given to men as a stewardship under God (Deuteronomy 6:10, 11), Saul would steal in order to increase his power and influence over the nation (cf. 1 Kings 21).

5. The king would demand a tithe in taxation—a sign of tyranny, for only God can require a tenth: "He will take a tenth of your seed and of your vineyards, and give to his officers and to his servants" (v. 15).

Eventually the people "will cry out in that day because of your king whom you have chosen for yourselves, but the LORD will not answer you in that day" (1 Samuel 8:18).

Even after Samuel warned the Israelites that the king would be a tyrant, the people still wanted a king: "Nevertheless, the people refused to listen to the voice of Samuel, and they said, 'No, but there shall be a king over us, that we also may be like all the nations, that our king may judge us and go out before us and fight our battles'" (vv. 19, 20). But God was supposed to fight their battles, not a human king: "The LORD does not deliver by sword or by spear; for the battle is the LORD's and He will give you into our hands [speaking to Goliath]" (1 Samuel 17:47).

Our modern State operates in a similar fashion. Taxes are above forty percent of national income: federal, state, and local. In some nations, taxes are above this level. In the United States, some states have a *sales tax alone* that approaches ten percent (e.g., Louisiana). Add to that a state income tax, property taxes, federal income tax, and the Social Security tax. Politicians use this tax money to bribe voters to vote for them. The poor are promised favors, governmental benefits through the tax, if they will only vote them into office. Of course, the Congress has the full force of its police power to require compliance.

Ruler of the Nations

The State's Job

What should civil government do? Are there specific tasks that the civil magistrate is required by God to perform? Certainly the State in the Bible is not pictured as a substitute father; rather, since the Fall, it is to be a judge "that does not bear the sword in vain" (Romans 13:4).

The family, church, and State are authorities ordained by God to perform tasks in their prescribed jurisdictions. The family has no authority or power to perform the tasks commissioned by God for the church and the State. The church is not called on to supplant either the family or the State in their appointed tasks. The State has no authority over families or churches as they perform their God-ordained duties. Of course, if a family member commits murder, is tried and convicted, then the State is duty-bound to execute the murderer. But the church has a task to perform as well; it must "restore the brother" (Matthew 18).

The State is God's "minister," taking vengeance out on those who do "evil" (Romans 13:3-4). Even if there were no Fall, however, the State would have been necessary as a ministry of social order. For example, the State probably has legitimate jurisdiction to build and keep up roads (Deuteronomy 19:3) and enforce local land use contracts (Numbers 35:1-8). But many believe we need a strong central government to guarantee the redistribution of income to provide for the economic welfare of all, the instruction of the citizenry through tax dollars and compulsory education laws, the subsidizing of failing business enterprises, and the capping of prices to "protect" the citizenry against "unfair" prices.

If we believe the State is to be a substitute parent, then we must recognize that those who desire to create a State with this in mind will use the sword to see that their goals are enacted. The power of the sword will be used to exact the needed money to pay for these "free services."

More often than not, the State becomes an advocate for highly influential political groups. The tax money of the many is used to establish the goals of the few. Promises are made to citizens. For votes from their constituency, political favors are granted by those running for office. Of course, it's usually done under the slogan of "taxing the rich in order to help the poor." These political step-fathers set a trap for the dependent. In time, the politically dependent get "hooked" on the favors from a supposed benevolent State. Slavery is the result. The dependency habit is hard to break. More and more promises are made, and fewer freedoms are secured by civil law. Where individuals, families, and churches had authority and power, the State has now moved in and supplanted their God-ordained jurisdictions, all in the name of freedom, security, and greater efficiency. This is why the Bible is very specific as to what the civil magistrate ought to do. Before a nation will have good *civil* government, a nation must have good *self*-government.

Civil Justice

Let's establish the Biblical guidelines for the operation of the State in society. First, civil government should operate *judicial systems* on the local, state, and national levels. The law of God, as outlined in Scripture, is to be the standard of justice. If the accused does not believe justice has been done, he can appeal his case to a higher court. He can move from a local jurisdiction to, say, the county, state, or a district court that encompasses a section of the nation. Finally, he can appeal to the Supreme Court. In each case, however, Scripture is to be the standard of justice.

A judicial system can operate only so long as the majority of the citizenry are self-governed. Our nation's courts would be swamped and justice perverted if the majority were lawless. We are now seeing the breakdown in law and order, a backlog of court cases, and bulging prisons. Self-government is being repudiated by a growing segment in our nation. The best courts and the most just judges cannot deal with the abandonment of self-government.

Weights and Measures

Second, the State must ensure the maintenance of "just weights and measures." God considers tampering with weights and measures to be "violence and destruction" (Ezekiel 45:9). Men are not permitted even to *own* false weights and measures: "You shall not have in your bag differing weights, a large and a small. You shall not have in your house differing measures, a large and a small" (Deuteronomy 25:13, 14). Again, a Biblical monetary system can only work when the people are self-governed, when they do not cheat, pilfer, falsely advertise, or appeal to their civil representatives to create laws that favor them in their business dealings.

When civil governments abandon basic Biblical laws relating to economics, the people suffer. Inflation of the currency, by abandoning gold and silver as the monetary standard and "creating" money to fund non-Biblical political projects, especially hurts the poor: "Your silver has become dross, your drink diluted with water. *Your rulers are rebels, and companions of thieves; every one loves a bribe, and chases after rewards. They do not defend the orphan, nor does the widow's plea come before them*" (Isaiah 1:22, 23).

Defending Christianity from Public Attack

Third, the Christian religion should be protected against those who would seek to destroy it. The State cannot be neutral toward the Christian faith. Any obstacle that would jeopardize the preaching of the Word of God and carrying out the Great Commission must be removed by civil government. Civil rulers should have the interests of "godliness" and "dignity" in mind as they administer justice. This is why Paul instructs Christians to pray for their rulers, so "that we [Christians] may lead a tranquil and quiet life in all godliness and dignity" (1 Timothy 2:2).

Many wish to maintain that the State must be religiously and morally neutral. The Bible makes no such suggestion. Even our Constitution assumes the protection of the *Christian* religion. The First Amendment had the specific purpose of excluding all rivalry among *Christian* denominations. Paul expected even the Roman civil government to protect him from those who threatened the Christian religion (Acts 23:12-31; cf. 25:11). This means civil government cannot be religiously neutral. If the Christian religion is not defended, then some other religion will be, usually a State religion that degenerates into secularism. The State cannot be neutral toward all religions because all religious views or philosophies necessarily entail uncompromising moral systems, and this guarantees conflict with those of other religious systems. If the State were truly "neutral," it would enact no laws, for each law would penalize someone's religion or religious view or religious practice.

National Defense

Fourth, the civil magistrate, given the power of the sword, is obligated to defend the nation against national and international aggressors. (See Albion Knight's book, *Chariots of God* in this series.) Peace, however, can only be realized through the life-transforming gospel of Jesus Christ. This is the element of self-government. Peace with God brings about peace with others: "Never pay back evil for evil to anyone. Respect what is right in the sight of all men. If possible, so far as it depends on you, be at peace with all men" (Romans 13:17, 18; cf. 5:1). Genuine and lasting peace will not come through law, force, political promises or compromises, the elimination of poverty, worldwide "public education," or the establishment of a one-world humanistic government.

Praying for peace, as an aspect of self-government, is no substitute for the preaching of the gospel so that the nations are discipled according to the Word of Jesus Christ (Matthew 28:18-20). Wars are not the result of environmental factors. Rather, they are the result of man's inherent sinfulness: "What is the source of quarrels and conflicts among you? Is not the source your pleasures that wage war in your members? You lust and do not have; so you commit murder. And you are envious and cannot obtain; so you fight and quarrel . . ." (James 4:1-2).

Does this mean that a nation should not defend itself against the sinful military advancements of aggressive nations? The Bible takes evil and the reality of war seriously (Nehemiah 4:7-18; Ecclesiastes 3:8; Joel 3:10; Matthew 24:6, 7; Luke 11:21, 22; 14:31, 32); it recognizes that if men will war with God they certainly will war with other men. Under certain circumstances the individual is given the authority to attack and kill an intruder (Exodus 22:2). The civil magistrate is God's "avenger who brings wrath upon the one who practices evil" (Romans 13:4). The civil magistrate's symbol of authority is the "sword," an instrument of death (Romans 13:4). Israel was commanded to have an army of armed men (Deuteronomy 20). While peace is what we all desire, war often is a reality we must face and prepare for.

Quarantine

Fifth, civil government has the power to quarantine, to protect human life. Plagues can race through whole populations because of the infectious nature of the diseases transmitted through casual and sexual contact. The individual with the infectious disease "shall live alone" (Leviticus 13:46). Even his home can be "quarantined" after "an inspection" (Leviticus 14:33-53). If the disease is not abated, then even his house can be torn down (vv. 39-42). The State is given legislative power to deal with plagues, epidemics, venereal diseases, and other contagious and dangerous diseases like Acquired Immune Deficiency Syndrome (AIDS).

Defining and Defending Private Property

Sixth, civil government has the duty to protect private property. When individuals, families, churches, and business establishments possess property, they have an area of liberty and dominion that is beyond the reach of men with greater power and influence. The Bible is explicit about how property is to be acquired. Confiscation through State power is not legitimate. The commandments "You shall not steal" (Exodus 20:15) and "You shall not covet" (Exodus 20:17) are meaningless unless there are prior owners who are secure in their right to hold the land. When Naboth refused to sell his land to king Ahab, the king devised a plot to kill Naboth in order to confiscate his land: "Arise, take possession of the vineyard of Naboth, the Jezreelite, which he refused to give you for money" (1 Kings 21:15).

The individual in self-government must assist the police pow-

ers by securing their homes against theft, developing neighborhood watch groups, and taking courses in self-defense. The "citizen's arrest" is also an aspect of self-government. A police State is
difficult to generate if the people take responsibility for their actions and do not look to the State as the only protecting agency.
Big Brother's influence increases when we fail to watch out for
ourselves and the well-being of our neighbors.

Off Limits

A careful reading of Scripture will show that the State, or civil
government, has almost no authority in the areas of education,
business, welfare, and ecclesiastical affairs. For example, the only
time education of children is taken on by the State is when the
people of God are held captive by a pagan government (Daniel
1:1-7). Jurisdiction of education is given to parents (Deuteronomy
6:4-9). A legitimate educational function of the State would be
military academies.

Caring for widows is another concern. The responsibility first
lies with family members. This is why Paul makes a distinction
between "widows indeed," or those who have no family or who
have families that refuse to care for them, and widows who have
family members who can help out: "Honor widows who are widows indeed; but if any widow has children or grandchildren, let
them first learn to practice piety in regard to their own family, and
to make some return to their parents; for this is acceptable in the
sight of God. Now she who is a widow, indeed, and who has been
left alone has fixed her hope on God, and continues in entreaties
and prayers night and day" (1 Timothy 5:3-5). The church is to
step in and help those widows "who are widows indeed." Their
hope is fixed "on God." The church is God's special representative
on earth. God's provision comes through the church in tithes and
offerings of the people. The State can best help widows by not taxing inheritances.

Some of Jesus' harshest words are for children who put their
parents' lives in jeopardy. He pronounces the death penalty on
unfaithful and self-righteous children who neglect caring for their

parents: "You nicely set aside the commandment of God in order to keep your tradition. For Moses said, 'Honor your father and your mother'; and, 'He who speaks evil of father or mother, let him be put to death'" (Mark 7:9, 10). The apostle Paul says that those who fail to care for their own family members are "worse than unbelievers" (1 Timothy 5:8).

The State is not called on to feed the hungry and clothe the naked except as wartime measures. You will not find instructions given to the State to establish a welfare system. What the State ought to do is keep the market place open. This would mean the abolition of minimum wage laws that keep the less skilled from entering the work force; the reduction of taxes at all levels; the elimination of Social Security taxes on those just entering the work force (this alone would add over 14% to their income); phasing out Social Security for employers and employees already in the system; and the elimination of all entitlement programs that keep the poor dependent on the Parent State.

Summary

The fifth basic principle in the Biblical blueprint for government is that the State is not our father, provider, or savior. We're all looking for security. Now, security is not a bad thing. God wants us to find security in Him. But when man rejects God as the only Sovereign Lord and Savior, he turns to some other "higher power" to fill the vacuum.

There are those who are convinced that a better society can be created and maintained by turning over nearly all authority, power, and jurisdiction to benevolent caretakers of our souls. "God is not needed," they say. And we begin to believe it. "Just give us a little more power. . . . A bit more jurisdiction. . . . All we need is a few more tax dollars. . . . After this, you'll see the difference."

We do see the difference. The merchants of promise have an insatiable appetite for control. There is never enough money to do want they claim needs to be done. So they're back again for more money. In all of this God is rejected as our Father. The State no longer wields the sword. Rather, it becomes a benefactor, buying votes with the slippery voice of the promise and the transfer of wealth from the "haves" to the "have-nots."

How do these merchants of promise remain in office? We, the people, keep them there. The nation has chosen its god, and it's not Jehovah.

Christians have fallen into the trap of looking to the State as a substitute father, looking for sustenance. God is our Father. He cares for us. Turning to the State for every provision is a form of slavery. Civil Government has a very limited role, defined by God in Scripture. To go beyond those Biblical limits turns the State into God's competitor.

In Biblical terms, the State is a "minister of God," serving God by promoting the good and punishing the evil doer. The State must ensure the maintenance of "just weights and measures." The Christian religion should be protected against those who would work to destroy it. The State has the responsibility to protect the nation against internal and external aggressors. The State has the power to quarantine.

The State, because it is limited by God, does not have unlimited jurisdiction. The State does not have Biblical authority to educate or to confiscate income to fulfill some ill-conceived social agenda.

In summary:

1. God is the source of our protection.
2. The State is not our ultimate protector.
3. The modern humanist State is worshipped today as the primary provider of safety.
4. God gives life and removes it.
5. God's Word sustains us.
6. Obedience to Biblical law is the basis of long-term prosperity.
7. The Israelites kept returning to the State for their protection.
8. God feeds us.
9. All men are either slaves or servants.

10. A servant to God is a free man spiritually.

11. A servant to Satan is a slave spiritually.

12. Slavery is Satan's imitation of servitude to God.

13. Modern men are increasingly slaves to the State.

14. Sin is the first step toward slavery.

15. Samuel warned Israel against the kingly State.

16. The State's job is limited: bearing the sword (vengeance).

17. It is to dispense God's justice: punishing criminals.

18. It is to enforce honest weights and measures.

19. It is to defend Christianity from public attack.

20. It is to defend the nation from invasion.

21. It is to impose medical quarantines.

22. It is to define and protect private property.

23. It has little authority over other spheres of government, especially in the area of welfare.

6

JESUS ALONE POSSESSES DIVINE RIGHTS

And on His robe and on His thigh He has a name written,
'KING OF KINGS, AND LORD OF LORDS' (Revelation 19:15).

When nations refuse to acknowledge God's rule (God = *theos*, rule = *kratos*), meaning God's universal government, He promises sure judgment: "Now therefore, O kings, show discernment; take warning, O judges of the earth. Worship the LORD with reverence, and rejoice with trembling. Do homage to the Son, lest He become angry, and you perish in the way, for His wrath may soon be kindled. How blessed are all who take refuge in Him" (Psalm 2:10-12). "Homage to the Son" has reference to the Lord Jesus Christ and to His written Word. Jesus instructed His disciples to "make disciples of all the nations" (Matthew 28:19). Jesus' great commission will result in the nations paying homage to Him, the Son, by observing all He commanded (v. 20).

Who is a king? In the Bible, the king is the one who lays down the law. He possesses the sovereign authority to require all those under his jurisdiction to obey. He tells them what they are allowed to do, and then he polices their behavior. The heavenly King is the only king who lays down the law to all men, and who is present with all men always, to see if they obey.

In the Old Testament, God did not reserve His commandments for just the nation Israel and the church. Scripture makes it clear that all kings in Israel were to *copy the law* in the presence of the Levitical priests, so the rulers would be careful to observe every word of the law (Deuteronomy 17:18, 19).

85

Even nations outside Israel were required to follow the law as it was given to the nation Israel. This is a controversial statement. If the nations of the Old Testament world were supposed to obey God's civil law, then it becomes more difficult to argue that nations of the New Testament world are not under the same obligation. But what is the evidence that nations in the Old Testament were to be governed by God's law? The best evidence is this: *God judged them.*

Sodom and Gomorrah were destroyed because they broke the law of God (Genesis 13:13).

God commanded the prophet Jonah to preach to the Ninevites (Assyrians) because their wickedness had come up before God (Jonah 1:2). The reason is clear: "There shall be one standard for you; it shall be for the stranger as well as the native, for I am the LORD your God" (Leviticus 24:22).

The prophet Amos set forth the coming judgment of God to Damascus, Gaza, Tyre, Edom, Ammon, and Moab. These non-Israelite nations stood accountable for their transgressions: "For three transgressions . . . and for four I will not revoke its punishment" (Amos 1:3, 6, 9, 13; 2:l). Non-Israelite nations were to be judged along with Judah and Israel (Amos 2:4, 6). There is one law and one Lawgiver. The One who gives the law is the sovereign Lord of history — all of history, not just Israel's history and not just the church's history.

The Law Established

The New Testament shows a similar emphasis, as we should expect. The God of the New Testament is the God of the Old Testament. We must not adopt a "two gods" view of history, with a mean, evil, tyrannical god in the Old Testament, and a sweet, kind, "devil may care, but I don't" god of the New Testament. God does not change (Malachi 3:6); therefore, His law does not change (Matthew 5:17-20).

Though Christians do not make blood sacrifices as remission for sins, we do keep this Old Testament law in Christ. We take holy communion, in which the wine becomes the sacrificial equivalent of His blood. The Bible states that "all things are cleansed with blood, and without shedding of blood there is no forgiveness" (Hebrews 9:22; cf. Leviticus 17:11). Shed blood is still required, but Jesus became our perfect and final sacrifice for sins: "[B]ut now once at the consummation of the ages He has been manifested to put away sin by the sacrifice of Himself" (Hebrews 9:26). All ceremonial laws, laws applied to the redemptive work of Christ, are fulfilled when an individual repents of his sin and unconditionally surrenders himself to Jesus.

The redemptive work of Jesus does not free us from an obligation to keep the moral and civil laws laid down in the Bible, however. Scripture shows no instance of an individual, Christian or pagan, who is free to ignore these laws. We are freed from the "curse of the law" (Galatians 3:13), but not from the guidance of the law: "Do we then nullify the Law through faith? May it never be! On the contrary, we establish the Law" (Romans 3:31). Of course, the non-Christian is free neither from the curse of the law nor from its demands: "He who believes in Him is not judged; he who does not believe has been judged already, because he has not believed in the name of the only begotten Son of God" (John 3:18).

Turmoil that reaches our newspaper headlines can be traced to repudiating the saving work of Jesus Christ and denying His law as a standard for the nations. Man first sinned by rejecting the absolute government of God. Adam and Eve attempted to interpret life by their own standards. What is true for individuals is multiplied for the nations.

Christianity threatens all totalitarian regimes because the Christian citizen's ultimate allegiance belongs to God, who rules all earthly kingdoms and who calls those who rule to rule according to laws set forth in Scripture, rather than by the whims of men.

Daniel's prophetic dream depicted the character of nations that opposed the ordinances of God and their eventual destruction. The kingdoms were humanistic, anthropocentric (man-centered), kingdoms: "You, O king, were looking and behold, there was a single great statue" of a man (Daniel 2:31). God brought an end to man's attempt to rule without His saving work and law structure by crushing the colossus: "Then the iron, the clay, the bronze, the silver and the gold were crushed all at the same time, and became like chaff from the summer threshing floors; and the wind carried them away so that not a trace of them was found" (v. 35).

The Conflict Over Kingship

The Roman Empire presents a classic historical example of the Messianic man-centered State, of the denial of God's Law, and of the implementation of humanistic law. The Caesars declared themselves gods, and their decrees were acknowledged as the laws of gods. Because of each Caesar's false claim of divinity, his limited reign was threatened by God's unlimited and universal reign. Peter declared confidently "that there is salvation in no one else; for there is no other name under heaven that has been given among men, by which we must be saved" (Acts 4:12). The gospel of Jesus Christ, with its claim of divine prescriptions, threatened the very nature of the Roman State. Rome had to submit itself to the position of "minister" *under* God or be crushed by the power *of* God. Rome did not submit.

Early Christians were accused of "acting contrary to the decrees of Caesar, saying that there is another king, Jesus" (Acts 17:7). There is no evidence that the early church advocated that people act contrary to the prevailing law-system, except when those laws prohibited them from worshipping and evangelizing. However, those who heard the disciples preach understood the implications of Jesus Christ's demands. If Jesus is truly the Messiah, then even the State must submit to His authority and rule: no middle or neutral ground exists. Jesus' words make it clear that only one master can claim absolute authority: "No one can serve two masters; for either he will hate the one and love the other, or he will hold to one and despise the other" (Matthew 6:24).

The State *and* God cannot both be the absolute sovereign. One must submit to the other. Obviously, the State must submit to the Lordship of Jesus Christ or perish in its attempt to overthrow His rule. Any attempt by the nations to oppose the rule of God is an act of futility. God laughs at and scorns their attempts to overthrow the advancing kingdom of Christ (cf. Psalm 2).

"The LORD reigns," declares Scripture. Notice that the reign of God is comprehensive; it knows no geographical limitation: "Say among the *nations*, 'The LORD reigns'" (Psalm 96:10). God's reign is not limited to the nation Israel. Every nation is responsible to acknowledge the reign of God. Any attempt to deny God's reign will be met with judgment:

> Why are the nations in an uproar, and the peoples devising a vain thing? The kings of the earth take their stand, and the rulers take counsel together against the LORD and against His Anointed (*Messiah*): "Let us tear their fetters apart, and cast away their cords from us!" He who sits in the heavens laughs, the LORD scoffs at them. Then He will speak to them in His anger and terrify them in His fury (Psalm 2:1-5).

The fact of God's reign terrifies those who seek to free themselves from His rightful position as the reigning monarch of all creation: "Now therefore, O kings show discernment; take warnings, O judges of the earth. Worship the LORD with reverence, and rejoice with tremblings" (vv. 10-11). No nation can claim the exclusive title reserved for the Messiah of God. All civil governments are subordinate to God and are *under* His jurisdiction.

The Bible makes it clear that "*the* government," the absolute *reign* of God, rests upon the shoulders of Jesus Christ (Isaiah 9:6, 7). This is not a future reign, but a present reality. The promise of government by the Messiah is realized at His birth: "For a child will be born to us, a son will be given to us; and the government will rest on His shoulders" (Isaiah 9:6a). Notice that "there will be no end to the increase of His government or of peace" (v. 7a). God then removes any nation standing in the way of the increase of the Messiah's government.

The nations do not influence God's decision on how He will evaluate them. The nations are in God's hands, and He controls them. Their conspiratorial desires to manipulate other nations are vain. Even Israel, God's chosen nation, is not favored when evaluated in terms of God's holy character. Because of Israel's disobedience, Jesus states that the kingdom will be taken from Israel and will be given to the Gentiles, that is, the true nation of Israel (Matthew 21:33-46; cf. Romans 9:6-8).

Isaiah describes the perspective we need when considering the actions of the nations: they are nothing more than a drop in the bucket and dust on the scales compared to the grandeur, glory, and holiness of God (Isaiah 40:15).

King by Nature

Jesus Christ is King because of Who He is. Jesus has not over-thrown another king to make His claim. He is King legally. God the Father has decreed Him to be king: "But as for Me, I have in-stalled My King upon Zion, My holy mountain" (Psalm 2:6). God has anointed and sealed Him to His regal office. God has set the crown upon His head.

Jesus has a kingly title: "He is Lord of lords and King of kings" (Revelation 17:14; 19:16). He bears the ensigns of royalty: a crown (Hebrews 2:9), a sword (Revelation 1:16; 2:16), a scepter (Hebrews 1:8), and a coat of arms (Revelation 5:5). He is called "the ruler of the kings of the earth" (Revelation 1:5). It is by Him that "kings reign" (Proverbs 8:15). His throne is everlasting (Hebrews 1:8). Even the angels worship Him: "And let all the angels of God worship Him" (Hebrews 1:6). He is the center of all a person, family, church, group, organization or nation does. He is God, the Creator and Preserver of the Universe (John 1:1; Colossians 1:17). He "upholds all things by the word of His power" (Hebrews 1:2).

Confession

Because all actions originate in the heart (Mark 7:20-23; James 4:1), acknowledging Jesus Christ as king also must begin in the heart. His kingdom is spiritual. He rules first in the hearts of men. This does not mean that He does not rule from on high, but the manifestation of His rule is supposed to be *in deep*. He sets up His throne where no earthly king does—in men's hearts. His sword, the Word of God, "is able to judge the thoughts and inten-tions of the heart" (Hebrews 4:12). No nation can survive unless

Jesus Christ is acknowledged as King and its citizens embrace Him as such personally.

The Bible emphasizes that all people are Christ's subjects in a variety of ways: *First*, Jesus speaks to Nicodemus about the necessity of a "new birth," a comprehensive transformation of the entire individual (John 3:5-7). Man is not considered "sick." He is considered *sinful*. The unregenerate sinner is "dead in trespasses and sins" (Ephesians 2:1). Only the regenerating power of the Holy Spirit can make a dead man live. The fundamental issue is ethical, not medical or psychological.

Second, the written Word of God is acknowledged as the only rule of faith and *practice*. Law is not found in the vote of the people, the decree of the courts or the pronouncement of rulers. The law of God is Christ the King's law; therefore, it must be obeyed. Moreover, being set free in Jesus Christ liberates neither citizen nor ruler from the guidance, obligations, and benefits of the law (Romans 3:31), only from the final *curse* of the law (Galatians 3:13). The consequences of broken law are well established (Deuteronomy 28:15-68).

Third, the regenerate mind is renewed (Romans 12:2). Every individual operates from a particular view of the world in mind, and evaluates all life from this perspective, meaning his chosen religious presuppositions. Prior to acknowledging Christ as King, all life is seen from man's perspective: "For as he [man] thinks within himself, so he is" (Proverbs 23:7). The new creature in Christ should evaluate life from the perspective of the Word of God, thinking God's thoughts after Him, "taking every thought captive to the obedience of Christ" (2 Corinthians 10:5).

Fourth, those who do not want Jesus as King "will wage war against the Lamb, and the Lamb will overcome them, because He is Lord of lords and King of kings, and those who are with Him are the called and chosen and faithful" (Revelation 17:14).

Separate Jurisdictions

The Bible reveals that the jurisdiction of the State and the jurisdiction of the church are to be separate, though the separation is not absolute. The Word of God transcends any absolute wall of separation some may seek to erect. For this reason, civil servants often are given religious titles. The king in Israel was the Lord's anointed set apart for a *civil* task in the same way the priest was set apart and anointed for his *ecclesiastical* (religious) task (Numbers 3:3).

David, who was to replace Saul as the Lord's anointed, respected the special office of the king: "Far be it from me because of the Lord that I should do this thing to my lord [Saul], the Lord's anointed, to stretch out my hand against him, since he is the Lord's anointed" (1 Samuel 24:6).

Those subordinates who served with David also enjoyed religious titles. His chief officers were called *priests* (2 Samuel 8:18). These were not temple priests or Levites; they were comparable to *ministers* of Romans 13:4. The reason for the title "priest" is not immediately evident until we understand that these "priests," in their governmental role, were to give *counsel* to the king. Only the title of "priest" was significant enough to give these counselors' role the importance it deserved: they were to counsel the civil minister in godly law and actions. The New Testament emphasizes a similar title for all rulers by designating them as "ministers of God" (Romans 13:4, 6).

King of All the Nations

Even outside Israel, rulers were given religious titles for civil functions. Cyrus is given the title of "shepherd." This title is usually reserved for God Himself (Isaiah 40:11; cf. John 10) and the rulers of Israel (Jeremiah 23:4), but God calls a non-Israelite "My shepherd" (Isaiah 44:28): "It is I who says of Cyrus, 'he is My shepherd! And he will perform all My desire.'" Cyrus is given an even more significant title: "Thus says the Lord to Cyrus His anointed, whom I have taken by the right hand, to subdue nations before him, and to loose the loins of kings; to open doors before him so that gates will not be shut" (45:1). The High Priest in Israel and the King are designated in the same way. Of course, it is the title for the coming deliverer, the "Messiah."

Hence, the rulers of the nations are given titles which clearly indicate that they are considered by God's Word to be *"ministers of God"* (cf. Romans 13:4, 6). Such special designations of "shepherd" and "anointed" tell us that even those rulers who do not seek to govern according to the law of God still are obligated to function in that capacity. Moreover, they will be held responsible for their actions.

The written Word of God is to be the standard for the king's rule: "Now it shall come about when he sits on the throne of his kingdom, he shall write for himself a copy of this law on a scroll in the presence of the Levitical priests. And it shall be with him, and he shall read it all the days of his life that he may learn to fear the LORD his God, by carefully observing all the words of this law and these statutes" (Deuteronomy 17:18, 19). The king, as well as his people, come under God's law.

The Divine Right of God Alone

No *Biblical* "divine right of kings," in which the king was a law unto himself, existed in Israel. To possess such a divine right means that your actions are autonomous; no one can appeal to a higher court for justice. The idea of the "divine right of kings" was challenged with great force three centuries ago by Samuel Rutherford, a Presbyterian minister who served as a commissioner at Westminster Abbey in London and rector of St. Andrew's Church in Scotland. His book *Lex, Rex* caused enough controversy to have him placed under house arrest and held for possible execution. Summoned to appear before Parliament at Edinburgh, he died before he could comply with the order.

The divine right of kings was the 17th century's version of judicial humanism. It placed the king under God, but there was no human institution to call him to account. Thus, the divine right of kings under God became a theory justifying the autonomy of the king from any other human jurisdiction. It made the king the civil manifestation of God walking on earth. There could in theory be no appeal beyond the king to God by means of any rival institution. But the theory claimed too much for the king, and it sparked a revolution. By the end of the century in England, this theory regarding kings was tossed into the historical dustbin. The "Glorious Revolution" of 1688 transferred the mythical divine right of kings to Parliament. Nine decades later, the American Revolution broke out in opposition to Parliament's taking seriously its own stolen theory.

One purpose of the civil law in the Old Testament was to see to it that the king's "heart may not be lifted above his countrymen" (v. 20). Citizens and king are to serve the same law. King Solomon prayed for "an understanding heart to judge [God's] people to discern between good and evil" (1 Kings 3:9). Solomon's standard of right and wrong was the Bible. Only when he ignored Scripture did judgment came to his kingdom. This is no less true in the New Testament, where Jesus is one with the Lord who gave Moses the law (John 10:30), and said that we are to keep His commandments (John 14:15; 15:14). By keeping Jesus' commandments, we keep the commandments of God, for Jesus is God (John 1:1).

God's standard of justice is the same for all His creatures. This includes nations that consider themselves non-Christian. Some people believe that because they do not acknowledge God as Lord and King, they somehow are exempt from following the law of God. Sodom and Gomorrah enjoyed no such exemption: "Now the men of Sodom were wicked exceedingly and sinners against God" (Genesis 13:13). This wicked city was destroyed for breaking God's law: in particular, the sin of homosexuality[1] (Genesis 19:4-5; Leviticus 18:22; 20:13). Jonah went to preach to the non-Israelite city of Nineveh because of their sins. If the Ninevites were not obligated to keep the law of God, then how could they be expected to repent (Jonah 3)? The stranger, an individual *outside* the covenant community, must obey the law of God: "There shall be one standard for you; it shall be for the stranger as well as the native, for I am the LORD your God" (Leviticus 24:22; cf. Numbers 15:16; Deuteronomy 1:16-17).

---

1. See Gary DeMar, "Homosexuality: An Illegitimate, Alternative Deathstyle," *The Biblical Worldview*, Vol. 3, No. 1, January 1987, Atlanta, Georgia: American Vision.

The law as given to Israel was a standard for nations surrounding Israel. When other nations heard of the righteous judgments within Israel, these nations remark with wonder: "Surely this great nation is a wise and understanding people" (Deuteronomy 4:6). The psalmist proclaims to the kings and judges of the earth "to take warning . . . and worship the LORD with reverence" and "do homage to the Son" (Psalm 2:10-11). Quite frequently, the other nations are called upon in the Psalms to honor God. The prophets insisted that the nations surrounding Israel would respond to His threat of historical judgment. God does not exempt other nations from the requirements of His righteousness. He holds them responsible for their sins (Amos 1:3-2:5).

The New Testament Emphasis

The New Testament presupposes the moral order laid down in what we call the "Old Testament." John the Baptist used the law of God to confront Herod in his adulterous affair: "Herod . . . had John arrested and bound in prison on account of Herodias, the wife of his brother Philip, because he had married her. For John had been saying to Herod, 'It is not lawful for you to have your brother's wife'" (Mark 6:17, 18; Leviticus 20:10; Deuteronomy 22:22). This was not mere advice. John lost his own head in the exchange.

In Romans 13, the civil magistrate is termed a "minister of God" who has the responsibility and authority to punish evildoers. As God's servants these rulers must rule God's way. Just as a minister in the church is obligated to implement the law of God as it touches on ecclesiastical matters, a civil servant must implement the law of God in civil affairs. *The determination of good and evil must derive from some objective standard.* In Hebrews 5:14, the Christian is instructed to train his senses "to discern good and evil." In Romans 13:4 the civil authorities are to wield the sword, punishing evil doers and promoting the good.

God certainly does not intend the standard of good and evil to be simply whatever a ruler autonomously desires or thinks it ought to be. The standard of good and evil is nothing less than that which the Creator, Sustainer, Ruler, and Judge of heaven and earth ordains, decrees, and declares it to be: the revealed Word and law of God.

The psalmist declares he "will speak of Thy testimonies before kings, and shall not be ashamed" (Psalm 119:46). These testimonies are the "commandments" that he loves (v. 47). Jesus informs His disciples that persecution will give them opportunity to speak "before governors and kings . . . as a testimony to them and to the Gentiles" (Matthew 10:18).

Civil servants approached John the Baptist regarding their obligations to the law of God: "Some tax-gatherers also came to be baptized, and they said to him, 'Teacher, what shall we do?' And he said to them, 'Collect no more than what you have been ordered to.' And some soldiers were questioning him, saying, 'And what about us, what shall we do?' And he said to them, 'Do not take money from anyone by force, or accuse anyone falsely, and be content with your wages'" (Luke 3:13-14). John was not appealing to them on the basis of some "neutral" law, but referred to the sixth, ninth, and tenth commandments of the Decalogue, though he did not name them as such.

An incident in Jesus' ministry shows that the Biblical laws of restitution are in force for tax thefts. Zaccheus, an unscrupulous tax collector, followed the laws of restitution by promising to pay back those he defrauded: "If I have defrauded anyone of anything, I will give back four times as much" (Luke 19:8; cf. Exodus 22:1; Leviticus 6:5). Christians are obligated to inform those who rule of the demands of the law and the consequences of disobedience. There is no area of life where man is exempt from the demands of the law of God.

Blessings and Curses

Because God's laws are a standard for all nations, consequences of disobedience affect pagan nations as well as godly nations. External blessings accrue to societies that conform to the laws of God, and there are curses for those societies that fail to conform externally to these laws (Deuteronomy 28:1-68). The laws of God that relate to blessings and curses are operative for all peoples. The prophet Amos made this clear when he denounced the nations surrounding Israel. Damascus, Gaza, Tyre, Edom, Ammon, and Moab incurred the curses of Deuteronomy 28:15-63 (Amos 1:3; 2:5). Those judges who fail to render verdicts according to the absolute standard of the law of God "will die like men, and fall like any one of the princes" (Psalm 82:7).

The Levites stood before the people to remind them of their sins and the reason for God's judgment on their nation: "For our kings, our leaders, our priests, and our fathers have not kept the law or paid attention to Thy commandments and Thine admonitions with which Thou hast admonished them. . . . Behold, we are slaves today, and as to the land which Thou didst give to our fathers to eat of its fruit and its bounty, behold, we are slaves on it" (Nehemiah 9:34, 36). Slavery, in which even our bodies are ruled by despotic leaders (v. 37), is the result of a nation's failure to keep the commandments of God.

Breaking God's commandments means "transgressors and sinners will be crushed together, and those who forsake the LORD shall come to an end" (Isaiah 1:28). Harlotry, injustice, murder, theft, taking bribes, and afflicting the helpless are results of a nation's repudiating the laws of God for the laws of men (humanism). Even the greatest kingdoms of the world will be reduced to dust if they fail to honor God's law (Daniel 2:31-35). One of the most sobering judgments of God is the one that falls on Herod for his humanistic government: "On an appointed day Herod, having put on his royal apparel, took his seat on the rostrum and began delivering an address to them. And the people kept crying out, 'The voice of a god and not of a man!' And immediately an angel of the Lord struck him because he did not give God the glory, and he was eaten by worms and died" (Acts 12:21-23).

God in His providence appoints and deposes all rulers. He, therefore, is never surprised about the development of the nations because the heads of foreign powers are His servants. For example, Pharaoh (Romans 9:17), Herod, and Pilate (Acts 4:25) were raised up by God to do God's will. The psalmist says that God "puts down one, and exalts another" (Psalm 75:7). God's dealings with Nebuchadnezzar surely are the most revealing actions of sovereignty brought upon an earthly ruler. Daniel acknowledges the sovereignty of God in the appointment and removal of kings by stating that God "changes the times and the epochs; He removes kings and establishes kings" (Daniel 2:21a).

The rule and authority that men in power enjoy come from the gracious hand of God: "The Most High is ruler over the realm of mankind, and bestows it on whom He wishes, and sets over it the lowliest of men" (Daniel 4:17). Nebuchadnezzar was reminded of his rightful position as a ruler *under* God (4:25, 32). When the king comes to his senses, *God* returns the kingdom to Nebuchadnezzar: "So I was reestablished in my sovereignty, and surpassing greatness was added to me" (4:36). This great lesson was not remembered, however. Some years later Belshazzar's mockery of God's rule (cf. 5:2-4) brought sudden destruction, but not before Daniel reminded him of the nature of his sovereignty: "O king, the Most High *God granted sovereignty*, grandeur, glory, and majesty to Nebuchadnezzar your father" (5:16). Belshazzar's kingdom was "numbered," "weighed," "divided," and "given" *by God* (vv. 25-28).

Summary

The sixth basic principle in the Biblical blueprint for civil government is that the lordship of Jesus Christ is universal. There are no exemptions from God's service. There is no "King's X" for human kings.

One of the greatest lies ever fostered in the church is that Jesus is King of the church but not of the State. The law of God is valid for individual believers, but non-Christians are supposedly not required to keep it. The nations are supposedly under their own jurisdiction—an assertion of their autonomy (self-law). The nations supposedly do not have to keep the law of God unless they wish to. God supposedly does not hold them accountable. Suppose,

suppose, suppose: the theory is all supposition and no fact. It is a lie perpetuated by the devil and his minions.

If it were true, then it would mean that men around the world can break God's law and get away with it. Or, if His law does not bind them, then this theory means that God is not sovereign over the nations. Legal theory of all societies recognizes this principle: *no law-no authority, no law-no sovereignty.* Those who argue that God's law does not apply are in principle denying the sovereign rule of God.

This must be Satan's favorite lie. It is certainly one of his most successful lies in Christian circles.

You cannot come away from a reading of the Bible with the conclusion that the nations are exempt from the commandments of God. If the nations are exempt as long as they do not submit to Jesus as their King, then how will they be held accountable on judgment day? According to this "new theology," there is no accountability. The atrocities of despots from the beginning of time are off the hook.

Our country's foreign policy makes it evident that we have forsaken the gospel for the nations. When is the last time (let alone the first time) that you heard that what our foreign policy really needs is the claims of Jesus Christ? Do our ambassadors call the Russians, the Czechs, the Chinese, the Japanese, the Iranians, the Poles, and the Jews to surrender unconditionally to the lordship of Jesus Christ? My friends, this is the only hope for the world. God will not honor our supposed religious neutrality for long.

God establishes nations by His eternal decree. All nations are accountable to God and His law. When God is rejected as the King, false king-messiahs claim to be saviors of the people. The State and God cannot claim to be the ultimate sovereign. All conspiratorial designs of men and nations are doomed to fail.

Jesus is King of kings because of who and what He is. For nations to submit to Jesus as King, the gospel must be preached and the Word of God proclaimed as law. Both church and State are obligated to keep the law of God. The State cannot exempt itself from keeping the commandments of God except at its own peril.

There is a jurisdictional separation between church and State but not a religious separation. Jesus is King of *all* the nations. There is no "divine right of kings." The New Testament repeats the fact that Jesus is Ruler of the Nations. There are blessings and curses attached to obedience and disobedience.

In summary:

1. God promises to bring judgment against nations that ignore His law.

2. New Testament nations are as bound by God's law as Old Testament nations were.

3. The God of the Old Testament is the God of the New Testament.

4. The Redemptive work of Christ has not freed us from obedience to God's law.

5. God's law threatens totalitarian nations.

6. God destroys all rival earthly kingdoms.

7. The Roman Empire fell because it opposed God and His church.

8. The early Christians were persecuted because they claimed that Christ was sovereign over all kings.

9. The State and God cannot both be equally sovereign.

10. The government rests on Christ's shoulders.

11. Christ is King legally.

12. The confession that Jesus is Lord must begin in the heart.

13. The jurisdictions of church and State are separate.

14. The civil magistrate is called by names that denote a religious function: priest, minister.

15. Only God possesses divine rights.

16. Divine rights means not being subject to a legal appeal for one's actions.

17. In the past, king and parliaments have claimed divine rights.

18. This doctrine leads to tyranny.

19. God alone is king.

20. The New Testament says that all magistrates are under God's kingship.

21. God's law rules magistrates, and they are supposed to rule their subjects in terms of God's law.

22. Armed with God's law, the early church challenged the State.

23. The Levites were to warn kings against transgressing God's law.

24. Slavery results when rulers ignore God's law.

25. God still appoints all rulers.

7

WE MUST RENDER APPROPRIATE SERVICE

> Render to all what is due them: tax to whom tax is due; custom to whom custom; fear to whom fear; honor to whom honor (Romans 13:7).

As we saw in Chapter Two, God has established a bottom-up system of multiple hierarchies: church, State, and family. This means that we must always be obedient *where obedience is required by God's law.* The appeals court system of Exodus 18 is to be our guide: we are free men only when we obey God, and we must subject our actions to scrutiny by lawful, God-ordained, *covenantal* authorities in church, State, and family. The Bible directs us to submit to *every* human institution. "Whether to a king as the one in authority, or to governors as sent by him for the punishment of evildoers and the praise of those who do right" (1 Peter 2:13). While Peter has civil authority in mind here, this text is inclusive enough to include family and church authorities. As Bible-believing Christians we must always remember that when we speak of authority, we mean more than *civil* authority.

The family has real authority that it exercises over its members: "Children, obey your parents in the Lord, for this is right" (Ephesians 6:1). The symbol of authority is the rod of correction: "He who spares his rod hates his son, but he who loves him disciplines him diligently" (Proverbs 13:24). It is in the family that children ought to learn the basics of Biblical authority and its relationship to church authority, the authority that an employer has over an employee, and the authority the police have over the citizenry within the confines of the law.

The church has real authority to discipline members:

> And if your brother sins, go and reprove him in private; if he listens to you, you have won your brother. But if he does not listen to you, take one or two more with you, so that BY THE MOUTH OF TWO OR THREE WITNESSES EVERY FACT MAY BE CONFIRMED. And if he refuses to listen to them, tell it to the church; and if he refuses to listen even to the church, let him be to you as a Gentile and a tax-gatherer. Truly I say to you, whatever you shall bind on earth shall have been bound in heaven; and whatever you loose on earth shall have been loosed in heaven (Matthew 18:15-18).

The apostle Paul goes so far as to put ecclesiastical authority on an equal par with the civil courts: "Does any one of you, when he has a case against his neighbor, dare to go to law before the unrighteous, and not before the saints? Or do you not know that the saints will judge the world? And if the world is judged by you, are you not competent to constitute the smallest law courts?" (1 Corinthians 6:1-11).

The symbol of the church's authority is the "keys of the kingdom of heaven" (Matthew 16:19).

As citizens of political jurisdictions, Christians must submit themselves to those who rule because God has established them in their positions of authority by His own sovereign will (Romans 13:1). Civil rulers, as well as family and ecclesiastical rulers, are called "ministers of God." The word "minister" in Romans 13:4 is the same word used for deacon—servant (see 1 Timothy 3:8). The symbol of the civil magistrates' authority is the "sword" (Romans 13:4). (The symbol of the parent's authority is the rod.)

Resisting Tyranny

Rulers should not be cursed by the people: "You shall not curse God, nor curse a ruler of your people [because he represents God]" (Exodus 22:28; cf. Romans 13:1). This does not mean, however, that the sinful practices and policies of rulers either represent God or should go unnoticed and therefore unchallenged (cf. Mark 6:18). Moreover, Christian citizens are under obligation to disobey those laws that prohibit worship and the proclamation of the gospel (Daniel 3; Acts 4:18; 5:29). In addition, a law that forces people to commit a crime, such as murder, must also be disobeyed (Exodus 1:15-22). Jesus made it clear that evil rulers must be exposed publicly as evil rulers (cf. Luke 13:32). The Bible shows that resistance to tyranny is legitimate and often commanded.

Old Testament Examples

The Hebrew midwives were commanded by "the king of Egypt" to put to death all the male children being born to the Hebrew women (Exodus 1:15-16). The Hebrew midwives disobeyed the edict of the king: "But the midwives feared God, and did not do as the king of Egypt had commanded them, but let the boys live" (v. 17). God shows His approval of their actions: "So God was good to the midwives, and the people multiplied, and became very mighty. And it came about because the midwives feared God, that He established households for them" (vv. 20-21).

Jochebed, Moses' mother, also disobeyed the edict of the king by hiding her child and later creating a way of escape so he would not be murdered by the king's army: "But when she could hide him no longer, she got him a wicker basket and covered it over with tar and pitch. Then she put the child into it, and set it among the reeds by the bank of the Nile" (v. 3). Jochebed even deceived Pharaoh's daughter into believing that she was in no way related to the child (vv. 7-9).

Rahab hid the spies of Israel and lied about their whereabouts. When a route for escape became available, she led them out another way from that of the pursuing soldiers. She is praised by two New Testament writers for her actions: "By faith Rahab the harlot did not perish along with those who were disobedient, after she had welcomed the spies in peace" (Hebrews 11:31). Rahab is listed with Abraham as one whose faith was reflected in her works: "And in the same way [as Abraham] was not Rahab the harlot also justified by works, when she received the messengers and sent them out by another way?" (James 2:25). By sending the spies out by another way, she subverted the king's desire to capture the spies.

Shadrach, Meshach, and Abednego refused to follow the command of the king to worship the golden statue: "These men, O king, have disregarded you; they do not serve your gods or worship the golden image you have set up" (Daniel 3:12). When the three were thrown into the furnace, the angel of the Lord came to their aid (v. 25).

King Darius signed a document that prohibited anyone from making "a petition to any god or man besides" himself (Daniel 6:7). Anyone refusing to obey the order "shall be cast into the lion's den" (v. 7). Daniel refused to obey. The Bible states that Daniel went out of his way to disobey the order: "Now when Daniel knew that the document was signed, he entered his house (now in his roof chamber he had windows open toward Jerusalem); and he continued kneeling on his knees three times a day, praying and giving thanks before his God, as he had been doing previously" (v. 10).

New Testament Examples

The New Testament has similar accounts of resistance to tyranny. When Peter and John were ordered by the rulers and elders of the people to stop preaching in the name of Jesus (Acts 4:18), the two apostles refused to follow the prohibition: "Whether it is right in the sight of God to give heed to you rather than to God, you be the judge; for we cannot stop speaking what we have seen and heard" (vv. 19-20). Peter and John could not stop speaking what they had seen and heard because they had been commanded by Jesus to preach in His name (cf. Matthew 28:18-20; Acts 1:8; 1 Corinthians 9:16).

On another occasion, some of the apostles were arrested for preaching and healing in the name of Jesus. Again, they were put in a "public jail" (Acts 5:18). During the night "an angel of the Lord . . . opened the gates of the prison" and commanded them to disobey the rulers of Israel: "Go your way, stand and speak to the people in the temple the whole message of life" (v. 20). When the apostles again were confronted with the command not to preach and teach, their response was quick and sure: "We must obey God rather than men" (v. 29).

The apostles' obedience to God conflicted with the laws of the State. This resulted in the first apostolic death: "Now about that time Herod the king [Agrippa I] laid hands on some who belonged to the church, in order to mistreat them. And he had James the brother of John put to death" (Acts 12:1-2). Peter was later arrested for similar "crimes" against the State (v. 3). God, at least, does not show His disapproval of rebellion against tyrants in these specific cases. He even sent one of His angels to release Peter from prison (vv. 6-8). There are several such cases where divine assistance released outspoken Christians from the hands of the State.

Thus, there can be no question of the legality of resistance to evil civil magistrates. But the Bible always specifies that such resistance is not to be autonomous (self-law), but rather based on God's call through another lawful authority, such as a local church, a local civil magistrate, or parents. This is a now unfamiliar doctrine of the Protestant Reformation called "the doctrine of interposition." John Calvin articulated it in his *Institutes of the Christian Religion* (Book IV, Chapter 20, Sections 22-32).[1] It also is one of the legal justifications for the American Revolution.[2]

Praying for Civil Servants

Our rulers need the prayers of Christians. *First*, to give them support for the difficult tasks that surely burden them. The work of the civil magistrate is multi-faceted. There are constant pressures that weigh heavily on the office of each civil representative. A minister in the civil sphere must keep his own house in order as well as the house of State. Family responsibilities are often neglected for the supposed urgency of civil affairs. There is the constant barrage of special interest groups wanting to turn the civil sphere of government into a vehicle to engineer society through power and coercion. The temptation to appease these groups is great.

1. Michael Gilstrap, "John Calvin's Theology of Resistance," *Christianity and Civilization 2* (1983): Symposium on "The Theology of Christian Resistance," pp. 180-217.

2. Tom Rose, "On Reconstruction and the American Republic," *ibid.*, pp. 285-310.

Second, to have God change their minds when they stray from the principles of Scripture. I can remember talking with a congressman about the abortion issue. He told me that he would not change his mind no matter what argument he heard. This is certainly presumption and arrogance. The Christian is assured that God is in control of the king's heart: "The king's heart is like channels of water in the hand of the LORD; He turns it wherever He wishes" (Proverbs 21:1). There is a Biblical precedence for this attitude. Pharaoh would not listen to the arguments of Moses. God made Pharaoh a believer (Exodus 3-15).

Third, to give them wisdom in applying the absolutes of God's Word to civil situations. This was Solomon's prayer (1 Kings 3).

Fourth, to pray for a well-ordered State so the church of Jesus Christ is protected and given freedom in preaching the gospel (1 Timothy 2:1-4). The State must protect the *Christian* religion. Any obstacle that would jeopardize the preaching of the Word of God in carrying out the Great Commission must be removed by civil government. The apostle Paul instructs Christians to pray for those who rule so "that we [Christians] may lead a tranquil and quiet life in all godliness and dignity" (1 Timothy 2:2).

In another place Paul appeals to the civil magistrate for protection from those who were threatening the Christian religion, and in particular, his own life (Acts 23:12-31; cf. 25:11). This all means that civil government cannot be religiously neutral. If the Christian religion is not protected and made foundational, then some other religion will be, usually a State religion that degenerates into paganism. The State must go beyond mere toleration (the acceptance of *all* religions as long as those religions do not conflict with the operations of the State) and maintain religious freedom for Christian churches.

Instructing Civil Rulers

Jesus told His early disciples that they would be "brought before governors and kings for His sake" (Matthew 10:18). The apostle Paul declared, "Woe is me if I do not preach the gospel" (1 Corinthians 9:16). When Paul was brought before the civil officials of Rome, he was obligated, for he was under compulsion by God, to preach the gospel. King Agrippa was confronted with the claims of Jesus Christ and responded by saying, "In a short time you will persuade me to become a Christian" (Acts 26:28). Paul responds by saying, "I would to God (lit., *I pray to God*), that whether in a short or long time, not only you, but also all who hear me this day, might become such as I am, except for these chains" (v. 29).

It is not enough to have "conservative" rulers who merely follow after the traditions of men. Christians should be working for *Christian* leaders whose lives are conformed to the image of Jesus Christ and who seek to make the Word of God the law of the land. Moreover, Christians must preach the whole counsel of God to all men — especially to civil rulers, to whom much has been given and of whom much will be required.

Civil governments have the responsibility to punish evil doers and promote the good. The task of civil government at all levels is to exercise its authority in its jurisdiction and settle disputes between conflicting jurisdictions. When disputes and/or crimes are committed, the State must act swiftly and justly. The standard of judgment is the Word of God, "for it [the God-ordained authority] is a minister of God to you for good" (Romans 13:4). Notice that Paul declares that the State is a minister to *you* for good. Paul has a Biblical moral order in mind when he speaks about the operation of the State as minister.

In the Old Testament, the priests who were experts in the law of God, instructed the king on how he should apply the details of the law to various civil issues (Deuteronomy 17). Unfortunately, the church no longer sees its calling as prophetic. Of course, there are those in the civil sphere who despise the absolutes of God's Word and anyone who would hold them accountable.

Pursuing Peace

Peace can only be realized through the life-transforming gospel of Jesus Christ. Genuine and lasting peace will not come through law, force, political promises or compromises, the

elimination of poverty, the establishment of a one-world humanistic government, or the military threat of Mutual Assured
Destruction (MAD). (On the last point, see the book in the Biblical Blueprints Series, *The Chariots of God*.) To pray for peace, as we
are instructed to do, can be no substitute for the preaching of the
gospel so that the nations are discipled according to the Word of
Jesus Christ (Matthew 28:20). Wars do not come because of environmental factors. Rather, they are the result of man's inherent
sinfulness: "What is the source of quarrels and conflicts among
you? Is not the source your pleasures that wage war in your members? You lust and do not have; so you commit murder. And you
are envious and cannot obtain; so you fight and quarrel . . ."
(James 4:1-2). If this is true of the Christian community, should
we expect anything less among non-Christians?

Humanist institutions deny the reality of sin; therefore, they
believe that man can save himself given enough time, money,
technology, and education. The following is an excerpt from The
Preamble to the Charter of the United Nations. It is an example
of man's attempt at peace without Christ: "We the peoples of the
United Nations determined to save succeeding generations from
the scourge of war . . . to unite our strength to maintain international peace and security, and to ensure, by the acceptance of
principles and the institution of methods, that armed force shall
not be used, save in the common interest . . . have resolved to
combine our efforts to accomplish these aims."

Peace then comes by and through the efforts of man. Of
course "peace" is defined in man's terms. The peace that the Lord
wants us to pray for and promote is His peace, not peace as men
define it. Jesus said that He came not to bring peace, but a sword.
The Word of God does not place the absence of physical conflict or
war as the highest value, but rather recognizes legitimate reasons
for men engaging in war—just grounds for defending family
members, neighbors, property, and the nation.

Rendering to Caesar

Because civil governments are ordained by God and act as *service* institutions, for they are ministers of God (Romans 13:4), they are in need of tax money to pay for the rendered services. Jesus states that Caesar is due tax money because he offers them protection against foreign enemies. Caesar renders a service: "Render to Caesar the things that are Caesar's; and to God the things that are God's" (Matthew 22:21). Jesus certainly was not endorsing the way Caesar governed in all cases, but He was, at least, upholding the Biblical institution of civil government and its authority to limited taxation. Of course, those "things that are Caesar's" are not his by edict. Rather, they fall within the parameters of God's ordination of Caesar's jurisdiction. Jesus was not giving *carte blanche* authority to Caesar as the civil representative of the State.

But what about those who maintain that the State is taking more than its God-ordained share? Should we still pay the tax? We can afford to pay. If we are faithful, God will provide. When Peter asked about the tax, Jesus provided a fish with a coin in its mouth (Matthew 17:24-27). Christians are on the winning side. In effect, we are paying the taxes to ourselves. We are maintaining an orderly society for the day when Christians will faithfully carry out the dominion mandate.

Of course, once Christian dominion is a growing reality, the need for taxes will decrease because the State will once again be a protector and not a provider. Some nations tax over 100% of income! While we should not be satisfied with our tax rate, we should thank God that it's not worse. At every opportunity we should work to cut taxes and reduce expenditures. There are more significant battles to fight (e.g., abortion, church-State relations, the building up of the church and family, and Christian education). For the most part, the courts are stacked against the tax protester. What happens if the court rules against you? You will still have to pay the tax as well as penalties and interest. You might even lose your house. This says nothing about what might happen to your family if you are put in jail for a year or two. I want to make it clear that there are certain non-negotiable items that the Christian cannot compromise on. These were discussed earlier in the chapter. Nowhere in Scripture is it a sin to pay a tax under compulsion.

For the Romans, lordship was personified in the Emperor. For the Jew, therefore, paying taxes was believed to be an acknowledgment of the Roman gods. This is made clear by the stamp of the emperor's face on the coin of the realm: "TI[berius] CAESAR DIVI AUG[usti] F[ilius] AUGUSTUS," or, in translation, "Tiberius Caesar Augustus, son of the deified Augustus." The Jews knew whose coin it was. It was used to pay taxes, and it was the medium of exchange throughout the Roman world. Israel participated in the Empire; it benefited from roads, a Mediterranean Sea free of pirates, and a common silver currency unit. Why, then, should the Jews refuse to pay taxes to the State that provided these benefits? The Jewish leaders were collaborators with the Roman authorities. Why shouldn't they pay the tax to their superiors? Why not admit that Caesar was the rightful civil ruler? It was from him that they derived their own civil authority. But the Jews, like so many tax protesters of our day, did not want to admit how economically dependent they had become on Caesar. They wanted these benefits free of charge.

They also did not want to admit that God had once again brought them under historical judgment, just as He had in the days of the judges, with the invasion by Assyria, and their captivity in Babylon. They had become spiritual rebels, as they proved when they crucified Jesus. Oppressive taxation always indicates that the people in general have rejected the God of the Bible. High taxes are a judgment of God, just like military defeats, pestilence, and economic crises. The only way to overthrow political oppression through taxation is to repent before God and acknowledge that He alone is Savior, Lord, and King.

But what of the faithful? They know that the State is not God. Two points should be kept in mind. First, it may be that the many Christians may not *believe* that the State is god, they may, however, *act* as if it is. Second, those Christians who do not believe that the State is god or act as if it is, are not admitting the State is god by paying a tax. Scripture tells us that "by nature" the State, or anything else, is not God (Galatians 4:8). We pay the tax "for conscience sake" (Romans 13:5), "lest we give them offense" (Matthew 17:27). The faithful Christian works for the day when the State will stop acting as a god and the people will stop living as if the State is a god.

Supporting Godly Leadership

The people have the responsibility to support godly leadership. Moses chose leaders who had already come through the ranks of family, business, and community leadership: "Choose wise and discerning and experienced men from your tribes, and I will appoint them as your heads" (Deuteronomy 1:13). The responsibility for choosing godly leaders rested with the people. Moses then chose from those presented to him as worthy leaders: "So I took the heads of your tribes, wise and experienced men, and appointed them heads over you, leaders of thousands, and of hundreds, of fifties and of tens, and officers for your tribes" (1:15). Judges were chosen with the same ethical and experiential considerations (1:16, 17).

In time, however, Israel rejected this procedure and chose a different standard for determining leadership. An autonomous (*autos* = self; *nomos* = law) choice was made. The people wanted a king "like all the nations," someone who would meet their needs rather than God's requirements (1 Samuel 8:5). They rejected Biblical law and voted for the "Law of the Nations," a distorted law that put man at the center of law-making. God warned them that such an allegiance would bring only tyranny, despotism, and eventual slavery (vv. 10-18). The rejection of Biblical law resulted in the State determining what is right and wrong. Long-term, the State is the law. All those who reject the king's law are either killed or enslaved (1 Kings 12:6-15).

Today, Christians have the freedom and duty to vote for responsible leadership using the standard of God's law as the measuring device for their political choice: "By the blessing of the upright a city is exalted, but by the mouth of the wicked it is torn down" (Proverbs 11:11). There is a direct relationship between those who rule and the condition of the nation: "When the righteous increase, the people rejoice, but when a wicked man rules, people groan" (Proverbs 29:2). The *people* chose a "king like all the nations." God gave them what they wanted. Christians who refuse to vote, for whatever reason, are getting what their non-vote brings.

Qualified to Lead

The qualifications for leadership are ethical and practical, that is, they are to have some leadership experience in the family, church, school, or business world. Rulers must be "men of truth, those who hate dishonest gain" (Exodus 18:21). The standard by which they are to rule is not to be their own, and no amount of monetary and political gain will move them from their allegiance to God and His Word. They are to "fear God." This is the ethical dimension.

The apostle Paul builds on these principles when he sets forth the qualifications of leadership in the church. Ethical considerations abound. Self-government must first be manifested in a potential leader. Leaders must be able to control their own appetites (1 Timothy 3:1-7); that is, they must be self-disciplined in all their affairs. Paul draws on the Old Testament system of government that applied to both church and State, and he carries these principles to the New Testament people of God.

In addition to ethical qualifications, there are practical considerations as well. The ethical leads to the practical. The individual who is scrupulous in personal, family, and business affairs will gain positions of leadership where experience is cultivated. Those who are faithful in small things (an ethical evaluation) will be entrusted with greater responsibilities (a practical result) (Matthew 25:23). This is why the young are discouraged from holding positions of authority without some supervision or accountability. New converts are susceptible to conceit because they have not gained the needed maturity to work out the implications of their new faith in Christ (1 Timothy 3:6).

Jethro's advice to Moses suggests that "able men" must rule (Exodus 18:21). Ability is cultivated through time as the Word of God is applied to life's situations. Of course, there are rare exceptions to this general rule. Timothy is told, "Let no one look down on your youthfulness . . ." (1 Timothy 4:12). Instead, he is to conduct himself in a way that reflects his faith in ethical terms. His life (ethical behavior) is to be an example (practical behavior) for others to imitate.

Civil leadership, like ecclesiastical leadership, is designed to be ministerial. Those in authority must follow the pattern of God as *ministers* rather than attempt to define the role of governmental leadership in terms of how others rule (Luke 22:24-30; cf. 1 Samuel 8:5).

Summary

The seventh basic principle in the Biblical blueprint for civil government is that those who rule in the civil sphere are God's servants. Those under their jurisdiction must serve the civil government faithfully, to the extent that the government is serving God faithfully by enforcing God's law. Faithful service upward is supposed to insure faithful service from subordinates.

Civil government is not a "necessary evil." God established the civil sphere of government like He established the family and church, for our good. What is missing in each of these governments is godly leadership. We're often faced with voting for the best of two bad choices. It's hard to find men of principle, men who "fear God rather than man."

But where is leadership cultivated? The family and church are the training grounds for developing true civil servants. The example of Christ as the servant par excellence is our model. Most governmental leaders are persuaded by their voting constituency. If the people back home want some law passed that will favor their district or them personally, their congressman will seek out their wishes and vote accordingly. Of course, if it's the majority view. Service in the Biblical sense means responsibility. Today, leadership so-called is really slavery. Politicians are slaves to the will of the people. Their impetus for action is not principle but pressure.

The Bible commands us to submit "to every human institution." Governments are established by God, therefore, they rule in God's name. This is why rulers should not be cursed by the people. The Bible, however, shows resistance to tyranny is legitimate and is often commanded. Christians are commanded to pray for those in authority over them.

Civil rulers must hear from the Christian citizenry. Christians are inheritors of the earth because we are "fellow-heirs with Christ." We have a stake in the way our world is being run.

Peace can only be realized when we recognize that we are first at war with God and need to be reconciled to Him. The State has the duty to collect taxes for its Biblically defined function.

Christians should support qualified Christian leaders.

In summary:

1. God has established multiple covenantal authorities.

2. These authorities are structured as appeals courts, as in Exodus 18.

3. Civil authority is only one authority among many.

4. The family and the church can lawfully discipline its members.

5. The symbols of the church's authority are the keys to the kingdom.

6. The symbol of the State's authority is the sword.

7. The symbol of the parent's authority is the rod.

8. We must disobey laws that prohibit the public preaching of the gospel.

9. The Hebrew midwives disobeyed Pharaoh.

10. Moses' mother disobeyed Pharaoh, and saved Moses in an ark.

11. Rahab disobeyed the laws of Jericho by hiding the spies and lying to the authorities.

12. The three young Israelites disobeyed Nebuchadnezzar's command to worship his statue.

13. Peter and John refused to obey the order to cease preaching.

14. Civil resistance must not be autonomous.

15. Christians are to pray for rulers: to guide them, to turn

their hearts from evil, to judge society in terms of Biblical law, and to achieve peace.

16. Christians are to instruct civil rulers in the law.

17. Civil government is required to enforce God's law.

18. Lasting peace can come only through the enforcement of Biblical law.

19. Man cannot save himself.

20. The State cannot save man.

21. Civil governments are service institutions: service to God.

22. We owe taxes to the State.

23. Caesar's claims on us are not unlimited, however.

24. High taxes are one way God judges sin.

25. Taxes also support the peace-keeping activities of the State.

26. Leaders should be elected because of their righteous behavior.

8

NEUTRALITY IS A MYTH

> No one can serve two masters; for either he will hate the one
> and love the other, or he will hold to one and despise the other
> (Matthew 6:24).

Two masters give conflicting orders. Both cannot be right. It is
our task to submit ourselves to the master who will give us righteous orders, according to righteous law, and who will judge our
responses righteously.

But what is the proper definition of "righteous"? The Bible gives
us the answer: whatever the Bible tells us. The humanists also
give us an answer: whatever the humanists tell us. Either way, we
are arguing in a circle. The question is: Is it a righteous circle or a
vicious circle?

To argue on the basis of righteousness is to argue on the basis
of *ethics*. Until we get ethics straight in our minds and lives, we
will remain confused. But one thing is sure: if the fundamental
issues of government are issues of ethics, then there can be no
neutrality. Passing a law hurts some people and benefits others.
Not passing this same law reverses the beneficiaries and victims.
So there is no escape: there must be beneficiaries and victims.
There can be no neutrality.

The Early Church

For example, the Roman Empire and the Empire's Jewish
officers were at war with the Church. The early Christians were
accused of turning "the world upside down" (Acts 17:6). In one
sense, those pagans who were negatively affected by the preaching

116

of the gospel were correct in their assessment of how Christianity changed their culture—their godless, humanistic, decaying world was revealed as empty through the gospel's consistent application to their way of thinking. These unbelievers understood the implications of the gospel. The Christians "act contrary to the decrees of Caesar, saying that there is another King, Jesus" (v. 7). Caesar or Christ? Man or God? The State or the Kingdom?

First-century humanists saw that their world was jeopardized by the claims and demands of Jesus Christ: "And His voice shook the earth then, but now He has promised, saying, 'Yet once more I will shake not only the earth, but also the heaven.' And this expression, 'Yet once more,' denotes the removing of those things which can be shaken, as of created things, in order that those things which cannot be shaken may remain" (Hebrews 12:26, 27).

In another sense, these first-century humanists were wrong. Their worldview assumed that a godly order must be upside down. In reality, a Christian world order is right side up. Society does not function properly unless the effects of God's Word permeate every corner of culture. At this moment, the world appears upside down—*ethically* upside down. The Christian's task, through God's powerful provision in the gospel, is to turn it right side up.

In and Over the World, but Not *of* the World

Many Christians have refused to bring the first-century Christian faith into the 20th century. Often they are confused when they read Jesus' words, "My kingdom is not of this world" (John 18:36a). Jesus did not say His kingdom does not operate *in* this world. He did not say His kingdom is not *over* this world. When Jesus states His "kingdom is not *of* this world," He emphasizes the *origin* of His kingdom's power and authority; it simply does not derive its authority from the world. His disciples had scattered. There was no army following Jesus. This should have been obvious to Pilate. "If My kingdom were of this world, then My servants would be fighting, that I might not be delivered up to the Jews; but as it is, My kingdom is not of this realm" (John 8:36b).

He in no way repudiated His own authority; He was not "internalizing" His kingdom, for He was God, the Creator who made the external realm. He simply pointed to the obvious: His kingdom does not come from this world.

Caiaphas, the high priest, interrogated Jesus on *religious* questions. Caiaphas wanted to know if Jesus was "the Christ, the Son of God" (Matthew 26:63). This did not concern Pilate. In fact, in order to have Pilate hear the grievances of the religious leaders, a *political* threat to the jurisdiction of Pilate or Rome had to be fabricated: "And they began to accuse Him saying, 'We found this man misleading our nation and forbidding us to pay taxes to Caesar, and saying that He Himself is Christ, a King'" (Luke 23:2). Unless Jesus was portrayed as a *political* threat to the Roman Empire, they knew Pilate would not hear their case.

Pilate's question about kingship and kingdoms concerned mere political power. Jesus was questioned from Pilate's perspective. Would Jesus bring an army? How large would it be? Since He was said to be "King of the Jews" (Luke 23:3), would Jesus incite a rebellion among the Jews to usurp Pilate's position of authority? What sort of weaponry would He use? Pilate believed, as did many Jews of that day, that armed conflict alone could extend a kingdom. It was a king's duty, Pilate thought, to use the power of the military against an enemy. Since Jesus was a king, Pilate assumed He must command an army. This was the Roman way. The *Pax Romana* was maintained through force. Jesus' response to Pilate shows that Pilate failed to understand the nature of Jesus' kingdom.

In John 18:37 Pilate says, "So You are a king?" Pilate understood that Jesus did not deny kingship, for Jesus answered Pilate's tentative question: "You say correctly that I am a king. For this I have been born [Luke 1:32, 33; 2:2], and for this I have come into the world, to bear witness to the truth. Every one who is of the truth hears My voice" (John 18:37). Later, Jesus informed Pilate that his position of political authority, and, by intimation, that of all who rule (cf. Romans 13:1), was subject to God's kingly rule: Jesus is "ruler of the kings of the earth" (Revelation 1:5).

When Jesus kept silent regarding Pilate's question concerning His origin (John 19:9), Pilate grew indignant: "You do not speak to me? Do you not know that I have authority to release You, and I have authority to crucify You?" (v. 10). Jesus' answer settled the matter about the operation of God's kingdom. Unless the kingdom of God operated *in* and *over* this world, what Jesus next said would be false: "You would have no authority over Me, unless *it had been given you from above* . . ." (v. 11).

Looking for Political Solutions

Confusion over Jesus' words develops from a false notion that the answer to man's problems is solely political. There were numerous occasions when the crowds wanted to make Him King (e.g., John 6:15). While there are political implications to Jesus' kingship, just as there are personal, familial, economic, business, ecclesiastical, and judicial implications, *the kingdom of God cannot be brought about politically.* Good laws do not make good people. They can at best *prepare* people to become good people by *restraining outward evil.* Only the sovereign work of the Holy Spirit in regeneration makes people good. The State has a God-imposed jurisdiction to perform kingdom activities related to *civil* affairs according to the specifics of God's Word.

The people in Jesus' day saw the kingdom of God in externals only. They visualized the kingdom of God as coming, not through regeneration, but revolution. Jesus said of His followers: "Truly, truly, I say to you, you seek Me, not because you saw signs, but because you ate of the loaves, and were filled" (John 6:26). It was Jesus' message about mankind's need for salvation and about Him as the Savior, the Messiah of God, that caused the religious and political establishments of the day to seek His death.

The kingdom of God never advances through political intrigue, backed by military power. Though power-directed, its power comes from above and works on and in the heart of man: "I will give you a new heart and put a new spirit within you; and I will remove the heart of stone from your flesh and give you a heart of flesh. And I will put My Spirit within you and cause you to walk in My statutes, and you will be careful to observe My ordinances" (Ezekiel 36:26, 27). Self-government, wherein God subdues the heart to teachableness, leads to godly family, church, and civil governments (cf. 1 Timothy 3:1-13).

Implements of war which deteriorate over time or become obsolete are only as reliable as those who manufacture and use them. Moreover, such weapons affect only externals. They can subdue a people, but they cannot regenerate those dead in their trespasses and sins (Ephesians 2:1). God's Word "is living and active and sharper than any two-edged sword, and piercing as far as the division of soul and spirit, of both joints and marrow, and able to judge the thoughts and intentions of the heart" (Hebrews 4:12).

The supernatural power that energizes God's kingdom is never bound by political rhetoric: "For the kingdom of God does not consist in words, but in power" (1 Corinthians 4:20). The battle against the kingdoms of this world is waged through the awesome power inherent in God's Word, energized by His Spirit: "For though we walk in the flesh, we do not war according to the flesh, for the weapons of our warfare are not of the flesh, but divinely powerful for the destruction of fortresses" (2 Corinthians 10:3, 4). As Christians, "we are destroying speculations and every lofty thing raised up against the knowledge of God, and we are taking every thought captive to the obedience of Christ" (v. 5). This is kingdom living, dominion living.

The kingdom of God advances by changing the hearts and minds of those who oppose Jesus Christ and His law. The kingdoms of this world are at war with the kingdom of Jesus Christ and it is the duty of all Christians to be involved in that war until the gates of Hades can no longer stand (Matthew 16:18).

Saved by Law?

Old Testament Israel was given what can be described as a full-orbed or comprehensive Biblical worldview. Every area of life was to be interpreted in terms of God's revealed law. The law was God's *standard* of righteousness; it was never designed to *make* a person righteous.

Too many Christians have been lead astray with the false notion that Israel was saved by the law (never its God-designed function) while New Testament believers are saved by grace through faith.[1] The false inference is made that since the law played such a major part in Israel's salvation and grace now plays the major part in the Christian's life, the law should be abandoned in favor of grace.

There is really no justification for such a belief.[2] The Israelites were to have circumcised hearts, equivalent to the New Testament's requirement to be "born again" (John 3:3): "Circumcise then your heart, and stiffen your neck no more" (Deuteronomy 10:16); and, "Moreover the LORD your God will circumcise your heart and the heart of your descendants, to love the LORD your God with all your heart and with all your soul, in order that you may live" (Deuteronomy 30:6).[3] This is regeneration. This is not justification through the works of the law. Regeneration makes the heart of stiff-necked and rebellious men and women submit willingly to their heavenly Father. When the heart is made new, it is able and ready to love. How do we show our love for God? By keeping His commandments. Isn't this what Deuteronomy 30:6 maintains? Isn't this what the New Testament tells us? (John 14:15). Israel's keeping the law was an expression of their love for God.

The proper ordering of society arises from regenerate individuals who move into the broader culture to be "salt and light"

---

1. When Paul sets forth the doctrine of justification by grace through faith in the letter to the Romans, he uses *Old Testament* examples, Abraham (before the giving of the law) and David (after the giving of the law) (Romans 4).

2. See Greg L. Bahnsen, *Theonomy in Christian Ethics* (2nd ed.; Phillipsburg, New Jersey: Presbyterian and Reformed Publishing Co., 1984); Greg L. Bahnsen, *By This Standard: The Authority of God's Law Today* (Tyler, Texas: Institute for Christian Economics, 1985); James B. Jordan, *The Law of the Covenant: An Exposition of Exodus 21-23* (Tyler, Texas: Institute for Christian Economics, 1984); Rousas J. Rushdoony, *The Institutes of Biblical Law* (Nutley, New Jersey: Craig Press 1973).

3. Notice the personal responsibility/divine sovereignty connection.

(Matthew 5:13-16). Salt is a preservative,[4] keeping the culture from experiencing social entropy, the inevitable decline of society as sin works out its rotting effects. The Christian also is light, pointing out the way to the spiritually blind.

> As Christian cultures develop toward [the final days], aren't we serving as *lights to all nations* in every case where the gospel becomes a shaping influence in any one nation? Shouldn't we strive to create a society which will *shine ethically* before other nations, just as we try to do in our families, our churches, and our businesses?
>
> Obviously, this passage applies both to individuals and to groups of Christians. Yet many Bible teachers draw an arbitrary line at politics and say, "Thus far, and no farther, Jesus. Your word does not speak to this area of life. Yes, Israel was supposed to shine, and Israel had less light then we do, for you have come. But Christians have *less* responsibility!"
>
> A godly society before pagans was an important aspect of evangelism in the Old Testament. Why not today?[5]

Many Christians contend that if enough people are saved, the broader culture will change automatically. On the surface this might seem reasonable. But it misses a vital element. While the regenerate person certainly has a new disposition to do right, he is often left without knowing what to do. The specific ethic of God's revealed laws has been reduced to the single ethic of "love." Of course, the Bible does command us to love, but love without specific guidelines is nothing more than sentimentality.

The Earth Is the Lord's

Restoration begins by realizing that we live in the midst of God's kingdom. God's pattern for godly living is established in

---

4. Salt can also season food. "Christians are to improve the world, in the same way that salt improves flavor in otherwise bland, tasteless foods. How are they to do this? With their *good works*, which is the focus of this passage [Matthew 5:16]. Remove a Christians good works, and he is no better than tasteless salt in the eyes of the world": Gary North, *75 Bible Questions Your Professors Pray You Won't Ask* (Tyler, Texas: Spurgeon Press, 1984), p. 145. Both metaphors teach similar truths: Our good works *preserve* society and our good works add *savor* to society.

5. *Ibid.*, p. 148.

heaven. In the Lord's Prayer we petition God, "Thy Kingdom come. Thy will be done, *on earth as it is in heaven*" (Matthew 6:10). God has not called us to forsake the earth, but *to impress heaven's pattern on earth*.

The Bible does not support the belief that Christians should abandon the world. Christians are to be "salt" and "light" (Matthew 5:13, 14). Salt is useless unless applied to potentially decaying material; light is not needed unless there is darkness (Matthew 5:15; Luke 2:32). Without involvement in the world, neither salt nor light are of any value.

Christians are to be in the world, but they are not to be of the world (John 17:14-16). They are not to be squeezed into the world's mold (Romans 12:2). They are not to be led astray by the "elementary principles of the world" (Colossians 2:8). They are to keep themselves "unstained by the world" (James 1:27). They are warned not to get entangled in the "defilements of the world" (2 Peter 2:20). Nowhere are they told to abandon the world (cf. Matthew 28:18-20; John 3:16).

The "world" is corrupt because people are corrupt. Where corrupt people control certain aspects of the world, we can expect defilement. But the world does not have to remain in decay. When individuals are redeemed, the effects of their redemption should spread to the society in which they live and conduct their affairs.

The world of pagan thinking and practice is to be replaced by Christian thinking and practice. It is a perversion of the gospel to maintain that the world, as the domain where evil exists, is inherently corrupt. We should remember that Jesus came to this world to give His life for its redemption (John 3:16). Christians must be transformed by God's Word and not be conformed to the world's principles. As Christians work in the world through the power of the Holy Spirit, the world will be transformed.

A Cleansed and Redeemed Earth

There is no inherent sinfulness in material things. Scripture says Jesus shared in "flesh and blood" (Hebrews 2:14). He who denies that Jesus Christ has come in the flesh "is the deceiver and the antichrist" (2 John 7; cf. 1 John 4:1-3). Man's body is not inherently sinful. We shall have bodies in the resurrection, as Jesus does (John 20:24-27). In the resurrection, we will be "raised imperishable" (1 Corinthians 15:52).

By denying the spirituality of God's created order, we neglect its importance and give it by default to those who deny Christ. *Worldliness* is to be avoided, not the world. God created everything wholly good (Genesis 1:31). Man, through the Fall, became profane, defiled by sin. Redemption restores all things in Christ.

Peter failed to understand the gospel's comprehensive cleansing effects. He could not believe the Gentiles were "clean": "What God has cleansed, no longer consider unholy" (Acts 10:15; Matthew 15:11; Romans 14:14, 20). We should not say that the Fall eradicated God's pronouncement that the created order "was very good" (Genesis 1:31). The New Testament reinforces the goodness of God's creation: "For everything created by God is good, and nothing is to be rejected, if it is received with gratitude; for it is sanctified by means of the word of God and prayer" (1 Timothy 4:4, 5).

These verses give Christians no license to sin. All things are good while the Word of God remains our standard. Scripture is our guide and not the Platonic view of matter as chaotic and imperfect. God "became flesh and dwelt among us" (John 1:14). Jesus worked in his earthly father's shop as a carpenter, affirming the goodness of the created order and the value of physical labor.

The Bible: A Political Textbook

The Bible is filled with "politics." Here are just a few examples of political concerns found in the Bible. Noah is given authority to execute murderers (Genesis 9:6, 7); Joseph is made ruler in Egypt (Genesis 41:38-49); Israel is kept in bondage by a political ruler who sets himself up to oppose the kingdom of God (Exodus 1:8-14:1-31); "case laws" are tabulated for family, church, *and* State (Exodus 21-23); God instructs both priests and kings to follow the law of God (Deuteronomy 17:14-20); the book of Judges shows the interrelationship between religion and government; 1 Samuel 8 shows how rejecting God as Israel's true King leads the people to substitute Him with an earthly king (an attempt to equate the State with the kingdom of God); the books of Samuel, Kings, and Chronicles tell of the rise and fall of kings and kingdoms, with individual kings singled out for special counsel by God's emissaries (e.g., Jeremiah 36-38). Daniel serves as one of Darius' three civil commissioners (Daniel 6).

The realm of "politics," or civil government, is given much attention in the Bible, in both the Old and New Testaments. Kenneth Gentry writes:

> That God is vitally concerned with political affairs is quite easy to demonstrate: it is God who ordained governments in the first place (Rom. 13:1; Rom. 2:21). He is the One who establishes particular kings (Prov. 16:12; Psa. 119:46, 47; 82:1, 2). Therefore, He commands our obedience to rulers (Rom. 13:1-3). Rulers are commanded to rule on His terms (Psa. 2:10ff.). Even in the New Testament activity of political import is discoverable. Jesus urged payment of taxes to *de facto* governments (Matt. 22:15-22). In response to reminders of King Herod's political threats against Him, Jesus publicly rebuked the king by calling him a vixen (Luke 12:32). He taught that a judge is unjust if he does not fear God (Luke 18:2, 6). John the Baptist openly criticized King Herod (Luke 3:19, 20). Peter refused to obey authorities who commanded him to cease preaching (Acts 5:29). The Apostle John referred to the Roman Empire as "the beast" (Rev. 13).[6]

Denial of political involvement repudiates most of the Bible. Paul makes it clear that the "saints will judge the world" (1 Corinthians 6:2). The context of this verse has to do with constituting "the smallest law courts." Christians at various times in history have "judged the world." The foundation of Western legal tradition is Christian. The demise of the West results from Christians' non-involvement in every sphere of life, the civil sphere included.

---

6. Kenneth Gentry, "The Greatness of the Great Commission," *Journal of Christian Reconstruction*, Symposium on Evangelism, VII, No. 2 (Winter, 1981), p. 45.

Legislating Either Morality or Immorality

Life's political sphere should not be used to change or reform men and women (though the fear of punishment does change people from considering criminal activity). The law's purpose as it relates to the civil magistrate is to punish and restrain evil, to protect human life and property, and to provide justice for all people, using God's Word as the standard. Only God can regenerate the heart. An individual cannot be made good by law-keeping.

The Bible exists as the State's perfect standard of justice. In fact, this truth remains primary in the establishment of justice. When the Bible speaks to *civil* affairs, *civil* government has a duty to heed its commands. How will civil government determine what is good or evil, unless God's law is consulted? Where God's law is not the standard, there can be no objective standard for man to follow.

We live in an era in which the Bible is rejected as the State's authority. Killing unborn babies is legal, and the State, through a corrupt tax system, uses the tax money to support this heinous crime. Religion, and in particular, Biblical law, cannot be separated from life in general and politics in particular.

For example, the speed limit was reduced from 70 mph to 55 mph for two advertised reasons. First, to save lives. Second, to cut fuel consumption. Both reasons are value-laden and rest on moral considerations. They presuppose that human life is valuable and that society at large is valuable (if the world runs out of fuel then everyone is hurt). Laws—political laws—were instituted to enforce these moral, value-laden concerns.

When reason or the will of the people determine what should become law, in time laws change to reflect the heightened reason of some, or the shifting opinions of others. If we divorce religion from politics, the only thing left is irreligion, which becomes a religion of its own: man is his own God, determining good and evil for himself.

Man bows, not to God's law, but to the will of the people. Why? The people give him power to rule. The relationship between religion and politics cannot be avoided. The question is not, "Do religion and politics mix?" Rather, it is, "Which religion will be mixed with politics, or form the basis for politics?" Israel was not judged because it mixed religion and politics, but because it mixed the wrong religion with politics. Today it is no different. The potential for judgment is the same.

Dirty Politics?

The first chapter of Genesis ends with this evaluation of God's creation: "And God saw all that He had made, and behold, it was very good" (1:31). Things in themselves are not necessarily evil. The "tree of the knowledge of good and evil" was not evil. Even as Adam and Eve ate the fruit, the fruit was not evil. The Garden where they committed their sin was not evil. The decision they made was evil. What they did with God's good creation was evil.

The political sphere is a created entity. So is the family order. So is the church order. God has instituted all governments. Anyone who would say that *on principle* he wants nothing to do with either church government or family government is clearly a covenant-breaker. The same is true of anyone who says that on principle he wants nothing to do with civil government.

Mankind images God. God is the Governor over all creation; He has called us to be governors under His one government. The civil or political sphere is an area of legitimate governmental activity. It is dirty (i.e., evil) when evil men practice evil schemes. So is every other area of human responsibility: business, law, education, labor, or whatever. Sin has affected every institution. This means that *God's law has called every institution into judgment*. In short, *no law-no sin* (Romans 7:7-12). The person who says that God's law does not judge every area of life and every institution is saying that these institutions are not sinful, not in rebellion, and clearly not dirty. But they *are* dirty. Christians therefore must insist that the gospel of Jesus Christ can cleanse every institution from sin. God has given us a *comprehensive gospel* that offers *comprehensive redemption*.

Salt and light are necessary because of the reality of sin. Christians should be involved in politics even if it is dirty. Who else has the means to clean up politics (or any other area of human activity)? If Christians do not, who will? Christians have stayed out of politics, making its corruption even more pronounced. The answer is not to consign politics to even more corruption by ignoring its potential as an area for redemption and restoration.

The Bible never condemns political involvement. John the Baptist does not rebuke Herod for his political position, but for his sinful actions as ruler. Jesus does not quarrel with Pontius Pilate over whether he should rule, but only reminds him *why* he rules and, implicitly, by what standard he rules. Paul calls rulers God's "ministers," servants in the political sphere (Romans 13:4). Paul appeals to Caesar, the seat of Roman *political* power, in order to gain a hearing.

The desire to retreat from political concerns is recent within our history. John Witherspoon, a minister in the Presbyterian church and the President of the College of New Jersey (which later became Princeton), was a signer of the Declaration of Independence. The framers of the Constitution, "with no more than five exceptions (and perhaps no more than three), . . . were orthodox members of one of the established Christian communions: approximately twenty-nine Anglicans, sixteen to eighteen Calvinists, two Methodists, two Lutherans, two Roman Catholics, one lapsed Quaker and sometime-Anglican, and one open Deist—Dr. [Benjamin] Franklin, who attended every kind of Christian worship, called for public prayer, and contributed to all denominations."[7]

Summary

The eighth basic principle in the Biblical blueprint for civil government is that there can be no neutrality or passivity in the advance of God's kingdom. It parallels Chapter Three, which deals with Biblical law and Biblical ethics (point three of the Biblical covenant).

For many Christians, evil times are evidence that the end is

---

7. M. E. Bradford, *A Worthy Company* (Marlborough, New Hampshire: Plymouth Rock Foundation, 1982), p. viii.

near, and Jesus is about to return to remove us from a steadily decaying world. Such "prophetic pronouncements" have been self-fulfilling. For generations, Christians have been saying, "This is it! Now is the time for the end!" Instead of Christians working out their salvation with fear and trembling, the church of Jesus Christ has retreated into passivity in fear and trembling.

In the process of retreatism, in the face of an advancing secularism, things have gotten worse. But what do we expect? We've removed the only preserving factor, the church of Jesus Christ, as the salt of the earth. Things will be even worse for the next generation. What will these Christians do? Will they too maintain that it's the end? Or will they see the errors of the past and work to preserve and reconstruct the world to the glory of God and the advancement of the Christian faith?

Christians ought to be turning the world "right side up" through the preaching of the gospel and the application of God's law to every area of life. This is all possible because Jesus' kingdom operates *in* the world although it does not derive its sovereignty, authority, and power *from* this world.

Jesus was a threat to the religious and political leaders of His day because He held them accountable to His law. On the other hand, others looked to Jesus as a political messiah, rejecting His saving work and the demand for repentance.

The earth belongs to the Lord and to those whom He gives it as an inheritance. The world has been cleansed by the blood of Christ; therefore, let us not call unholy what God now calls holy. God ordained government. Government, even *civil* government, is good. The Bible is filled with politics. For example, there are two books in the Bible titled "Kings."

Politics is not inherently sinful. Politicians may be, but so are fathers, mothers, children, teachers, businessmen, ministers, and doctors. God calls His people to act out the redemption Jesus has accomplished for the whole universe. Remember, Jesus is the Savior of the *world*.

In summary:

1. No man can serve two masters.

2. We need to serve a righteous master who gives us righteous law, and who judges righteously.

3. The Bible must provide our definition of "righteous."

4. The issue therefore is ethics.

5. The fundamental issues of government are ethical issues.

6. A law says yes to one group and no to another.

7. In the early church, the issue was: Christ or Caesar?

8. The humanists of the Roman Empire were threatened by the church.

9. That first-century world-transforming Christian faith has not been brought into this century.

10. Jesus' kingdom did not originate in this world, but it was always intended to change this world.

11. The kingdom of God cannot be brought in politically.

12. The people followed Jesus because He fed them by the miracle of the loaves.

13. The kingdom of God is powerful: the power of the Spirit.

14. A war is in progress between Christ's kingdom and the kingdoms of this world.

15. We are to pray that God's kingdom impresses itself on the institutions of this world.

16. The world can be progressively molded by Christ's kingdom.

17. The world can become cleansed progressively.

18. The Bible does establish guidelines for politics, although it is not a political book.

19. The denial of political involvement is the denial of many portions of the Bible.

20. Law legislates either morality or immorality.

21. There is no such thing as neutral legislation.

22. Religion and politics *are already* mixed.

23. The question is: Which religion?

24. Politics is dirty because Christians have abandoned politics.

25. God's law has called every institution under judgment.

26. Retreatism is not Biblical.

9

JUDGES NEED JURISDICTION

Let every person be in subjection to the governing authorities. For there is no authority except from God, and those which
exist are established by God (Romans 13:1).

The word is plural: *authorities*. The frame of reference in
Romans 13 is civil, but not exclusively so. Even civil authority is
to be manifested through plural offices. This is a fundamental
aspect of Biblical government. Power is not to be concentrated in
any single office.

The most important division is between the office of king and
priest. The power of one office is to be augmented by the other,
but also checked when it becomes tyrannical. Both are offices
under God. Both represent God. Neither exclusively represents
God.

When judgment is brought in God's name, it must be within a
lawfully designated jurisdiction. Churches do not physically punish evil doers, and civil governments do not excommunicate people, denying them access to the Lord's Supper. Civil governments
do not possess the authority to cast people to the edge of the pits of
hell, as the church does, turning people's bodies over to Satan in
order that they might be brought back inside the covenant
(1 Corinthians 5:5).

Because men today do not fear God or God's eternal judgment, they do not fear excommunication. Churches that do not
honor (at least by a careful investigation of the facts and trial) the
excommunications of other churches are adding their authority to
the skepticism of the covenant-breakers.

So what do men fear today? They fear an institution that can punish them physically and economically: the State. As men lose faith in God, they gain new respect for the State. This is a great temptation for officers of the State to usurp their God-given authority and extend their jurisdiction beyond what God has delegated.

But judgment eventually comes. In the Old Testament, it sometimes came in the most feared form of all: *leprosy.*

Leprosy and Jurisdiction

Leprosy! The word strikes terror in those who know its disfiguring work. We are not sure that the disease we call leprosy today is the same as the one called leprosy in the Bible. Lepers were placed under quarantine in the Bible (Leviticus 13), isolated from family, work, and worship. It was considered the ultimate curse. Victims were not merely sick; they were "unclean." Leprosy was like sin; its infection would slowly consume its prey. There was no known cure other than divine intervention. *It was considered the special judgment of God, and only God could remove it.* This is one reason why anyone cured of leprosy had to offer sacrifices to make atonement (Leviticus 14).

When we raise the subject of leprosy, we raise the subject of lawful jurisdiction. (Law = *juris*; declare = *dictio*.) In the Old Testament, the priests had jurisdiction over quarantine for leprosy. They would declare a suspected person either leprous or clean. Their word was sovereign.

There are a number of Biblical accounts where God vented His wrath by inflicting the rebellious with leprosy. The important point to bear in mind is that in the two cases surveyed here, God inflicted leprosy as a judgment on people for having rebelled against God's lawful authority. They violated the office of another God-ordained ruler. Again, the focus was jurisdictional. The question is: Who has the lawful authority to judge? Who speaks for God in any given instance? In short, who has *jurisdiction?*

Miriam

Miriam, Moses' sister, was struck with leprosy when she and Aaron challenged God's choice of Moses as His mediator. "So the anger of the LORD burned against them [Miriam and Aaron] and He departed. But when the cloud had withdrawn from over the tent, behold, Miriam was leprous, as white as snow. As Aaron turned toward Miriam, behold, she was leprous" (Numbers 12:10). Their challenge was a serious offense. Aaron was the high priest, the supreme religious leader in Israel. Miriam was a prophetess and head of the spirit-filled women (Exodus 15:20, 21). Though they each held high *religious* positions in Israel, their authority was limited by God. Any attempt to usurp the mediatorial position given to Moses by God was met with judgment.

Uzziah

God's laws are not to be tampered with. King Uzziah is said to have been "proud" (2 Chronicles 26:16). His pride lead him to go beyond his jurisdiction. While he was "chief of State," being the king in Judah, he was not a priest. King Uzziah could not assume the role of a priest and perform ecclesiastical functions. He had no jurisdiction in the Temple, the Old Testament equivalent of the New Testament Church. Uzziah ignored God's law and "acted corruptly, and he was unfaithful to the LORD his God, for he entered the temple of the LORD to burn incense on the altar of incense" (2 Chronicles 26:16).

Is God serious about this jurisdictional separation? Apparently He is. The king was struck with the most feared disease: leprosy! "And king Uzziah was a leper to the day of his death; and he lived in a separate house, being a leper, for he was cut off from the house of the LORD" (v. 21). He lost access to the Temple, was isolated from the general population, and lost his kingdom to his son, Jotham, who "was over the king's house judging the people of the land" (v. 21).

The Priests

Azariah the priest was not passive in this whole affair. He knew the limitations of the king's power. He, along with "eighty priests of the LORD" (v. 17), took action against the king. Notice that they "opposed Uzziah the king" (v. 18). They informed him that "it is not for you, Uzziah, to burn incense to the LORD, but for the priests, the sons of Aaron who are consecrated to burn incense" (v. 18). The priests commanded Uzziah to "get out of the sanctuary" (v. 18).

These "ecclesiastical officials" are called "valiant men" (v. 17). Why? They acted with great risk. While there were eighty of them, the King still commanded an army. He could have put them to death. There was a precedent for this, when Ahimelech the priest helped David against King Saul (1 Samuel 21-22). King Saul called on Doeg the Edomite to attack the priests, after the King's own servants refused. "And Doeg the Edomite turned around and attacked the priests, and he killed that day eighty-five who wore the linen ephod" (1 Samuel 22:18). Doeg the Edomite, one who despised the covenant, had no qualms about killing the priests. In our day, if our nation moves further from its Biblical foundation, we'll see similar despisers who will rape the Bride of Christ, the Church. King Uzziah had Saul's hate in his eye: "Uzziah, with a censer in his hand for burning incense, was enraged" (2 Chronicles 26:19).

The priests were not casual about their duties. Too often the church has been passive as the State has increasingly encroached on the jurisdiction of the church. While they knew their lives were at stake, they were more concerned with the "honor of the LORD" (2 Chronicles 26:18).

Back to Basics: Family, Church, and State

The leprosy of Uzziah is a dramatic scene. It brings out the essence of church/State relations. Let's go back and study the Biblical relationship between church and State. The easiest way to understand this relationship is to begin with the family. It, too, is a government with a specific jurisdiction. The infringement on the church by the State is paralleled by a similar encroachment against family authority, usually for the same reasons: *the secular humanist State will not endure competition.* Once the State repudiates God, it becomes a god unto itself. It will not tolerate the worship of other gods. The family, because it is a God-ordained government, competes with the secularized State. The family has rulers, laws, and subjects.

The Bible establishes multiple covenantal jurisdictions: family, church, and State. Each has a specific *limited* jurisdiction where a *limited* amount of authority and power operate. While the jurisdictions may differ, the same law is to be used for each. While the standard for each is the Bible, the application of Scripture differs as an individual moves from one jurisdiction to another. For example, a father has authority to discipline his own child for an infraction, but he cannot discipline another parent's child. Parental *authority* and *power* operate within this specified *family* jurisdiction. Parents can delegate jurisdiction to other parents, say, in a school setting. Authority, however, is not usurped nor claimed by the school; it is delegated and transferred by the parents.

The father, who may also be an elder in his church, has ecclesiastical jurisdiction, along with other elders within his own church, to discipline an erring member according to the guidelines laid down in Matthew 18 and 1 Corinthians 6. He cannot, however, go to another church and exercise discipline there unless formally and officially appealed to. His *authority* and *power* to exercise discipline is *limited* to a specified ecclesiastical jurisdiction.

A man who is a father in family government and an elder in church government may also be an elected official in *civil* government. (Because of the church/State jurisdictional separation, an elder who becomes a civil official would have to demit the ministry. He certainly should not *exercise* both offices simultaneously. Only Jesus wears the crowns of Priest and King.) As soon as he acts as a civil representative, his area of jurisdiction is limited to *civil* government. He cannot use his *authority* and *power* as a *civil* governor to infringe upon family and church governments with the sword. He must stay within the bounds of civil affairs when he is acting as an elected official.

It should be pointed out, however, that there is a qualitative difference between family government and church and civil governments. Fathers are not ordained with oil (Zechariah 4:14 in context of chapters 3 and 4). Thus, the family as an institution is not in all ways parallel to State and church. This is why the family cannot by itself lawfully resist the State; Biblically, only the church has been ordained to do so. The family ought to find protection under the church.

Family-Worshipping Revolutionaries

This is one very good reason to reject the revolutionary radical segments of the so-called "identity movement." Members of numerous radical religious groups claim that they have a lawful right to rebel against civil authority because of their supposed link to the ten lost tribes of Israel. They are trying to make family or tribal authority supreme over civil authority. This is anti-Biblical to the core. The family is not the church, nor is it an alternative to the church. Paralleling the decline in Christianity in our day has also been the rise of a new humanist familism which is proposed as the only lawful alternative to the humanist State. Such a choice is inherently unlawful and anti-Biblical. The church is the protector of the family. It is the God-ordained government that alone can lawfully authorize and therefore legitimize family resistance to the State.

In short, from a Biblical perspective: *no church-no lawful family resistance.* Anyone who teaches otherwise is a covenant-breaker, a revolutionary, and should be avoided. He will eventually be smashed by the State, and any association with him will produce unpleasant consequences. If the church is corrupt, then the State's tyranny is simply God's lawful judgment, just as it was when Assyria and Babylon carried away the Israelites. Tyranny in such a case is a step toward repentance, revival, and reform.

What the Church Can Do

First and foremost, the church can preach. It can set forth God's permanent standards of right and wrong: for individuals, families, churches, and civil government. Preaching applies God's standards to this world. A church that refuses to preach the whole counsel of God has become an accomplice of evil in every area of life not touched upon by its preaching.

Second, it administers the sacraments. Baptism places people under the covenant structure of God, and therefore under God's protection. The Lord's Supper is God's way to commune formally with men. We come into the presence of God in a unique way. This is a way of spiritually empowering the church.

Third, the church can begin to preach the psalms of judgment, sometimes called the *imprecatory psalms*. The church formally and judicially calls God's external wrath down upon the heads of public officials who are publicly disobeying God's law. Psalm 83 is a good example of these psalms:

> O my God, make them as the whirling dust;
> Like chaff before the wind.
> Like fire that burns the forest,
> And like a flame that sets the mountains on fire,
> So pursue them with Thy tempest,
> And terrify them with Thy storm.
> Fill their faces with dishonor,
> That they may seek Thy name, O LORD.
> Let them be ashamed and dismayed forever;
> And let them be humiliated and perish (vv. 13-17).

Of course, pagans believe that the God of the Bible is a myth. They believe that He is incapable of judging anyone in history, and probably not in eternity. Therefore, they believe that the church is impotent, prayers of Christians are impotent, and they can safely ignore God's Bride.

This is what a lot of Christians believe, too. For them, imprecatory psalms are not good enough. The Lord's Supper is not powerful enough. No, they say that we need guns and ammo. We need Army surplus camouflage garments and weekend war games in the woods. We need all the tools of the power religionists. Or else they take the other approach and conclude that we need to become doormats in the name of Jesus, wimps for Christ. Instead of the power religion, they adopt the escape religion.

Both groups reject the Biblical alternative: the *dominion religion*. They do not want to do covenantal work in God's way.

The Limits of Jurisdiction

The Bible defines the *limits* of jurisdiction; it must also be used to prescribe the *specifics of operation* for each jurisdiction. The Bible is a blueprint for family government, for church government, and for civil government. If the Bible is the blueprint for only the family and church and not the State, then immediate jurisdictional infringements take place. For example, according to the Bible, parents have educational jurisdiction of their children. If the State repudiates the Bible as a blueprint for State-craft, children will be seen as wards of the State and thus under its jurisdiction. Taxes will be raised by the State, teachers will be certified by the State, schools will be accredited by the State, and students will be compelled by the State to be educated by the State.

What if the State decides that more taxes are needed to fund some of its programs (programs that must be defined by the Bible)? Can the State legitimately tax the church to raise the needed revenue? The State certainly has the authority and power to tax (Romans 13:7; Matthew 22:15-22). But can it tax any way it wishes? Can it tax the church? If the Bible is not a blueprint for taxation and the limits of civil jurisdiction, then the State is free to tax as it pleases.

God has established both church and State. They are not, in principle, hostile toward one another. But because each is a government, with a certain amount of authority and power, we should expect power struggles. Sometimes the power struggle is the church attempting to impose its will on the State. The church grows, then, not by the regenerating work of the Holy Spirit, but by the power of the sword.

More often than not, the State imposes its will on the church because it sees the church as a competing government. This occurs because the State has already become secularized. It has repudiated the Bible as its standard. Of course, the State is secularized due to the secularization of the nation. By the time the State rejects the Bible, the nation as a whole has already rejected the Bible as a blueprint for life. Civil government reflects self, family, and church governments.

Church/State Cooperation

The Bible portrays church and State as cooperating governments. Most people are aware that the Bible is the standard for the priests as they carry out their priestly duties. But what of the king? Was he obligated to follow the Bible as well? The Bible makes it clear that he was.

> Now it shall come about when he [the king] sits on the throne of his kingdom, he shall write for himself a copy of this law on a scroll in the presence of the Levitical priests. And it shall be with him, and he shall read it all the days of his life, that he may learn to fear the LORD his God, by carefully observing all the words of this law and these statutes, that his heart may not be lifted up above his countrymen and that he may not turn aside from the commandment, to the right or the left; in order that he and his sons may continue to live long in his kingdom in the midst of Israel (Deuteronomy 17:18-20).

While church and State as *jurisdictions* are separate, religion is not. Both priests and kings are commanded to follow the same standard of government, even though not all laws apply to each in the same way. We can go so far as to say that the presence of the priests was a reminder to the king that they were to help him interpret the law as it related to civil affairs. This is precisely what Azariah and the eighty priests were doing when they confronted King Uzziah; they were reminding him of his limited jurisdiction.

Moral Criteria for Rulership

The criteria for leadership in both church and State is the same. When Jethro, Moses' father-in-law, counseled Moses to decentralize the judicial arm of the civil government and choose lesser magistrates, he laid down the qualifications for those who would rule. They were to be "able men who fear God, men of truth, those who hate dishonest gain" (Exodus 18:21). In Deuteronomy 1:9-15, Moses recounts the circumstances of Jethro's counsel and adds that these leaders were to be "wise and discerning and experienced men," not showing "partiality in judgment" (Deuteronomy 1:13, 17).

Church leaders in the New Testament are to exhibit similar ethical qualities and real life experience (1 Timothy 3:1-7). Being "above reproach" can be compared to "men of truth." "Those who hate dishonest gain" is similar to being "free from the love of money." An "experienced" man is someone who is "not a new convert."

Parallel Jurisdictions

Moses became the chief judicial officer in Israel, assisted by numerous lesser magistrates (Exodus 18:17-26). Aaron, Moses' brother, became the chief ecclesiastical officer as High Priest, assisted by numerous lesser priests (Leviticus 8).

In the days of the Judges, Othniel, Ehud, Shamgar, Gideon and Samson served as political officers (Judges 1-13), while the son of Micah, Phineas, Eli, and the Levites served in an ecclesiastical capacity (Judges 17; 20:28; 1 Samuel 1-8).

During the period of the monarchy, King Saul served in a civil capacity while Ahimelech ministered as the chief ecclesiastical leader in the nation (1 Samuel 10 and 21). There was King David and Priest Abiathar (1 Chronicles 15:11), King Solomon and Priest Zadok (1 Kings 1:45), King Joash and Priest Jehoiada (2 Kings 11), and King Josiah and Priest Hilkiah (2 Kings 22:4).

Even after the return from exile, church and State as parallel institutions operated with Governor Nehemiah (Nehemiah 7) and Priest Ezra (Nehemiah 8). This jurisdictional cooperation culminated in the priestly office of Joshua and the civil office of Zerubbabel (Zechariah 4:14).

All Are Ministers

The New Testament describes leaders in the church and State as "ministers" (Mark 10:42-45 and Romans 13:4). Even when describing the role of the civil magistrate, the Greek word for "deacon" is used.

The word underscores the ruler's duty to *serve*, rather than to "lord it over" those under his authority. Dominion comes through service. The civil "minister" rules for our "good" and he is "an avenger who brings wrath upon the one who practices evil"

(Romans 13:4). How does the civil magistrate determine what is "good" from what is "evil"? As God's "minister," he must consult God's Word.

Jurisdictional Usurpation

There is always the danger of jurisdictional usurpation, when, say, civil government removes the jurisdictional framework of the church. The Bible cites a number of examples of how the king sought to overrule the authority and function of the church. King Saul assumed for himself the duties of the priests when he offered sacrifices rather than staying within the bounds of his kingly duties (1 Samuel 15:9-15, 22). In another place, King Saul killed the godly priest Ahimelech because he would not fulfill the king's political goals (1 Samuel 21:1).

King Jeroboam established his State religion in Bethel and Dan. Non-Levites of the worst character were appointed to serve as priests (1 Kings 12:26-31). Of course, we've already seen how King Uzziah was struck with leprosy for usurping the priestly function of burning incense in the temple (2 Chronicles 26:16).

But there are times when the church forgets its God-ordained role. The church can deny its prophetic ministry when it is seduced by politics, having lost faith in our Transcendent God, putting trust in human action. Isn't this what happened when the people wanted to crown Jesus as King, to make Him their political ruler? They had given up hope in the transformation of man from the inside out. They denied the transforming work of the Holy Spirit to regenerate the dead heart of man. Man's salvation would come through political power. Jesus rebuffed their desires to make Him a political savior. While politics has a role to play, it is only one role among many.

Summary

The ninth basic principle in the Biblical blueprint for civil government is that lawful jurisdiction for any government is established by God in the Bible. To violate these God-ordained jurisdictions is to become rebellious. It brings on God's judgment in history.

God judges those who tamper with His law. There is a *jurisdictional* separation between church and State. The Bible defines the limits of jurisdiction. Church and State were established to cooperate, not compete. Leadership in both church and State is based on *ethical* considerations. Church and State are *parallel* governments bound by the same law. Leaders in both church and State are given the title "minister." The Bible condemns jurisdictional usurpation.

God establishes multiple government jurisdictions, and therefore multiple hierarchies, in order to reflect His own plural nature, but also to restrain the sinfulness of man. He brought judgment in history against the builders of the Tower of Babel because they proposed to build a one-world messianic State. They wanted to give their own name to themselves, defining themselves without reference to God, and to establish their own jurisdictions.

The criteria for serving as a judge, in church and State, is morality. Men are not to use their offices to pursue personal economic gain or power. They are to execute judgment as God's delegated representatives. This representative character of all civil and ecclesiastical offices is basic to every human government.

God brings His people freedom. One means to this freedom is a system of potentially competing delegated sovereignties. When men sin, and overstep their limits (the meaning of sin), they often try to extend their authority over others. Parallel governments help to reduce the extent of such lawless behavior. This is the meaning of federalism, of checks and balances.

Most Americans are confused when it comes to church/State relations. If they were asked to choose between the language of the First Amendment of our Constitution and the language of the Soviet Constitution, few could tell the difference. The critics of Christ and His law have done a masterful job in rewriting history. (See Chapter 13 and the Appendix for details.)

In summary:

    1. All authority is delegated from God.
    2. Obedience to God-authorized judges is required.
    3. There is no single human authority; human authority is always plural.

4. King and priest are the most obvious examples of divided authority.

5. When judgment is brought in God's name, it must be within a lawfully designated jurisdiction.

6. Men mainly fear the State today because they do not fear God or excommunication.

7. Leprosy was an Old Testament judgment from God.

8. King Uzziah was judged with leprosy because he refused to honor the sanctification (set-apartness) of the sanctuary.

9. The secular humanist State refuses to honor the other jurisdictions: family and church.

10. Fathers possess God-given limited authority over wives and children.

11. The church is the primary protector of the family.

12. The family is not "the key" institution; the church is.

13. The church's weapons are preaching, the sacraments, and prayer (for example, imprecatory psalms).

14. The Bible establishes the jurisdictional limits on each institution.

15. Church and State should cooperate.

16. Both are under Biblical law; both must rule (judge) in terms of Biblical law.

17. The criteria are moral for both the civil and ecclesiastical offices.

18. The jurisdictions are parallel.

19. The officers of both are ministers of God.

10

REBUILDING TAKES TIME

For who has despised the day of small things? (Zechariah 4:10).

Depression can easily set in when you consider how far behind the humanists today's Christians are in various areas. We have a lot of lost ground to recover. For example:

- The three major networks are run by hardcore humanists.
- Most major publishing companies refuse to publish a genuinely Christian book.
- Christian schools often have to settle for curriculum materials developed by secular companies.
- Christian parents are often left with few choices when their children are ready to attend college.
- 86% of the news media personnel seldom or never attend religious services and yet they are the primary source of news.
- The courts are hostile to religion in general and Christianity in particular.

These facts could depress even the most optimistic Christian. We have lost a tremendous amount of ground over the last 150 years. It is going to take a long time to get it back. The only events that might speed up this timetable would be a mass revival — a revival of self-government under God (we have yet to hear of such a revival in modern history) — or a terrible catastrophe: a lost war, a plague, or both. In either case, Christians will be called upon to exercise responsibility under God as never before. But how will they train themselves in advance to exercise such responsibility in a culture that promises continued benefits without revival? What if they are not prepared to take responsibility? As the publishers of the Biblical Blueprint Series asked themselves before they began the project: *How do you sell responsibility to modern Christians?*

What if a group of dedicated Christians were to buy their nation's most prominent newspaper? What difference would it make? Not much. Where would they find the reporters who understand Biblical principles and who will write their articles from this perspective? Where would they find the advertising people who would recognize the pagan symbolism of advertisements? Would the editor even be willing to risk dropping the daily astrology column? Without an army of dedicated, well-trained, Biblically self-conscious professionals, the ownership of the newspaper (or television network, or whatever) would not mean very much. In fact, it would probably mean financial losses, as the new owners floundered with the responsibilities of management.

But we need to do more than buy a newspaper. We need to win the whole world to Jesus Christ—to get the whole world to acknowledge what is in fact the case, that Jesus Christ is King of kings and Lord of lords. We have a big job ahead of us. But what encourages me is Zechariah 4:10. Beginning to do something is the main thing. Being big enough to do something is never an issue in the Bible. The giants did not seem to bother Joshua and Caleb; Goliath was no problem for David; and faith the size of a mustard seed is all the Christian needs to move a mountain.

Civilizations come and go, but the kingdom of God goes on forever. This is the point of Nebuchadnezzar's dream of the human colossus. Kingdoms built on the shaky foundation that man is sovereign cannot last. Pick up any history book and you can read about the demise of every empire-building civilization. They are dust on the cosmic scales of God's justice.

Christians have lost sight of the stone cut without hands that became a mountain that filled the earth (Daniel 2:35). For some reason we just cannot seem to believe that Jesus, through His redeemed people, is the fulfillment of that prophecy (cf. 1 Peter 2:5). We have convinced ourselves that defeat is the only option for the church. The only hope is retreat in the face of a creeping secularism. Maybe if things get real bad God will rapture us out of this mess

Unbelief and Defeat

It is interesting to note that every time there was any consideration of retreat in the face of opposition, the people of God were rebuked for their unbelief. For example, when the 12 spies were sent out to Canaan, God had promised them that the land would be theirs: "Send out for yourself men so that they may spy out the land of Canaan, *that I am going to give to the sons of Israel*" (Numbers 13:2).

You know the story: Ten of the spies came back with a report steeped in unbelief. Joshua and Caleb believed God. Sure, there were giants in the land. Joshua and Caleb never denied this. So what? God is the Lord. The promise was made, the land was theirs. Giants are nothing more than a minor and temporary inconvenience.

Forty years were wasted in the wilderness because the people chose to believe the report of the unbelieving spies. The giants turned out to be whimpering dogs. When two spies were sent out to Jericho forty years later, Rahab told the real story:

> I know that the LORD has given this land to you and that a great fear of you has fallen on us, so that all who live in this country are melting in fear because of you. We have heard how the LORD dried up the water of the Red Sea for you when you came out of Egypt, and what you did to Sihon and Og, the two kings of the Amorites east of the Jordan, whom you completely destroyed. *When we heard of it, our hearts sank and everyone's courage failed because of you, for the* LORD *your God is God in heaven above and on the earth beneath* (Joshua 2:8-11, New International Version).

There is little difference between the humanists of Rahab's day and the humanists of our day. They are just as frightened as the residents of Jericho were. But today's Christians are unwilling to believe this, any more than Joshua's generation was willing to believe it. And so Christians have sat on the sidelines of life, waiting for God to bail them out. Do you remember what God did to Joshua's generation? He did not bail them out. He waited for them to die, and then He allowed Joshua and Caleb to lead the next generation to victory (Numbers 14:21-23; Joshua 15:13-19).

Selling Fear

There is an old rule for fund-raising letters: you need to sell either greed or fear. Most cause-oriented groups find it easier to sell fear, or its corollary, outrage. You can tell a great deal about any organization by finding out what sorts of fears motivate the people who send it money. You can do this by reading the organization's fund-raising letters.

What is scaring humanists in the United States these days? Nuclear war? AIDS? The Republican Party? No, for the first time in this century, *Christians* are scaring them. A recent fund-raising letter from author Isaac Asimov, President of the American Humanist Association, shows that humanists are running scared: "Humanism is an ethical, rational outlook that has time and science on its side. If there is to be a future for humanity it will be *because* our outlook [humanism] kept back the present tide of irrationalism and superstition [Christianity]." The AHA wants to raise $100,000 to fight Christianity! "This is money that can be used to spread the message of Humanism further than it has been spread before, bringing in thousands of new members. . . . Our philosophy has reason on its side."

Why are these fund-raising letters being sent out? Yes, that's right: *to raise funds.* Bureaucracy lives! But what I really mean is: What is the *official reason* that the fund-raisers are using to justify people's sending in money to them? For the first time in over a century, humanists are facing the disintegration of their man-centered worldview. They need "thousands of humanistically minded people . . . [to] make the AHA the strongest possible force for the rational human mind we have in the Americas." *They realize that they may be on the way out.*

The Democrats are afraid of the Republicans, right? Not quite. They are afraid of Christians who are getting into politics, and who apparently are joining the Republican Party instead of the Democrats. A Democratic National Committee fund-raising letter, written by Paul J. Kirk, Jr., wrote this about Christian involvement in the political arena. This letter stated the following:

1. The idea that a Christian like Pat Robertson was running for President was "very frightening."
2. Pat Robertson is "an ultrafundamentalist."
3. Pat Robertson is "one of the most radical right-wing leaders in America."
4. Pat Robertson is *"one of the most powerful public figures in America today."*
5. According to Mr. Kirk, "Pat Robertson is beginning to worry the leaders of *both* the Democratic and Republican parties."

Mr. Kirk writes that he "couldn't believe that this relatively unknown man could be a major, if not leading, candidate for President." Yet this "unknown" is somehow "one of the most powerful public figures in America today." How can an unknown be so powerful? What bothers him is that someone powerful is a *political* unknown. This is what scares the humanists to death. They see that a Christian leader has gained what appears to be national political power, but he has done this *outside the normal secular humanist channels to power.* When Jimmy Carter ran for President in 1976 people were saying, "Jimmy Who?" But Jimmy Carter was hand-picked, a member of David Rockefeller's Trilateral Commission. He only appeared to be a political unknown. But Pat Robertson really *is* an unknown — unknown to the ways of political compromise, special deals, and political debts to be paid. He hasn't paid his political dues, and what worries the professional politicians is the possibility that he will pay his dues mostly to Bible-believing and morally conservative voters. He might vote their way, not humanism's way. This scares them.

Pat Robertson is the head of a major satellite television network, the president of a university, and his book *The Secret Kingdom* was on the *New York Times* bestseller list. But he is not yet "politically tested," meaning *politically screened.* This is what scares them. Power is only supposed to come to those who have played within the political system by the present leaders' rules.

After listing the impact that Pat Robertson has through his donor list, television network, Mr. Kirk makes this statement: "But his greatest threat is not his powerful organization. It is the enormous political muscle of the Religious Right." So then, Pat Robertson is not the only perceived threat. *All Christians who hold to certain fundamental beliefs are the enemies of the dominant humanist political faith.*

Why are these self-described humanists frightened when they learn that Christians are getting active in every area of life? There are probably as many reasons as there are people opposed to Christian activism. But at the heart of all the reasons there is one: those who deny the regenerating work of God's Holy Spirit as the Transformer of men and women from the inside-out see politics and their common allies, the courts and the public schools, as the new gods. *For the humanist, politics is the new messiah.* When the Christian says, "There is another King, Jesus" (Acts 17:7), he is accused of blasphemy, and worse, unbelief.

Why Christians Should Get Involved

The people in Gideon's day saw politics as the solution to their problems (Judges 8:22, 23). If they just had a powerful king to rule over them, their problems would be solved. When Abimelech murdered his opposition (9:1-6), he promised the people security if they would only follow him. While there is the offer of shade (salvation), it is an illusion that brings with it a choking tyranny (v. 15).

When the lack of personal holiness corrupted the family (Judges 14-16) and priesthood (1 Samuel 2:12-17, 22-36), the people turned to the State for salvation (1 Samuel 8).

The Christian calls politics into question, *not* because it is an illegitimate sphere of Christian activity, but because it is too often seen by people as the fundamental activity. Politics was never meant to save mankind, and it cannot save. While Christians are to redeem ("buy back") politics and the civil sphere of government, we are never to view political action as the sole solution to all our problems, or even the main solution.

The purpose of Christians' involvement in politics ought to be more than the mere replacement of non-Christians with Christians. There are numerous things that civil government should not be doing that it is doing — and doing with the support of most voters. A civil government based on Biblical law would mean a drastic reduction in its size and power and a return of jurisdiction to individuals, private enterprise, families, churches, and local civil governments.

The church has awakened (at least some of the church has) to her responsibilities in the area of world view thinking. Christians are beginning to realize that the Bible has answers, that the Bible addresses the world with specific solutions to seemingly perplexing problems. For the Christian, the Bible is a blueprint for building a Christian civilization.

There are many Christians and non-Christians who do not like to think of the Bible in these terms. In fact, many are horrified at any suggestion that the world is in any way redeemable. They are content to ignore verses like "God so loved the world" (John 3:16); "God was in Christ reconciling the world to Himself" (2 Corinthians 5:19); Jesus is "the light of the world" (John 8:12), "the Savior of the world" (4:42), and "the Lamb of God who takes away the sins of the world!" (1:29). And how about this one?: "The kingdom of the world *has become* the kingdom of our Lord, and of His Christ; and He will reign forever and ever" (Revelation 11:15).

Now, don't get me wrong. To say that the world is redeemed is not to say that the world can be made perfect. For example, the dead sinner is redeemed, but he is not perfect. Judicially, the sinner stands before God as perfect because he has the perfect righteousness of Christ *imputed* to him. He is not made righteous; he is declared righteous. This, however, does not exempt him from conforming his life more and more to the image of Jesus Christ. This process is called sanctification.

God expects the redeemed sinner to conform his behavior to the commandments of God, though the effects of his sin nature will not be eradicated until he is raised "imperishable" (1 Corinthians 15:42). The implications of such a life are evident. If the redeemed sinner can change his life through sanctification, then how can we deny that the world is destined for corruption? Isn't the redeemed sinner both salt and light in the world? Let's face it, wherever the gospel has changed individuals it has changed civilizations. Just compare the Christian West with the paganism and cultural decline of other nations.

But what about the advance of humanism? The answer is quite simple: the *advance of humanism* is the result of the *retreat of Christianity*. Just as a neglected garden will be overwhelmed by weeds, so a neglected area of responsibility will be overwhelmed by evil.

Does Satan Have More Power Than Christians?

But what about the rise of demonic activity in our day? Many Christians point to this and say that this is proof that we're coming to the end of the world, meaning the end of the "Church Age." But there was also heightened demonic activity during Jesus' public ministry. Was this the end of the world? Yes! But not the end of the *Christian* world; it was the end of demon-sponsored humanism, Pharisaism, legalism, and Romanism. The pagans better understood the implications of Christianity than do many modern critics of civilization building: "These men who have upset the world have come here also" (Acts 17:6).

Gary North's analysis of occultism and New Age Humanism shows that "[t]he rise of occultism takes place at the end of civilizations. . . . This humanist civilization has spent spiritual capital, and its checks are bouncing. The decay of humanism has led to the revival of occultism. What we are witnessing is *occult revival and cultural disintegration*. What we may very well be witnessing is *humanist civilization's dying gasp*."[1]

The collapse of humanism and the stench of occultism bring with them certain opportunities for Christians. The world is look-

---

1. Gary North, *Unholy Spirits: Occultism and New Age Humanism* (Ft. Worth, Texas: Dominion Press, 1986), pp. 15 and 379.

ing for answers. The Christian, if he truly believes the Bible, has answers. Setting the agenda as we approach the 20th century should be the priority for all Christians. This will mean involvement.

We are too often occupied with what man has done, and the whole time we deny what God is doing. The way Christians think and act, you would suppose that Satan is more powerful than God. Satan has power, but it is limited by God. Even in the Old Testament era, Satan was restricted in the influence he could exert. Before Satan could afflict Job he had to seek God's permission: "Behold, all that he [Job] has is in your power, only do not put forth your hand on him" (Job 1:12; cf. 2:6). Through it all God received the glory and Job was finally restored (Job 42:10-17).

During Jesus' earthly ministry, the disciples had authority and power over demons because Satan's power was partially grounded. When the seventy disciples returned from their mission they remarked that "even the demons are subject to us" (Luke 10:17). How could this be?: "And He said to them, 'I was watching Satan fall from heaven like lightning. Behold, I have given you authority to tread upon serpents and scorpions, and over all the power of the enemy, and nothing shall injure you'" (vv. 17-18).

Jesus tells the Pharisees that His casting out demons is the sign that the kingdom of God has come, displacing the enemy territory of Satan: "But if I cast out demons by the finger of God, then the kingdom of God has come upon you. When a strong man [Satan] fully armed guards his own household, his possessions are undisturbed; but when someone stronger [God] than he attacks him and overpowers him, he takes away from him all his armor on that he had relied, and distributes his plunder [Satan's kingdom]" (11:10-22).

When Jesus was about to go to the cross He made reference to the effect that Satan will have on His work: "I will not speak much more with you, for the ruler of the world is coming, and he has nothing in Me" (John 14:30). All the powers of Hell would not be able to deter Jesus in the task that would soon energize the church to such an extent that the gates of Hell will not be able to stand against her power: "Upon this rock [the sure testimony that Jesus is the Christ, the Son of the living God] I will build My church; and the gates of Hades shall not overpower it" (Matthew 16:18).

The apostle Paul, aware of the power of Rome and that many Christians would suffer at the hands of the State, strengthened them with these words: "And the God of peace will soon crush Satan under your feet" (Romans 16:20). These Roman Christians could expect this "soon" by praying for it and carrying out their dominion task in every area of life. The Christian is able to spoil the works of the devil because of the limited power that Satan has over believers. He cannot "touch" a Christian (1 John 5:18); his works have been destroyed (1 John 3:8); he must flee when resisted (James 4:7); and he has been rendered powerless over believers (Hebrews 2:14).

The above Scriptural evidence is of no use if Christians assume incorrectly that Satan is now in control, and that his controlling influence will continue. Of course, if Christians do nothing we can expect Satan's kingdom to advance. The whole world lies in the power of the evil one (1 John 5:19) as long as Christians refuse to plant and water the seeds of the gospel in the world. The power of Satan over the world is temporary until the nations are discipled (cf. Matthew 28:18-20). Moreover, to say that Satan is in control of the governments of the world is to say that Christians have been irresponsible in transforming the civil realms of power according to the commandments of God. Christians have no excuse because God has "disarmed the rulers and authorities [and] made a public display of them, having triumphed over them through Him [Jesus]" (Colossians 2:15).

The crucifixion brought the false powers to light. Jesus has exposed the powers of darkness (cf. Luke 1:79; 1 Corinthians 4:5, 6; Colossians 1:13). They are, in fact, powerless over the kingdom of Jesus Christ. When the kingdom of God is compared with the kingdom of Satan there is a radical difference. Satan's mask of deception has been torn from him. What looked like triumph for Satan and his followers, the resurrection showed to be folly. The gates of Satan's kingdom are vulnerable and will be battered down by the advancing church of Jesus Christ under the power of God's

Holy Spirit working through obedient, dominion-oriented Christians (Matthew 16:18). Victory for the people of God is certain: not because of their own strength, but because of the strength of the One whom they serve, even Jesus Christ, unto whom all power in heaven and earth has been given, and who is with His people always, even unto the end of the age (Matthew 28:18-20). The Christian's hope is found in the resurrected Jesus Christ who sits at the right hand of His Father. Present-day Christians are to know the present-day power of that resurrection and act upon it (cf. Philippians 3:10; Romans 6:5).

If Satan doesn't have as much power as God does, then Satan's human followers also cannot have as much power as God's human followers do, unless the latter voluntarily renounce their responsibilities. If God's people are faithful, power will flow to them (Deuteronomy 28:1-14).

It is time that we start to build a Christian civilization.

The Question of Time

One of the most debilitating "doctrines" of the church is the belief that Jesus is coming back soon—meaning *man's* concept of "soon"—and that the world is headed for inevitable destruction. There is nothing Christians should do to try to stop the inevitable.

When Jesus' disciples asked Him at the ascension if at that time He was "restoring the kingdom to Israel," Jesus diverted their attention from final restoration to the work at hand: "It is not for you to know times and epochs which the Father has fixed by His own authority; but you shall receive power when the Holy Spirit has come upon you; and you shall be My witnesses both in Jerusalem, and in all Judea and Samaria, and even to the remotest part of the earth" (Acts 1:6-8). In effect, Jesus was saying, "Do not worry about God's timetable; it is already fixed. Busy yourself with the affairs of the kingdom."

Some of the Thessalonian Christians were "leading an undisciplined life, doing no work at all, but acting like busybodies" (2 Thessalonians 3:11). While this may have little to do with a preoccupation with "the day of the Lord" (1 Thessalonians 5:2), it reminds us that *God requires us to work, regardless of external circumstances.* Faithfulness is evaluated in terms of kingdom work: "Who then is the faithful and sensible slave whom his master put in charge of his household to give them their food at the proper time? Blessed is that slave whom his master finds so doing when he comes" (Matthew 24:45, 46). Jesus goes on to hint at the time and circumstances of His coming: "the master of that slave will come on a day *when he does not expect him and at an hour which he does not know*" (v. 50).

Nowhere does Scripture intimate that we should cease any aspect of kingdom work, even if we *think* Jesus' coming is near. George Ladd, a premillennial scholar, writes, "*The delay of the master made no difference to the true servant:* he busied himself about his Lord's business. . . . But the master's delay induced the false servant to a sinful course of action. *The Lord's delay brought out the true character of his servants.*"[2]

Jesus related a parable to His disciples when "they supposed that the kingdom of God was going to appear immediately" (Luke 19:11). In Jesus' day, many of His disciples assumed the kingdom would arrive through a cataclysmic event with no effort on their part. Jesus told them through the parable, "do business until I come back" (v. 13). When the master finally returns he will take an accounting. Those who made a profit on the money given by the master will "be in authority over ten and five cities" (vv. 17-19). The one who put the money "away in a handkerchief" (v. 20), not being industrious enough to "put the money in the bank" to collect "interest" (v. 23), loses everything (v. 24).

Charles Haddon Spurgeon (1834-1892), the great Baptist preacher and evangelist of the nineteenth century, shows how pessimism robs the church of its vitality and stunts its growth.

> David was not a believer in the theory that the world will grow worse and worse, and that the dispensations will wind up with general darkness, and idolatry. Earth's sun is to go down

---

2. George Eldon Ladd, *The Blessed Hope* (Grand Rapids, Michigan: Eerdmans, 1956), p. 106.

amid tenfold night if some of our prophetic brethren are to be believed. Not so do we expect, but we look for a day when the dwellers in all lands shall learn righteousness, shall trust in the Saviour, shall worship thee alone, O God, *"and shall glorify thy name."* The modern notion has greatly damped the zeal of the church for missions, and the sooner it is shown to be unscriptural the better for the cause of God. It neither consorts with prophecy, honours God, nor inspires the church with ardour. Far hence be it driven.[3]

"Therefore, my beloved brethren, be steadfast, immovable, always abounding in the work of the Lord, knowing that your toil is not in vain in the Lord" (1 Corinthians 15:58).

Our Inheritance Grows

Until Christians began to spread the gospel into the Roman Empire, the ancient world had never heard of linear (straight line) time. The ancient pagan world, from savages to sophisticated philosophers, believed in circular time. Time is cyclical, they argued. It is going nowhere. There was no beginning; there will be no end.

Christians challenged this view of time. They preached Christ, and Him crucified. Christ came in the midst of time, they said. God created the world; Adam rebelled; and now Christ has come in the midst of time to die and rise from the dead, overcoming sin. His resurrection points to a future resurrection, Paul writes in his first letter to the Corinthians, chapter 15. Thus, we have hope for the future; only Christians had such hope; therefore, *only Christians had enough confidence in the future to preach a doctrine of linear time.*

God told His people that their earthly efforts have meaning in time and eternity. What we think, say, and do has consequences for us, and also for history. And we know that the good that we do becomes a legacy to other Christians who follow us. *Because we have legitimate faith in the future, we can confidently use other people's gifts to us*

---

3. *The Treasury of David* (Grand Rapids, Michigan: Guardian Press, [1870-1885] 1976), IV:102.

out of the past. And we know that in the future, our good gifts will be put to good use by our spiritual heirs.

Not so the God-haters. Their gifts will either be cut off, or else be inherited by God's people. "The wealth of the sinner is stored up for the righteous" (Proverbs 13:22b). Our God shows loving-kindness to thousands of generations, to those who keep His commandments (Exodus 20:6). The text in Exodus 20 says that He shows lovingkindness to thousands, but most commentators agree that the comparison is between the three or four generations that He patiently endures sinners (Exodus 20:5) and the thousands *of generations* of kindness that He shows to the righteous.

We can build up spiritual capital, economic capital, educational capital, and political capital over many generations. This is our task before God. Slow growth over many generations is the proper approach. What is God's way for His people? Hard work and thrift. Satan, knowing that his time is short (Revelation 12:12), recommends a different program for his human followers: huge risks, borrowed money to fund "big deals," and going for broke. A few generations is all he can expect, *unless Christians voluntarily give him more time by retreating into cultural irrelevance.*

What we need now is not a string of miracles. Miracles are helpful, but what we need is a revival. We need to preach (and believe!) *the whole counsel of God.* We need a full-orbed gospel that offers *comprehensive salvation.* We need healing—not just spiritual and physical healing, but *cultural healing.* We need the doctrine of the resurrection—the resurrection, restoration, and reconstruction of every area of life, to the glory of God. We need to fulfill the dominion covenant of Genesis 1:26-28: to subdue the earth to the glory of God. We need the fulfillment of the great commission: the discipling of the nations.

And how can we get this? By simple covenantal faithfulness, by doing our normal daily jobs well, and then by doing a lot more. We have God's law, the tool of dominion. We have His Holy Spirit to empower us. We have Calvary behind us, which dealt a mortal blow to Satan. After all, can we Christians seriously believe that Satan is more powerful after the Cross than before it? That makes no sense.

No, if we do our work, we will be blessed. So Satan blinds us. He tells us we don't have enough time to get our work done. He persuades us that Christians' efforts are not sufficient to please God. He somehow has convinced a whole generation of Christians that they will leave nothing to their children and grandchildren because the Church will be "Raptured" out of the world and out of history before their children and grandchildren can inherit, or at least put their inheritance to work. Satan has won a temporary cultural victory by shortening the time perspectives of his enemies.

The best example that I can think of is the one Gary North always cites. The Communists believe that an overnight revolution is the only event that can save society from evil capitalism. But they work patiently for generations, eroding their enemies' faith in capitalism, subverting every institution, and planning for revolution, nation by nation.

In contrast, those Christians who have spoken for the church historically have usually believed in the steady progress of the gospel. They have opposed radical revolution. They have had faith in the future. Nevertheless, in our day they have dreamed of miracles and prayed for the Rapture to remove them from their misery. They have adopted Satan's faith in short-run miracles, national political miracles ("We must elect a Christian leader who will throw the rascals out, once and for all!"), and the miracle of the Rapture. Christians have shortened their time perspective, and Satan has convinced his followers that they have all the time in the world.

Satan has been winning for two centuries because of this. It is time to call a halt to this temporary period of Christian defeat. The way we do it is to lengthen our time perspectives and then get to work.

Summary

God tells us that it is our task to subdue the earth to His glory. This will take the cumulative efforts of all His people. No single generation will get all the credit. Step by step, line upon line, here a little and there a little, His kingdom in heaven marches forward, steadily manifesting itself in the kingdoms of this world. We are to pray, "Thy kingdom come. Thy will be done, on earth as it is in heaven." Because we have stopped praying that prayer, or no longer believe its words, we have given up too much ground and authority to the satanic enemy.

We have in effect despised the day of small beginnings. We have looked at the task ahead of us and have given up, overwhelmed by its magnitude. We have forgotten that after we do our work and die, there will come generations after us.

The battle for the universe takes place here on earth, not in the grave or in heaven. The battle is *spiritual* and *ethical*. It is fought *in history*. How is it to be fought? Not by power alone, certainly. Not by politics alone. *By the preaching of the gospel and obedience to His law.*

In summary:

1. Christians are far behind the humanists in every area of life.

2. Short of major catastrophes, it will take a long time to regain this lost ground.

3. Christians are not ready to exercise responsibility in the major institutions: education, entertainment, government.

4. Nevertheless, the kingdom of God goes on.

5. Retreat by Christians is a sign of unbelief.

6. Joshua and Caleb alone recommended an offensive against the Canaanites; they alone entered the land 40 years later.

7. The "giants of the land" (humanists) can be defeated.

8. Humanists' fund-raising letters now reveal their fear of Christians in politics.

9. Christians are the main enemies of the humanists today.

10. Politics is too often seen as the fundamental activity.

11. The State's authority and operations should be drastically cut back.

12. The Bible should be our guide in this chopping block process.

13. Many Christians don't want to think of the Bible as a guide to government.

14. Non-Christians are equally hostile.

15. The redeemed sinner is to be salt and light to the corrupt culture.

16. Humanism has advanced as Christianity has retreated.

17. Satan doesn't have more power than God.

18. Satan's followers don't have more power than God's followers, unless God's followers abdicate.

19. God requires us to work, no matter how little time we have remaining.

20. Pessimism concerning the future has robbed the church of its vitality (Spurgeon).

21. The Bible teaches growth over time, generation after generation.

22. The ancient pagan world believed in historical cycles.

23. The Christian should believe in the earthly future, so he should be able to pass on the gifts of the past.

24. The God-haters will be cut off before they see the full development of their culture.

25. Capital in the broadest sense is to be built up over many generations.

26. Satan's followers cannot expect to succeed for many generations, unless Christians hand over the civilization to them.

27. We need revival, not miracles.

28. We need the whole counsel of God.

29. We can get this if we work hard and long, so that God can safely send our culture a spiritual awakening.

30. The Communists believe in overnight revolution, and they work for decades to bring it about.

31. Christians say they believe in the long haul, but give up politically after a short time, trusting instead in an overnight victory in a national election.

32. We are to subdue the earth one step at a time, one generation at a time.

CONCLUSION

The Bible is very clear: Men can attain freedom only under bondage to Christ. We are bondservants by nature as creatures. The only question is: To whom will we be in bondage? To be outside of Christ is to be in slavery. The world today is outside of Christ, and never has slavery been more widespread or more scientific.

When the true God is rejected as the ruler of men and nations, men seek out other gods. Self, family, church, and civil governments are corrupted. Civil government ends up with an inordinate amount of power and authority. The people cannot govern themselves—in fact, do not want to govern themselves, and they turn all government over to the State. The State becomes their messiah. A brief look at a slice of Israel's history will make this clear.

Once the people rejected God from ruling over them, they immediately "did evil in the sight of the LORD, and served the Baals" (Judges 2:11). What is the recurring theme in the book of Judges? "Every man did what was right in his own eyes" (17:6; cf. Deuteronomy 12:8). Self-government under God was abandoned. The men are weak in battle and will only go to war if Deborah, a woman, leads them: "Then Barak said to [Deborah], 'If you will go with me, then I will go; but if you will not go with me, I will not go'" (Judges 4:8).

The *economic order* was disturbed. Gideon has to hide his produce "in a wine press in order to save it from the Midianites" (6:11). God commanded His people to be "fruitful and multiply,

161

and fill the earth" (Genesis 1:28). The people of God are to have dominion. Instead, we find Israel hiding from the Midianites in "the dens which were in the mountains and the caves and the strongholds" (Judges 6:2). You can't have dominion when you're hiding.

Families were corrupt. Gideon is said to have had "many wives" (Judges 8:30). Gideon's descendants were murdered by one of his sons, Abimelech: "He went to his father's house in Ophrah, and killed his brothers the sons of Jerubbaal, seventy men, on one stone" (Judges 9:5). Gideon's family was beset by idolatry. This idolatry "became a snare to Gideon and his household" (8:26). "All of Israel played the harlot to" the idol set up by Gideon (v. 27).

Worship was corrupted through this pagan link to God. It didn't take long before the people had returned to worshipping idols with reckless abandon: "Then it came about, as soon as Gideon was dead, that the sons of Israel again played the harlot with the Baals, and made Baal-berith their god" (8:33).

Time alone did not change these conditions. The nation steadily declined. Once the dominoes of self-government and family government fell, the church, represented by the priesthood, was easy prey: "Now the sons of Eli were worthless men; they did not know the LORD and the custom of the priests with the people" (1 Samuel 2:12, 13). This was a continuation of the priesthood's corruption that festered during the period of the Judges where "Micah had a shrine and . . . made an ephod and household idols and consecrated one of his sons [a non-Levite], that he might become a priest" (Judges 17:5). When Micah did find a Levite, he paid him to stay in his house thinking God would "prosper" him (v. 17). True worship turned to a belief in magic.

When the people recognized Israel's corruption, especially the corruption of Eli's sons, the people turned to Eli for relief. Eli in turn confronted his sons, but to no avail: "No, my sons; for the report is not good which I hear the LORD's people circulating" (1 Samuel 2:24). But, instead of returning to godly self-government, family government, and church government, the people cried out for a king like all the other nations (1 Samuel 8:5). They saw the answer to their problems as solely political. Of course, this was not new. It had occurred in Gideon's day (Judges 8).

The Bible Has the Answers

We have surveyed some of the basic principles of government in the Bible. We found that God is King of Kings, the ruler of the nations. He is transcendent above His creation, yet He is present (immanent) with it. He rules it sovereignly, yet He grants men the blessings of freedom when they obey His law.

God has established a bottom-up hierarchy through various appeals courts: ecclesiastical, civil, and familial. He has established multiple hierarchies, thereby reducing the power of any one human institution. Each court system is to be governed by God's law for each. Each has its own lawful jurisdiction.

In contrast, humanist empires seek to create and impose a top-down bureaucratic structure, with elite planners serving as the substitute gods of the age. This is Satan's way: to imitate God. He is not all-knowing, all-seeing, and all-powerful, as God is, so he substitutes a tyrannical bureaucracy.

We need a law structure to govern us, but this law structure must be God's revealed law. Natural law is a myth. So is Neutrality. There are only two kinds of law: God's law and man's laws. We should side with God's law, not autonomous (self-law) humanistic law. Men cannot forever serve two masters. They cannot forever obey rival law systems. Pluralism in ethics and laws points to pluralism of gods; or, to turn this into a slogan, "polylegalism means polytheism."

There must be judgment in life, beginning with self-judgment. There will be a final judgment, so there must also be judgments by men. God gives blessings and cursings, depending on men's faithfulness to His covenant. Human judges must do the same in their respective spheres of jurisdiction. But their standard of judgment must be the Bible.

God promises victory. He gives it to His people, if they remain faithful over time. He gives defeat to those who rebel, generation after generation. There is continuity: a continuity of faithfulness. The stability men seek in their lives can be found in government, as well as in other areas of life. Christians are to pray for peace. The secret of peace is covenantal faithfulness in every area of life.

Where Do We Begin?

Where should we begin? Political solutions by themselves are of little value. They often do more harm than good. In fact, it is blame shifting, similar to what Adam and Eve did after they rejected God from ruling over them. Ultimately, they blamed God: "The woman whom *Thou gavest to be with me*, she gave me from the tree, and I ate" (Genesis 3:12).

God is our starting point. He is the Sovereign. He has ordered society. Our governments (family, church, and State) must be built on His all-embracing government.

First, there is *church government*. "Saints will judge the world" (1 Corinthians 6:2). How can we expect *civil* government to change when the church has so much trouble governing herself? This is why Paul makes it clear that there is a direct relationship between self and family governments and church or ecclesiastical government: "But if a man does not how to manage his own household, how will he take care of the church of God?" (1 Timothy 3:5). The family and church are training ground for judging the world. Paul chastises the church of Corinth, first, for their immorality and how it affected self and family government (1 Corinthians 5), and, second, for their inability "to constitute the smallest law courts" within church government (1 Corinthians 6:2).

Second, *self-government* supports all other forms of government. Christian *self-government* requires God's grace in regeneration. The far reaches of civil government will not be changed until rebels against God are turned into faithful subjects. This is God's work: "I will give you a new heart and put a new spirit within you; and I will remove the heart of stone from your flesh and give you a heart of flesh. And I will put My Spirit within you and cause you to walk in My statutes, and you will be careful to observe all My ordinances" (Ezekiel 36:26, 27). Notice the progression: God changes the heart, a new spirit is put inside the once-dead rebel, a teachable heart is implanted, *then* we will walk in His statutes, and *then* we will observe all His ordinances. The fruit of regeneration is personal holiness toward God and love of our neighbor, the sum of the great commandments: "And you shall love the Lord your God with all your heart, and with all your soul, and with all your strength" and "You shall love your neighbor as yourself" (Mark 12:30). There can be no love for God and our neighbor without a new heart. See also Psalm 139, Psalm 141:4, Ephesians 2:1-10, and Titus 3:1-8.

Third, there is *family government*. If you can't govern yourself, you won't be able to govern in the home. King David is a perfect example of the relationship between poor self-government and the breakdown of family government. His personal sins affected his entire family. One of the requirements for an elder in the church is that he be able to "manage his own household well, keeping his children under control with all dignity" (1 Timothy 3:4). Parents in family government are responsible for (1) the education of their children: "For I have chosen [Abraham], in order that he may command his children and his household after him to keep the way of the LORD by doing righteousness and justice; in order that the LORD may bring upon Abraham what He has spoken about him" (Genesis 18:19; cf. Deuteronomy 4:1, 9, 10, 40; 6:1-8, 20-25; Psalm 78; Ephesians 6:4); (2) the control and discipline of their children: "Discipline your son while there is hope, and do not desire his death" (Proverbs 19:18; cf. Exodus 20:12; Hebrews 12:3-11; Psalm 89:30-32; Proverbs 10:13; 13:1, 24; 15:5, 10, 32; 22:6, 15); (3) and the general welfare of the family: "But if any one does not provide for his own, and especially for those of his own household, he has denied the faith, and is worse than an infidel" (1 Timothy 5:8). Too many have turned to the State to provide these family duties.

Fourth, there is *civil government*. Civil government will not change until people change from within. The gospel must be preached; personal holiness must be required; families must begin to govern themselves and care for their own members;

churches must once again work as a legitimate and effective government under God; and the State must submit itself "as a minister of God" (Romans 13:4). We will see no change at the top until there is change at the bottom. Finally, as Christians, we will not be good governors in the civil sphere if we fail to establish the church as the government God ordained it to be.

The basis of Christian reconstruction is regeneration. Then there must be the preaching of the whole counsel of God. Only after this can we seriously expect to see God's *comprehensive redemption:* the healing of all areas of life by the power of the Holy Spirit through the application of God's law. It is an inside-out process, a bottom-up process, not a top-down process.

Part II
RECONSTRUCTION

11

RECONSTRUCTING CHURCH GOVERNMENT

The church increasingly has come under attack by the State. The church is a God-ordained government, with leaders, courts, a law-book, discipline, a mandate from heaven to take dominion, and a covenantal hierarchy. It is a government that will outlast the other God-ordained governments: family and State.

Obviously, there are dozens of reforms that need to be made in church government in order to reconstruct it to conform to Biblical standards. Equally obviously, each denominational group has its own special view of just how this reordered church should look. These views do not agree. Thus, the church on earth has been divided, unlike the unified church in the courts of heaven. But that unity of faith is more fundamental than the divided claims of men, and before Christ returns in power and glory, a degree of unity will be achieved to reflect what is in principle a unified government.

So far, Christians have failed in their attempt to bring unity to the church. Much of what we have been doing for almost 2000 years has been wrong. So we should look to new approaches. The fundamental approach is to recognize the reality of the five-point covenant structure, and to work with it and work within it as much as we can. If we refuse to begin where God tells us to begin, then we can hardly expect success in history.

Remember God's two principles of government: decentralism and a bottom-up hierarchy. We will not be able to achieve our goals through a top-down imposition of power. That is Satan's way, not God's.

Transcendence/Presence

First, we begin with the truth that God alone is absolutely sovereign, not man. Thus, He alone is all-seeing (omniscient), all-
powerful (omnipotent), and everywhere present with His creation
(omnipresent). No creature, including Satan, possesses any of
these attributes of God. They are incommunicable attributes.

Thus, we can have faith that "God causes all things to work
together for good to those who love God, to those who are called
according to His purpose" (Romans 8:28). We do not need to impose power over others to achieve good. God does this through
His direct control over history and His direct meeting with each
person. He alone is truly transcendent (above everything, and
distinct in being from His creation) and truly immanent (truly
present next to each creature, yet not part of His creation). We
must avoid *deism* (a totally distant god) and *pantheism* (a god totally
immersed in the creation, and not different from it).

The church in many respects has lost its vitality and manifests
corruption, compromise, and retreat. Scripture tells us: "For it is
time for judgment to begin with the household of God" (1 Peter 4:17).

This means that true worship must be restored. Adam and
Eve rebelled, choosing to serve the creature rather than the Creator (Genesis 3:1-7; Romans 1:18-32). Jesus rebuked Satan and in
the process taught the true purpose of life: "You shall worship the
Lord your God, and serve Him only" (Matthew 4:10; cf. Deuteronomy 6:13). Robert Rayburn writes:

> The worship of God is at once the true believer's most impor-
> tant activity and at the same time it is one of the most tragically
> neglected activities in the average evangelical church today. In
> the preaching and teaching of the churches, in conferences and in
> seminars, individual Christians have been encouraged to have
> their own daily "quiet time," for a period of personal devotion is
> an important part of every Christian life. They have been ad-
> monished to pray for their own needs and the needs of others.
> They have been taught to study the Bible for their own spiritual
> growth and for use in guiding and instructing others. There re-
> mains, however, among sincere believers today a woeful ignor-

ance concerning the significance of true worship and the means of attaining the blessing of rich, rewarding corporate worship.[1]

The gospel must be faithfully preached to the world as mankind's only hope. Preaching the gospel should be so comprehensive as to affect every individual, group, institution, and nation. The curse of sin and death is removed as more and more people come under the preaching of the gospel (Romans 8:18-25). We recite John 3:16, which tells of God's love for the world, but limit that love to parts of the world, meaning only individuals *in* the world. David Chilton writes:

> *That the world should be saved!* Here is one of the most oft-quoted passages of all the Bible, and so often we miss the point. Jesus Christ came to save the *world*—not just a sinner here, and a sinner there. He wants us to disciple the *nations*—not just a few individuals. The Lord Jesus will not be satisfied in the success of His mission until the whole earth is singing His praises. On the basis of God's infallible promises, the Church must pray and work for the expansion of the Kingdom, with the expectation that God will fill His Church with "a great multitude, which no one can count, from every nation and all tribes and peoples and tongues" (Rev. 7:9).[2]

Authority/Hierarchy

Second, the church is established by God, not by man, either through the State or the family. This denies both statism and familism, both of which are popular heresies in today's humanist world. The church exists first and foremost to worship God; secondarily, it exists to meet the spiritual needs of men. Third, it exists to perform works of charity, first with those in the household of faith, and second to those outside.

Today's all-embracing State seeks to eradicate any institution

---

1. Robert G. Rayburn, *O Come, Let Us Worship* (Grand Rapids, Michigan: Baker Book House, 1980), p. 11.

2. David Chilton, *Paradise Restored: A Biblical Theology of Dominion* (Fort Worth, Texas: Dominion Press, 1985), p. 218.

that competes with its perceived areas of authority and jurisdiction. One way this is done is by redefining the church. The church is no longer viewed as a *religious* institution, a government under God, but as a *charitable* institution similar to the United Way. As a charitable institution, the church becomes the creature of the State, subject to its laws regarding taxation and public policy. The State is blind to religious considerations. The extension of the church as a charitable institution is found in the State-created doctrine of "public policy." The modern State wants to be bound to no law except its own created law. "Public policy" is synonymous with statist law. R. J. Rushdoony writes:

> Whatever is contrary to public policy is thereby not entitled to tax exemption, nor to a free exercise of its faith, i.e. to any legal existence. Thus, if abortion and homosexuality are held to be public policy, no group has any "right" to tax exemption, or to maintain its legal freedom to pursue and uphold its "discrimination," but must assent to these policies. No better blue-print for totalitarianism has ever been devised than this public policy doctrine.[3]

With such doctrine the State assumes the power to define the church and to establish the church's policies. The church no longer answers to Christ, only to the State.

One way for a church to get out of this trap is to abandon incorporation. If the church ever received tax-exempt status as a Internal Revenue Code 501(c)(3) organization, it should reconstitute itself and become a church, not a charitable trust or foundation. The grant of tax exemption to churches is automatic (though the Internal Revenue Service agent may not admit this). The church may not be able to receive educational rate mailing privileges, but so what?

The church must continue to speak and act. The pulpits must resound with the clear preaching of the Bible. Preachers should not fear the unauthorized authority of the State and its real power, nor should the church forsake the preaching of the gospel, fearing the removal of tax exemption and the possible arrest of its pastor.

---

3. "The War Against Christ's Kingdom," A Special Chalcedon ALERT No. 1.

The apostles were imprisoned and some murdered because they refused to be silenced (Acts 4:1-31; 5:17-42; 12). Those tyrants are dead but the church of Jesus Christ remains.

Ethics/Law/Dominion

Third, the church must be a "boot camp" for the saints in the war with humanism. The "whole counsel of God" (Acts 20:27) must be marshalled against the whole counsel of humanism: "And He gave some as apostles, and some as prophets, and some as evangelists, and some as pastors and teachers, *for the equipping of the saints for the work of service, to the building up of the body of Christ*" (Ephesians 4:11, 12). Archie Jones states:

> As a consequence of Christians' abandonment of the study, preaching, hearing, and doing of the whole counsel of God, *we have neglected the scope of the spiritual warfare* between the army of Christ and that of Satan, neglected the subtlety of the Serpent, the Adversary, *and retreated from our created, re-born, and commanded purpose of dominion for Christ*, under His lordship. Consequently, Christians today find themselves unmistakably embattled. Due to our neglect of God's word, however, rather than being on the offensive and the attack, American Christians find themselves under attack by humanists in high places.[4]

Elders, required to meet certain moral qualifications before being considered for office, also must be "able to teach" (1 Timothy 3:2). Basic doctrine certainly should be taught, from theology proper (the doctrine of God) to eschatology (the doctrine of the last things). The church should take care to include doctrines pertaining to inflation, abortion, foreign affairs, education, welfare and the poor, philosophy, and economics.

Finance represents an area of neglect within much of the church. Paul tells us to "owe no man anything" (Romans 13:8). Too many of us spiritualize this to mean "owe no man a spiritual

---

4. Archie Jones, "The Imperative of Christian Action: Getting Involved as a Biblical Duty," *Journal of Christian Reconstruction*, Symposium on Social Action, edited by Gary North, Vol. VIII, No. 1 (Summer, 1981), p. 110-11.

debt." That is nonsense. In the previous section Paul sets forth Christian requirements for payment of taxes to the civil magistrate. In like manner, financial debts, of money or some commodity, should be avoided, or at least limited.

> Pastors must equip the saints for the work of service in terms of God's word as it covers every area of life. I would single out economics and finance as spheres where much of the church has manifested studied indifference. Many of our seminaries and churches have done very little to prepare leaders for this aspect of their ministries. As a result the people in the pews have suffered. Instead of approaching these subjects in terms of God's word, our people have been forced to rely on the secular financial advisors and economists for understanding. In addition, I believe that many working men and women grappling with financial problems drop out of church life because they do not get answers or directions in this area.[5]

Judgment/Sanctions

Fourth, the church must restore its status as a court. One of the true marks of the church is the discipline of its members (Matthew 16:18, 19; 18:15-20; 1 Corinthians 5). The church leadership should not allow sin to go unchecked. An unrepentant member should be excommunicated from fellowship and from receiving the sacraments. Churches should respect the government (discipline) of another church. The purpose of discipline is to "restore our brother" (Matthew 18:15); discipline is not an end in itself. The church has developed an inferiority complex in neglecting its role as a legitimate court of law. Paul instructs us that conflicts between church members should be handled within the jurisdiction of the church. With the collapse of civil court justice, the church has a tremendous opportunity to witness to the world that Jesus is indeed the Lord (cf. Deuteronomy 4:1-8).

The church must stand against Statist encroachment. One way the State controls the church is by restricting its activities.

---

5. "Fiscal Fitness: an interview with Joseph McAuliffe," *Pastoral Renewal*, Vol. 9, No, 8 (March 1985), p. 123.

The church comes under attack in every nation that believes in the ultimate State. The church preaches another King, another Kingdom, and another way of salvation. The Christian owes allegiance to Jesus Christ and subordinately to Caesar or the modern State. Only in Christ do earthly rulers have legitimacy. This frightens and subverts the Messianic State. The apostles preached that "there is salvation in no one else; for there is no other name under heaven that has been given among men, by which we must be saved" (Acts 4:12). This early creedal statement countered the Roman belief that the Caesars were personifications of the gods. Jesus is the only truly independent King. All other kings derived authority and power from Him. Christians were accused of acting contrary "to the decrees of Caesar, saying there is another king, Jesus" (Acts 17:7).

The modern messianic, ultimate-State exhibits many of first-century Rome's characteristics, wherein all religions were tolerated so long as they acknowledged the ultimacy of the State.

> Leftism does not like religion for a variety of causes. Its ideologies, its omnipotent, all-permeating state wants undivided allegiance. With religion at least one other allegiance (to God), if not also allegiance to a Church, is interposed. In dealing with organized religion, leftism knows of two widely divergent procedures. One is a form of separation of Church and State which eliminates religion from the marketplace and tries to atrophy it by not permitting it to exist anywhere outside the sacred precincts. The other is the transformation of the Church into a fully state-controlled establishment. Under these circumstances the Church is asphyxiated, not starved to death. The Nazis and the Soviets used the former method; Czechoslovakia still employs the latter.[6]

Nazi Germany remade the church in its own image. Churches could exist so long as National Socialism was preached from the pulpits: "The National Reich Church of Germany categorically claims the exclusive right and the exclusive power to control

---

6. Erik von Kuehnelt-Leddihn, *Leftism* (New Rochelle, New York: Arlington House, 1974), pp. 40-41.

churches within the borders of the Reich; it declares these to be national churches of the German Reich."[7]

Inheritance/Legitimacy/Continuity

Fifth, the church must recognize that it is the true heir of God. It is the source of historical continuity. The wealth of sinners is stored up for the just (Proverbs 13:22). The mercy of God extends to thousands of generations to those who are faithful to Him (Exodus 20:6). This process of inheritance goes on, generation after generation because the church of Jesus Christ is the true heir of God. There is an unbroken continuity. In every generation, the gospel is preached, the sacraments are given, and the church develops its authority.

The church has lost much influence in society because it turned its calling over to the State, which has tried to become a substitute parent. The church can help the poor through tithes, gleaning, lending, job training, and financial instruction. Church members should be taught that the Bible knows nothing of a welfare State where taxes are levied against the more prosperous to care for the less prosperous. They should be taught about the *limited* duties of the State as well as the duties of the church — both as an ecclesiastical organization and as the body of believers in Christ — and be taught to act in accordance.

But Christians do not appear to possess much influence of power. What can we do? Everything. We *must* do everything. We must set the pattern for righteous living and lawful inheritance, the building up of spiritual and earthly capital over long periods of time. Little by little, we build, for we leave an inheritance behind. We lay up treasures in heaven, but these are also reflected on earth, for by our fruits men will know us. Thus, we can begin with very little, for we know that faithful living over time leads to growth, and growth, if continued, eventually multiplies and fills the earth. It is only Christians who can legitimately have faith in this compound growth process.

---

7. Quoted in William Shirer, *The Rise and Fall of the Third Reich* (New York: Simon and Schuster, 1960), p. 240.

Where to Begin

To get "from here to there" is not easy, but it is possible. Here are only a few practical steps that churches can take, as an expression of their covenantal faithfulness to God. Churches must keep working, and trust in God for the blessings.

Transcendence/Presence

Our creedal statements neglect vital social issues. The great creedal formulations of the past were developed in the heat of religious and political conflict. For example, the Council of Chalcedon (A.D. 451) established that the State was not divine. The Roman emperors had established themselves the "saviors of the world," the only link between heaven and earth. R. J. Rushdoony writes about the importance of Chalcedon:

> The Council of Chalcedon met in 451 to deal with the issue as it came to focus at the critical point, in Christology. If the two natures of Christ were confused, it meant that the door was opened to the divinizing of human nature. If the human nature of Christ were reduced or denied, His role as man's incarnate savior was reduced or denied, and man's savior again became the state. If Christ's deity were reduced, then His saving power was nullified. If His humanity and deity were not in true union, the incarnation was then not real, and the distance between God and man remained as great as ever.[8]

The drafting of creeds was serious business. The safety of the church depended on their clarity and comprehensiveness. The State knew where the church stood on any issue because the creeds directed their attention to the particulars of the faith.

The word creed comes from the Latin *credo* and simply means "I believe." If a contemporary creed does not include a particular item then one can assume that this item is either of little or no importance for the life of the church. If a group of churchmen really

---

8. R. J. Rushdoony, *Foundations of Social Order: Studies in the Creeds and Councils of the Early Church* (Fairfax, Virginia: Thoburn Press, [1969] 1978), p. 65.

believed in something it would find itself in the church's creed. This is one of the reasons the Amish have been able, up until recently, to practice their faith without the long-arm of government interference. On the new Social Security bail-out scheme, the Amish are exempt. Their creedal formulations and their consistent practice substantiates their claims of seeking no government aid. Prior to the new tax ruling, nearly 80% of all churches had voluntarily chosen to pay into the Social Security System.

This is an indication that the "whole purpose of God" is not preached from the pulpits. These church employees could have gotten a raise (employees must remember that the employer does not pay an equal share of Social Security. This is money that would have gone to the employee in the form of wages. By putting the money we now pay into private pensions and savings programs the pay off would be substantially higher than it could ever be under Social Security. Moreover, this investment capital could be loaned out for greater economic expansion.)

I've been told that "This is not a creed-writing age." No age is a creed writing age until the need for a creed arises and someone decides to write a creed. The last great creedal formulation was in 1647 when the Westminster Confession of Faith was written. That was over 300 years ago. A lot has happened since then. We didn't have statist schools, the NEA, Social Security, and the IRS. A. A. Hodge writes about the need for creeds as a preservative from external and internal hostilities: "The Church is forced, therefore, on the great principle of self-preservation, to form such accurate definitions of every particular doctrine misrepresented as shall include the whole truth and exclude all error; and to make such comprehensive exhibitions of the system of revealed truth as a whole that no one part shall be either unduly diminished or exaggerated, but the true proportion of the whole be preserved."[9]

The Westminster Confession of Faith, for example, says nothing about Christian education or the tax question. When the State

---

9. A. A. Hodge, *The Confession of Faith* (Edinburgh: The Banner of Truth Trust, [1869] 1978), p. 2.

imposes its laws upon the church, the church must scramble to develop what it believes. I've been in a number of informal meetings with Christians over the tax and school questions. This is creedal formulation. It is the beginning of what we desperately need today.

I see little hope of various denominations getting together under one Confession of Faith. While this would be nice, it's just not likely. But various denominations and independents (who should work with some type of denominational affiliation for survival's sake) could hammer out appendices to their own confessions. They could then be added without cutting out their denominational distinctives.

If the church does not begin to develop new creedal formulations (at least additions to present creeds) then we can expect continued statist encroachment. Our creeds are a witness to the world, including the State. Rev. Kenneth L. Gentry writes:

> Creeds witness to the truth to those outside the bounds of the covenant community by: clearly outlining and explicating the fundamental assertions of Christianity, seriously warning against misbelief, vigorously defending the truth from corruptions, witnessing to the unity and order of the Christian system, demonstrating the continuity and immutability of the historic Christian faith, showing the rational, objective content of Christian truth (as against misperceptions such as a belief that Christian faith is a mystic, blind leap), and so on.[10]

If the church fails to draft the necessary creeds and confessions then we can expect the State to do it for us. The question is not whether we should develop new creeds and updated confessions but *who* will develop the new creeds and updated confessions. Creedalism is inescapable. The future of the church depends on them.

Authority/Hierarchy

There must be a recovery of the idea of the covenant. This book is one step in this recovery. People must know that they report to church officers. There can be no followers without lead-

---

10. Ken Gentry, *The Usefulness of Creeds*, p. 9.

ers, and no leaders without followers. Men must learn to obey before they can successfully lead. This is why Paul establishes as *the* criterion for church office, elders and deacons, that the candidate must rule his family well (1 Timothy 3). If he has not learned to do this, he has not proven his capacity for leadership?

Does this mean that unmarried and never-married men should not ordinarily be ordained? If we are to take seriously the words of the apostle, this is what it means. But this also insures that creative, disciplined men will become leaders. They will understand the needs and problems of congregation members. They will be far less bureaucratic in their rule, and far more familial.

The Roman Catholic Church a thousand years ago made celibacy the basis of ordination, precisely because the leaders recognized that a man who worries about wife and family cannot be a bureaucrat whose obedience can be commanded. Protestants recognized early that this mandated celibacy favored a top-down hierarchical church that is unbiblical. What is needed is a bottom-up appeals court system, with judges who understand the lives of those under them. This means family men. To the extent that unmarried men, especially young unmarried men, are placed over congregations, to that extent one of the major insights of Protestantism is lost. If the seminary degree continues to be the major criterion for access to the pulpit, rather than family leadership, hospitality, and godly behavior, then the church will continue to flounder. On this point, the Reformed tradition of an educated ministry became the bureaucratic emphasis on academic training and academic degrees. Thus the church has suffered from this improper emphasis for over nine centuries.

Ethics/Law/Dominion

A continuing theme in this book is the idea that people must learn to govern themselves before they govern others. But self-government must be in terms of law. What law? Whose law? Until Christians get this clear in their own minds, they will not be able to exercise dominion in society.

The revival of Biblical law in our day is a crucial aspect of the revival of dominion theology. R. J. Rushdoony's book, *The Institutes of Biblical Law* (Craig Press, 1973), was the most important document in the revival of dominion theology. It sets forth the requirements of the Ten Commandments in many areas of society.

One of the crying needs today is "good counsel." The Bible tells us that as Christians, we are competent to counsel and "able to admonish one another" (Romans 15:14). But counsel must always be in terms of law and morality. It can never be neutral. There is no neutrality in life. Counsel must be in terms of God's law.

Instead of sending mentally disturbed and desperate church members to godless, humanistic psychologists and psychiatrists, a number of people in the church ought to become equipped to counsel.[11] This will mean studying the works of Jay E. Adams. Here's a list of just some of his books:

- *Competent to Counsel*
- *The Christian Counselor's Manual*
- *Matters of Concern to Christian Counselors*
- *Insight and Creativity in Christian Counseling*
- *More Than Redemption*
- *The Christian Counselor's New Testament*

Warning: your pastor may need counselling insurance. There are civil lawsuits against pastors these days for "bad counselling." It is not worth getting licensed, but an insurance policy might be a wise idea.

Judgment/Sanctions

The church should be an established court to handle disputes between brothers (1 Corinthians 6:1-11): "Actual studies conducted

---

11. On humanistic psychology, see William Kilpatrick, *Psychological Seduction: The Failure of Modern Psychology* (Nashville, Tennessee: Thomas Nelson Publishers, 1983), Martin and Deidre Bobgan, *The Psychological Way/The Spiritual Way: Are Christianity and Psychotherapy Compatible?* (Minneapolis, Minnesota: Bethany Fellowship Inc., 1979), and Nelson E. Hinman, *An Answer to Humanistic Psychology* (Irvine, California: Harvest House Publishers, 1980).

by the Christian Conciliation Service of New Mexico have shown that in Albuquerque, New Mexico, with a population of approximately 500,000 people, there were more than 8,000 lawsuits annually with church members on both sides. That amounts to 16,000 Christians suing each other annually and spending an average of $1,500 each in legal fees and court costs. In short, a total of $24,000,000 annually is being spent by Christians in Albuquerque for litigation prohibited by 1 Corinthians 6."

In Atlanta, Georgia, to cite another example, "Christians are spending roughly $96,000,000 annually suing each other contrary to Scripture." The individual is instructed: "make friends quickly with your opponent at law while you are with him on the way, in order that your opponent may not deliver you to the judge, and the judge to the officer, and you be thrown into prison" (Matthew 5:25).

While the judge, appointed by the State, has authority to settle disputes, those who are involved in the dispute can reach a settlement before the case even reaches the ear of the civil court. Moreover, the innocent party is duty bound to confront an erring brother: "If therefore you are presenting your offering at the altar, and there remember that your brother has something against you, leave your offering there before the altar, and go your way; first be reconciled to your brother, and then come and present your offering" (vv. 23, 24).

In another place, Jesus instructs us to reprove our brother in private before we involve others in the dispute (Matthew 18:15).

> It is not insignificant that the Scriptures suggest that his first step should be in private. Before others are brought into the conflict, before witnesses or the church are included, the parties should seek a reconciliation on a personal and private basis. In such initial meetings, friends or advisors may, in fact, impede reconciliation. Others who wish to rush in quickly might note the counsel of Proverbs 26:17: "He who meddles in a quarrel not his own is like one who takes a passing dog by the ears" (Revised Standard Version).[12]

---

12. Lynn R. Buzzard and Laurence Eck, *Tell it to the Church: Reconciling Out of Court* (Elgin, Illinois: David C. Cook Company, 1982), p. 31.

When disputes cannot be settled between two individuals or among family members, the church can (must) operate as a legitimate judicial authority. When individual and group confrontation fails to bring about a just decision, Jesus commands us to "tell it to the church" (Matthew 18:17). The church is a gifted body of believers (1 Corinthians 12-14) who have the Word of God as the final voice of authority for all matters of faith and practice (2 Timothy 3:16, 17).

If the church is not equipped to handle disputes then what institution is?

While Paul discouraged lawsuits between believers, he did establish the principle that the people of God are capable of handling disputes among the brethren: "Does any one of you, when he has a case against his neighbor, dare to go to law before the unrighteous, and not before the saints?" (1 Corinthians 6:1).

Inheritance/Legitimacy/Continuity

Establish an educational center at your church. Most families cannot afford to build a substantial library. And most Public Libraries will not carry the books you'll want to read. Start a book fund to purchase hard-to-find books. A room should be set aside for study. Tapes, magazines, newsletters, and Bible courses can be made available.

Your church could work with Christian schools in the area and set up teacher enrichment programs. Why send your teachers back to the State schools for indoctrination? Develop your own program and funnel any tuition money that would have gone to the colleges back through the church's study center.

If your church doesn't have a Christian school, and there isn't a good one in the area, help to get one started. When modern-day church-schools are harassed by the State today, the State sees no such creedal prescription. There is nothing written that expresses the convictions of the denomination. It's interesting to note that *independent* churches are most susceptible. Their "No creed but Christ" rhetoric gets them into trouble. Moreover, their independency leaves them vulnerable. Do you think the State would fool around with the Roman Catholic Church, the United Methodists, or the Southern Baptists if they had taken a strong stand on the Social Security issue?

Caring for the poor is not the duty of civil government. A basic poverty ministry ought to be started in your church. This will mean an *effective* poverty ministry and not a hand-out program for anyone who asks. The best book available on the subject is George Grant's *Bringing in the Sheaves*, published by American Vision, P.O. Box 720515, Atlanta, Georgia 30328.

Summary

"Change the world!" should be the rallying cry of every Christian. The early church was known for its world-changing gospel. When the gospel was preached, these first-century Christians were rightly accused of "turning the world upside down" (Acts 17:6). Their preaching affected all of life (Acts 20:27). Today's church is again believing the world can be changed. Christians are no longer content to see the world transformed into a nightmare by those who deny Jesus Christ and His Word.

The belief that the world can be changed has been adopted and perverted by Communism, militant Islam, and secular humanism. Karl Marx, for example, concluded his *Communist Manifesto* with the words "You have a world to win." This vision fired the imagination of millions of idealistic but misguided young Communists. Communists around the world understood that it was not enough to *interpret* the world. They worked to *change* it. Of course, theirs is a world without Christ; a movement without any chance of success (see Psalm 2 and Proverbs 8:36).

Christians must be obedient to the mandate God has given to extend His Kingdom to every sphere of life, to every corner of the globe (Genesis 1:26-28; Matthew 28:18-20). Communism, militant Islam, and secular humanism have had their day. The world can be changed through the preaching of the Gospel and the application of Scripture to every area of life. The time is now! Christians around the world are beginning to realize that Jesus is indeed Lord of heaven *and* earth.

12

RECONSTRUCTING FAMILY GOVERNMENT

The family is a divinely ordained institution that is not instituted or controlled by the State (Genesis 1:26-28; 2:24). The State does not create the family and, therefore, cannot define it. There are, what Alvin Toffler calls, "a bewildering array of family forms: homosexual marriages, communes, groups of elderly people banding together to share expenses (and sometimes sex), tribal grouping among certain ethnic minorities, and many other forms coexist as never before."[1] These counterfeit families attempt to restructure the family around an evolving order rather than a Biblical model. Whoever defines the family controls it.

The family is the original and primary God-ordained society from which church, school, business, State, and every other enterprise and association arise. The family serves as a societal force, extending dominion through the establishment of additional families (Genesis 2:24). The many family units work throughout society to establish churches, schools, business establishments, and various voluntary associations, all under God's one government, using Scripture as the blueprint for activity and order.

The monolithic, centralized State sees the decentralized family order as a threat. The State seeks centralization while the Biblical family's ordained structure represents decentralization. The scene at the construction of the tower of Babel in Genesis 11 depicts an attempt to centralize family, church, and political entities. Many family and tribal names were merged into one "name" designated by the builders of Babel. Genesis 10 lists the

---

1. *The Third Wave* (New York: William Morrow, 1980), p. 212.

many nations by their names. The building of the tower and the consolidation of the nations were acts of rebellion against God's original dominion mandate to be "fruitful and multiply" according to families (cf. Genesis 1:26-28; 2:24).

How can the family restore Christian civilization? We must recognize the binding character of God's covenant structure for this lawfully ordained system of government. Each institution is separate from the others, yet each is dependent. All are sovereign, but none is absolutely sovereign. We must assert the family's separate yet dependent existence from both church and state.

Hierarchy

Second, the family must maintain itself as a God-ordained authority structure (1 Corinthians 11:1-15; Ephesians 5:22-24; 6:1; Colossians 3:20). The family can exercise its authority by disciplining its members. Unfaithful children can be disinherited.

The totalitarian State works for the breakdown of family authority by abolishing the Biblical concept of headship. Many states have legislated the abolition of the Biblical concept of the "head of household." Many special interest groups want to make children equal authorities with their parents. This effectually makes the State the real home where children are to be nurtured and educated. If parents are found to be "unfit" (a condition solely defined by the State) the State can remove children and make them wards of the State. Rushdoony writes:

> Man is responsible to God for his use of the earth, and must, as a faithful governor, discharge his calling only in terms of his Sovereign's royal decree or word. His calling confers also on him an authority by delegation. To man is given authority by God over his household and over the earth. In the Marxist scheme, the transfer of authority from the family to the state makes any talk of the family as an institution ridiculous. The family is to all practical intent abolished whenever the state determines the education, vocation, religion, and the discipline of the child."[2]

2. R. J. Rushdoony, *The Institutes of Biblical Law* (Nutley, New Jersey: Craig Press, 1973), p. 163-4.

With the collapse of the family or the denial of the family's authority, a nation rapidly moves into social anarchy. God, as the source of the family's authority, has located immediate authority in the father or husband (1 Corinthians 11:1-15). When the father abdicates, or certain "interest groups" deny his authority, social rebellion, as described in Isaiah 3:12 results. Women become rulers and children are looked upon as authority equals with the same rights and privileges as their parents. Parents are oppressed in such a view of authority. A crisis in leadership forms (cf. Judges 4). The result is social collapse and captivity (Isaiah 3:16-26). For women, it is a time of "reproach" or "disgrace" (Isaiah 4:1).

The first government we recognize as children is the family. If parents lose the respect and obedience of their children within the family, they most certainly are going to lose them to the broader culture. Some of what I'm suggesting might not seem to relate to "Jesus as Ruler of the Nations," but I assure you it does. We're talking about family *government*. What your children learn in the home will be taken to the work place and the political arena. Our job is to produce leaders, not followers.

Family discipline is essential to good government. Children must learn Biblical principles relating to self-government so that they eventually will not reject family government for the proposed security of the State. One primary way we can discipline children is by teaching them Biblical truth about private property. Too often we ask the State to confiscate money from the more productive members of society to redistribute it to the less productive members, presumably in the name of fairness and justice. Gary North writes, "If the concept of private property is worth defending, and if personal responsibility is the moral basis of private property, the family must be the scene of the child's introduction to the responsibilities of ownership."[3] Money received in transfer payments comes from other families. In effect, some families use State power to plunder other families.

---

3. Gary North, "Ownership, Responsibility, and the Child," *The Freeman* (September 1971), pp. 515-21.

The family provides a training ground for world leadership, for it is the first institution in which people learn "followership." Church leadership is also to be cultivated in the family. The church leader "must be one who manages his own household well, keeping his children under control with all dignity (but if a man does not know how to manage his own household, how will he take care of the church of God?)" (1 Timothy 3:4-5).

Civil leadership also develops out of family leadership. The choice of rulers in Israel was based on prior leadership in the family and tribe: "Choose wise and discerning and experienced men from your tribes . . ." (Deuteronomy 1:13; cf. Exodus 18:17-26; 1 Samuel 2:12-17, 22-36). Paul gives us a hint of the extension of godly leadership into the world: "Do you not know that the saints will judge the world?" (1 Corinthians 6:2).

Ethics/Law/Dominion

Third, parents must teach their children the law of God. The Bible is very clear about this:

> And these words, which I am commanding you today, shall be on your heart; and you shall teach them diligently to your sons and shall talk of them when you sit down in your house and when you walk by the way and when you lie down and when you rise up (Deuteronomy 6:6-7).

Without an understanding that it is God who has "laid down the law," children will not clearly recognize the nature of family authority. They will be tempted to rebel, or to transfer their loyalty to the gang, the State, or some rival institution.

As they get older, they will no longer be impressed with the answer, "Because I say so," to the question, "Why should I do what you say?" This is why God first lays down the law to parents, as we have seen: "And these words, which I am commanding *you* today, shall be on *your* heart." Family government begins with self-government. God's government is *inside-out government*.

As Gary North demonstrates in his economic commentary on the Bible, *The Sinai Strategy* (1986), the Eighth Commandment,

"You shall not steal" (Exodus 20:15), is placed under the third point in the Biblical covenant, meaning the law and dominion section. This law against theft establishes the legality of, and the mandatory nature of, the institution of private property. The family must therefore hold to the Biblical pattern of private property. The family is closely tied to private property (Exodus 20:12), and the abolition of private property requires the destruction of the family (1 Kings 21). Private property is attached to the Biblical mandate of dominion.

Judgment/Sanctions

Fourth, the Bible teaches that God's covenant places all men under dual sanctions: blessings and cursings. Sometimes this system is called the carrot and the stick. The family is the first institution that brings to the attention of children the inescapable reality of this dual covenant sanction program.

God uses this system of punishment against mankind. It is called heaven and hell. It has earthly manifestations that are to remind us of the eternal consequences of both covenantal faithfulness and covenantal disobedience. The longest list of these dual sanctions is found in Deuteronomy 28: blessings (1-14) and cursings (15-68). God brings the rod of correction to adults, and the Bible even speaks of these punishments in the language of spankings: "On the lips of the discerning, wisdom is found, but a rod is for the back of him who lacks understanding" (Proverbs 10:13).

Parents are to train their children in the knowledge of God. This is why they are to use the rod of correction on their younger children. Parents are told that "He who spares his rod hates his son, but he who loves him disciplines him diligently" (Proverbs 13:24). "Foolishness is bound up in the heart of a child; the rod of discipline will remove it from him" (Proverbs 22:15). "Do not hold back discipline from the child, although you beat him with the rod, he will not die" (Proverbs 23:13).

These guides to proper child-rearing are all governed by the general principle of the love of God for His people. We deal with our children as He deals with us: "But when we are judged, we are disciplined by the Lord in order that we may not be condemned along with the world" (1 Corinthians 11:32). This verse appears in the middle of the section on self-judgment prior to taking the Lord's Supper in church. "But if we judge ourselves rightly, we should not be judged" (v. 31). Self-judgment should replace external judgment as we mature in the faith. It is the substitution of self-judgment for external judgment that is the mark of maturity, and therefore the mark of freedom under Christ. This is why spankings no longer work with older children who have not learned self-government, and why church officers and even civil officers need to be called in to judge chronic juvenile delinquents (Deuteronomy 21:18). This is why the family is not an independent institution, but a dependent one. But it was never intended by God that it be dependent solely on the State.

Inheritance/Legitimacy/Continuity

Fifth, the family is to care for its own members (1 Timothy 5:8). Rita Kramer writes, "We have asked institutions—the government, the schools—to undertake to direct human nature. The paradox is that as our aims have become increasingly humanitarian, our means have become increasingly controlling."[4] If we control our own families, we must take responsibility for family affairs and not turn over family government to another family, or to the church, the school, or the State. Too many families willingly sacrifice their children to such statist institutions as the public schools, day care centers, and welfare agencies.

The family must be the child's first school. The family must provide basic Christian teaching rather than turning all education over to the church or the school. This means daily instruction in the Bible, prayer, and worship. School and church should supplement these family activities, not replace them. Parents must be overseers of their children's education. North writes, "[E]ducation is the moral responsibility of parents. They are the ones who must

---

4. Rita Kramer, *In Defense of the Family* (New York: Basic Books, 1983), p. 19.

determine whether or not their children are being taught the truth. They are responsible before God for the rearing of their children. They are held responsible even for the content of their children's education. This is why it is a great responsibility to bring children into the world."[5] Unfortunately, many parents turn over their educational responsibility to the State. Parents must start schools and take a *direct* stake in their children's education. This means paying for the services directly. Where parents are dissatisfied with the quality of education presently received, they can demonstrate their displeasure by enrolling their children elsewhere. This is not an option in the "public school" (i.e., "State school" monopoly).

The family is a welfare institution. Parents should prepare for the time when they may be unable to work. Government retirement funds should not be considered. Children should share financial hardship within the immediate family and, where possible, within the extended family. For this reason, the first-born son is entitled to a double portion of the family's estate (Deuteronomy 21:17). He has the responsibility of caring for his incapacitated parents. North states, "The State, in modern times, has become the 'eldest son.' Estate taxes in some nations will take virtually the whole of very wealthy estates. Families are forced to sell off lands and family heirlooms in order to pay estate taxes. *The State has asserted its position as the pseudo-family, and now it demands payment for its services.*"[6] The family, therefore, should be future-directed. We should make decisions with our "children's children" in mind (Psalm 78:1-8). "A good man leaves an inheritance to his children's children" (Proverbs 13:22).

Where to Begin

The family is in disarray today, which is why society in general and politics specifically are also in disarray. The covenantal

---

5. *Unconditional Surrender: God's Program for Victory* (Tyler, Texas: Institute for Christian Economics, 1982), p. 94.

6. *Ibid.*, p. 97.ff.

administration of God is a unit; a breakdown in just one area is
called to a halt before it can affect everything else. Only when society reaches a crisis stage are all the institutions in crisis, because
men are in *comprehensive sin and comprehensive rebellion*. They therefore
need comprehensive salvation and comprehensive restoration.

The family must be reconstructed alongside of the church and
the State.

Transcendence/Presence

It must be made clear to all children that God is the head of
the household. The father is a priest who conducts family worship
services daily. The family must become God-centered in every
way, including family ritual.

It is the God-centered nature of the family which teaches children about the God-centered nature of reality. Their primary
reality for many years is the family. If this environment is not self-
consciously God-centered, then they will not learn to think in-
stinctively of all aspects of reality as God-centered. God-centered
thinking must be taught, now that men are born sinners and
under the curse.

God is far above man in terms of His being—power, mind,
and vision—but He is also present. Nothing escapes His view.
Children must be taught early that God sees, even if parents
don't. God remembers, even if parents don't. God brings judgment, even if parents don't. Understanding this is the first step to
achieving self-government under God.

Authority/Hierarchy

Fathers are to exercise final authority in the family. This
means that wives must be visibly in subjection to husbands. If
they aren't, then the children learn fast that the father's authority
is not enforceable in the household. Wives who challenge their
husbands in word and deed are setting the pattern for their own
children, who will learn the subtle and not-so-subtle arts of moral
and institutional rebellion from the mother. This is why Paul
begins his instructions regarding family authority with a warning

to wives to obey their husbands (Ephesians 5:22-24). Then he goes on to warn children to be obedient to parents (Ephesians 6:1-3).

The familiar phrase of mothers, "Wait till your father gets home!" is proper. Fathers must back up the threats of mothers. As soon as the father walks through the door at night, the wife must immediately inform him of any major infraction of the rules. Judgment should not be delayed. This may not please fathers, who want a little peace and quiet at home, but peace and quiet are not automatic benefits given by God to those whose work is not yet done. The child who is to be dealt with must not learn that he can avoid punishment by becoming an instant nice person when he hears father's car in the driveway.

Mothers are not to defer all judgment to fathers. The normal transgressions of children, especially younger children, must be dealt with immediately, or they will forget. They have very short memories. Only as they grow older, can they fully appreciate the threat of father's arrival hours later. Furthermore, the judgment of fathers is traditionally more severe, so children may spend the day worrying. They should worry this way only when infractions are major. But if they really are major, then the day of worrying is appropriate. Had Adam and Eve worried more before God's return, they might have come to repentance before full judgment was handed down.

Mothers, if they do not *have* to work, should try to stay home during the child's pre-school years, especially if the children will have to be put in day-care centers. Fathers should take extra care in spending time with the children after work. The old adage of "quality time, not quantity time" does not hold water. Children like to be around their parents. Make it easy for them.

Do things as a family. Husbands should not exclude wives, and mothers and fathers should not exclude their children. This will mean taking your children to a variety of activities. Children eventually get used to being left out. When they get into their teen years, they will often start leaving you out.

Ethics/Law/Dominion

Have children. God commands this as part of the dominion covenant (Genesis 1:26-28). Don't let the Population Explosion People (PEP) lead you astray. The populations of Western industrial society are threatened by falling birth rates. The replacement rate is 2.1 children per family. In virtually no West European nation, the U.S., or Canada is it above 1.8 children per family. In Italy, it has collapsed to about 1.5. If you have any questions about the nonsense of the PEP, I suggest you read *The Myth of Overpopulation* by R. J. Rushdoony and *The Economics and Politics of Race* by Thomas Sowell.

The humanists are killing their future through abortion. Many are not having children or are limiting the size of their families. This is a great opportunity for Christians to overwhelm them with numbers. The following anti-child statements will give some idea of the opportunity we have of winning the future by default if we only have more children:

- "We could not lead the kind of life we have if we had kids."

- "I'd rather buy a vacation home than funnel a large chunk of our income into a trust fund [for our children]."

- "We've made our choice for freedom and spontaneity. Our cats can take care of themselves, and we're free."

- "I've seen other couples lose a closeness they had before deciding to have children."

- "I guess I'm selfish. I'm just not ready to sacrifice my time to a kid."

- "This world is a crazy place to raise a kid."

- "I find the whole idea of pregnancy repugnant . . . I'm not wild about children."[7]

Begin educating your children at an early age. Teach them the Bible. There are numerous Bible "trivia" games that will make learning interesting. If you're not able to teach the Bible to your

---

7. "Three's a Crowd," *Newsweek* (September 1, 1986), pp. 68-74.

children, then insist that your church begin a course to help parents teach the Bible. I also recommend that you take an active part in your children's learning at a very early age. Don't wait until they're in kindergarten before you teach them how to read and write.

As soon as your children are born, you should begin to teach them that they are children of God and thus responsible to Him for all things. You can make your children responsible by not doing everything for them. They should pick up their toys — yes, the same day! — and say "please" and "thank you," "yes, sir" and "yes, ma'am." They should be given responsible work around the house. Mom should not be left with all the housework. Let the children pitch in and help. This is where self-government begins. They can learn at an early age to set the table, put the flat ware away, clean up after meals, help dad with the yard work, wash the car, and a host of other chores.

Read to your children daily. Let them see you read. Teach them difficult words. They need to hear words like government, epistemology, metaphysics, and presuppositions. Go through the dictionary and let your children pronounce words as you read them aloud. Children should have their own books and begin a library of their own. This means teaching them to care for books. In the end, children should be more interested in buying a new book than the latest top forty album or designer jeans. Of course, don't overdo it. Children are still children. But they should appreciate reading books and education in general.

Set up weekly family meetings to discuss concerns, goals, problems, and potential problems. This is a way of keeping your children informed on the many activities you're involved in. As your children get older, these meetings will keep you abreast of their growing activity calendar. Discuss and agree on plans and goals. This meeting is not to be democratic. You aren't "The Brady Bunch" or "Eight is Enough." You are "Father Knows Best" (at least the father should be after counsel with his wife). Of course, daily communication with your children is a must if you don't want to lose them to the latest ideology.

Judgment/Sanctions

One phrase should never become part of any parent's vocabulary: "Do as I say, not as I do." All government begins with self-government. God so loved the world that He placed His only begotten Son under the terms of the covenant, and punished Him with the punishment we deserve by nature, so that we will not suffer eternal separation from God in the lake of fire (Revelation 20:14-15). From the beginning, He placed Himself under the terms of His own covenant when He moved through Abraham's cut-up animals in the form of a smoking oven and a flaming torch (Genesis 15:17). God did as He said. We are to do the same.

Children are to be punished with punishments that fit their disobedient behavior, just as in civil government, the punishment should fit the crime. Furthermore, the punishment should be specified in advance. As in civil government, punishments should not be imposed without warning. Parents have to think through the life of a child, and say in advance what must not be done. Children are entitled to at least one warning. But warnings endlessly repeated and seldom enforced are self-defeating.

Specified punishments should be sure. They are not to be imposed only when the parent feels like it. The parent's word is law; if a parent knows that he will not be consistent in enforcing a specific infraction with a specific penalty, he should impose a different penalty. As in civil justice, the predictability of the judgment is of greater effect in controlling crime than the magnitude of the punishment.

The parent's word must be respected. If the parent does not respect his own word by fulfilling what he has promised, then the children will not learn to respect the parent's word. They will learn how to wheedle their way out of judgment. There will be no wheedling on God's day of final judgment. Children should not think of law as a system that can be beaten by manipulating the emotions of parents.

As children grow older, the rewards and punishments must change. Punishments more and more must take the form of removing desirable benefits, rather than the imposition of physical sanctions. For example, supervise the use of the automobile. It should become an earned privilege, not an automatic benefit. Set rules as to who will pay for gas, automobile insurance, and general maintenance. Be sure all family members wear a seat belt *at all times*. This is an aspect of self-government.

Supervise dating. Dating is another earned privilege. You should always know where your children are. If plans change, then they should call. Stiff discipline should be imposed when the rules are broken. Make the punishment fit the crime.

Inheritance/Legitimacy/Continuity

Start a family business. This will help you work together as a family, diversify your income, bring in extra income, help with taxes, and teach your children a trade that could turn into quite a business enterprise.

Encourage your children to set daily, weekly, monthly, and yearly goals. They must become future-oriented. This is the essence of upper-class thinking. It is the foundation of upper-class income and responsibility.

Take your children to libraries, museums, historical sights, anti-abortion rallies. Encourage them to visit the sick and help the poor.

Give them an appreciation for good art, music, literature, and poetry. Keep the radios in the house tuned to classical stations. The upper-class cultural achievements of Western civilization should be in front of them on a regular basis. This means, of course, that parents must learn to appreciate and understand this heritage.

Apprentice your older children during the summer months, if possible. The experience and skills they will pick up will be their pay. Let them try their hands at carpentry, plumbing, farming, computer programming, auto maintenance, journalism (neighborhood newspapers, church newsletters, etc.), small appliance repair, etc. Every child should learn how to type and operate a computer.

Teach your children how to spend money and the principle of

deferred gratification. What does it *really* cost to play a video game? Get them started saving for college. Let them see you pay the bills each month. Teach them the principles of debt-free living or at least short-term debt living. Take them shopping to teach them how to look for the best deals, not the cheapest items. You get what you pay for.

Teach your children that welfare begins in the home. They must learn to care for themselves. This will mean working for a living. Even if you have money to lavish on your children, don't. If you must give them something expensive, give them a useful *tool*. Make it clear that you are doing everything in your power to care for yourselves as you approach old age but if anything unforseen happens, your children are going to be responsible, not the State.

Teach them to tithe ten percent of their money income (including gifts). Teach them to save ten percent, too. It doesn't seem fair or reasonable to force them to tithe and save the equivalent money value of Christmas and birthday presents, but they can tithe and save Christmas and birthday *money*. Since they have been given the authority to spend this present as they please, they have been given a new degree of responsibility.

The primary wage earner should prepare for the possibility of a premature death. A *term life insurance* policy of at least $250,000 is necessary. You should be able to decrease the amount as you get older and your responsibilities decrease. Also, leave an inheritance to your children. Disinherit the unfaithful.

Work for the elimination of the Social Security program. Look what a family could do on its own: a wife can buy a $250,000 term life insurance policy for her 25-year-old husband for under $20 a month. This will protect her family in the event of his death. While the husband is still alive, and his wife and family are protected by the policy on him, the family could save nearly $2,500 plus interest that would have gone to the Social Security program. All in all, the family would be much better off financially. As he gets older the cost of term insurance increases but the need for such coverage decreases if an individual has saved a percentage of his income every year.

Low-Cost Annual Renewable Term Life Insurance

AGE	$100,000	$250,000	$500,000	$1,000,000
35	120	200	375	725
40	149	253	480	935
45	186	320	615	1205
50	231	403	780	1535
55	333	593	1160	2295
60	556	998	1970	3915

If the average worker at age 25 saved $2,549 per year and invests it at 6 percent interest after taxes, he will accumulate $394,483 by the time he is 65. This is for funds compounded annually. If interest were compounded quarterly, as many private institutions compound in order to be competitive, the effective interest rate would be 6.14 percent, and the savings total at age 65 would be even greater. There are many investment opportunities that pay more than 6 percent. Each year $2,549 saved and invested at 7 percent would produce $508,857 in 40 years. At 8 percent, the total would be $660,344.

- $2,549 per year for 40 years @ 6% interest = $394,483
- $2,549 per year for 40 years @ 7% interest = $508,857
- $2,549 per year for 40 years @ 8% interest = $660,344

With a sum of $394,483 invested at 6 percent, the retired individual could draw $1,972 monthly, or $23,664 per year. Compare this with the *maximum* monthly payment of $981 that a couple could receive under Social Security. Now it is important to take note of another important difference under this private savings plan versus Social Security. The $1,972 per month under the private plan is an *interest* payment. They can go on drawing interest at this rate (six percent) until they die. And they can follow the injunction of Proverbs 13:22: "A good man leaves an inheritance to his children's children, and the wealth of the sinner is stored up for the righteous" (Prov. 13:22).[8]

---

8. The above material on Social Security is taken from Tom Rose, *Economics: The American Economy from a Christian Perspective* (Mercer, Pennsylvania: American Enterprise Institute, 1985), pp. 100-111.

Do not depend on Social Security for retirement. Vote for those who will phase out the system. Why? In 1937 the Social Security tax was 2% of a maximum 3,000 yearly income. The maximum tax that could be collected from any one citizen was $60 per year. In 1973 the taxable wage base was $10,800. In 1974 it was $13,200. In 1980 it went up to $25,900; and in 1985 the total was $42,000. As we'll see, even the percentage of tax taken has gone up from 2% to over 7% for both employees and employers.

Stay out of debt, especially long-term debt. The Bible tells us that the debtor is a slave to the lender (Proverbs 22:7). There is little peace of mind and your creditors determine your financial priorities. When investment opportunities arise money is not often available because it must go to pay debts. The debtor is tied to the past. When emergencies arise, money is not available.

Most indebtedness is for *depreciating* items. If financed items must be liquidated in an emergency to pay unforseen expenses, great losses are the result. For example, most automobiles lose value *immediately* after you drive them off the lot.

Real estate is a possible exception to long-term indebtedness. Real estate is *usually* an appreciating item. Buying a house as an *investment*, in anticipation of increased inflation and therefore an appreciation in the price of your house so you can sell your house in order to purchase a more expensive house, is a mistake. Betting on a State-manipulated economy will leave you holding a house that you may not be able to sell.

We all have to live somewhere. A family can either rent for a certain amount per month, and have nothing after 30 years, or buy for slightly more money than a rental price, and acquire property. The risks are not that great for the lending institution. If you happen to default, the lending institution takes possession and can sell it. Of course, this does not help your credit rating.

The 30-year mortgage is not ideal, however. There is a psychological burden that goes with a 30 year debt. There are some alternatives to the 30 year mortgage. For example, a 15 year mortgage can save a bundle of money. This might mean purchasing a smaller home than you would like to have. Here are some of your alternatives on a $70,000, 13 percent fixed-rate mortgage:[9]

LOAN TYPE/ PAYMENT FREQUENCY	REGULAR PAYMENTS DUE	EFFECTIVE TERM	TOTAL INTEREST PAID
30-year/monthly	$774	30 years	$208,762
30-year/biweekly[10]	$387	18 years	111,970
15-year/monthly	$886	15 years	89,421

Here are some advantages to a "quick-pay loan":

1. A young couple with, say, a 15-year loan will create enough value to refinance the house, when their children reach 18, and pay for college.

2. Homeowners who quick-pay will find it easier to trade up to a better house, because they'll get more cash when the old house is sold.

3. Only a quick-pay loan can guarantee that a middle-aged couple will have a paid-up house when they retire.

4. Extra savings put into your house instead of the bank will build up tax-deferred.[11]

Be aware of legislation directed at the family. There are laws on the books where your underage daughter can get an abortion without your consent. Know the law and work for its defeat. Read your state's laws concerning parents' rights. A number of parents, or a group of parents, could hire a lawyer or ask someone to speak to you about what the law says. Under no circumstances should you "volunteer" information to state or local officials who are sent to your home to "investigate." Refer them to your lawyer, either retained by you or a group of concerned parents. Lobby your legislators on crucial family issues. Read John W. Whitehead's *Par-*

---

9. Jane Bryant Quinn, "The Rise of Quick-Pay Mortgages," *Newsweek* (December, 10, 1984), p. 72.

10. "Your payments are figured as if the loan were going to last for 30 years. But instead of paying once a month, you make one-half of the monthly payment every two weeks. Over the year, that equals 13 monthly payments instead of 12, a small change that brings surprisingly big savings in interest costs" (Jane Bryant Quinn, "The Rise of Quick-Pay Mortgages," *Newsweek*, December 10, 1984, p. 72).

11. *Ibid.*

ents' Rights and Mary Pride's *The Child Abuse Industry*, both published by Crossway Books, Westchester, Illinois 60153.

Education is the responsibility of parents. (See Robert Thoburn, *The Children Trap*, in this series.) You might want to educate
your children at home during the first few years. You'll need at
least two books: Mary Pride, *The Big Book of Home Learning: The
Complete Guide to Everything Educational for You and Your Children*
(Westchester, Illinois: Crossway Books, 1986) and John W. Whitehead and Wendell R. Bird, *Home Education and Constitutional Liberties* (Westchester, Illinois: Crossway Books, 1984).

Take your children out of the public schools. Start a private
school of your own, either for profit or parent-controlled, but as-
sociated with a church. Since you are paying for the schooling
directly, you will pay more attention to the kind of education your
children are getting or not getting, whatever the case may be.
Money talks. Yank your children out if you can't get any satisfac-
tion or movement with the administration. Encourage the school
to teach foreign languages, public speaking, philosophy, apologet-
ics, and ethics. Utilize talented parents to teach specialized
courses as "mini-courses."

Make sure your home school network is "under" some church,
and is considered a "Christian School." This is to put the Church
as a buffer between the family and the pagan State. Moreover,
such an arrangement makes you accountable to someone.

Summary

Humanism has given up on the family. Humanists are literally destroying their future through abortion. By just having children, the world could be ours in the next 20 years by default.

But we must use the family setting as a training ground for the
future. Our children must be given hope that there is a future. They
need skills. They need leadership qualities. The State is not a substitute for the family. It cannot care for us. The State has no heart.

The home is a child's first school, his first business, his first
church, and his first government. From the family he will gain the
experiences necessary to encounter and engage life. The world is
looking for leaders. The family is the place to turn them out.

13

RECONSTRUCTING CIVIL GOVERNMENT

What will it take to reconstruct our society? What rival faith offers us a legitimate hope in long-term dominion? None.

How about the political faith of the two major political parties in the United States? Should we join with them? The liberal end of the political spectrum promises a just society but only with more of *your* tax dollars, fewer freedoms, mediocrity in nearly everything, and more political control. The conservatives have their own brand of false hopes, believing that justice finds its wisdom in common sense, that natural law is a handy substitute for Biblical law, and that progress in a free market society is inevitable. For all of them, politics is the answer. "Vote for me and I'll see to it that all will be right with you and the world," goes the political promise. This is the political faith.

The Bible calls us to faith, but a faith that takes us to the God who created heaven and earth, to the God who sent His Son Jesus Christ to make the restoration of a fallen world a reality. This same faith will be a beacon to the nations, a light to the world that lies in darkness. This is God's purpose for His people, that they might be a "city on a hill." Not a light for the political faith, but a light that shines bright on *the redemptive work of Jesus Christ*, the only hope for the world. Where is the source of the light found? In the Bible.

The reconstruction of civil government begins with the Bible. Jesus wants us to return to the standards of God's law so the whole world will marvel and follow. First, to show men everywhere that they are sinners and are in need of redemption. Second, to set forth a blueprint for living in a world of contrary opinions. This was Israel's task (Deuteronomy 4:1-8) that has now fallen upon the church, the New Israel, to be "a city set on a hill" (Matthew 5:14), to give "the people who were sitting in darkness . . . a great light" (Matthew 4:16; cf. Isaiah 9:2).

So Jesus calls us *to restore the broken foundations*, not to become revolutionaries for a misguided political faith. This was the vision of our Puritan forefathers, given expression by John Winthrop in his "Model of Christian Charity" in 1630 aboard the *Arabella* as they sailed for New England, and also in numerous charters and documents drafted by men who understood that Jesus indeed is ruler of the nations. Let us make Winthrop's vision of the future our vision:

> The Lord will be our God and delight to dwell among us as His own people. He will command a blessing on us in all our ways, so that we shall see much more of His wisdom, power, goodness, and truth than we have formerly known. We shall find that the God of Israel is among us, and ten of us shall be able to resist a thousand of our enemies. The Lord will make our name a praise and glory, so that men shall say of succeeding plantations: "The Lord make it like that of New England." For we must consider that we shall be like a City upon a Hill; the eyes of all the people are on us.

Transcendence/Presence

God spoke the world into existence: "Then God said, 'Let there be light'; and there was light" (Genesis 1:3). The ten commandments are called the "ten *words*" in Deuteronomy 4:13. Scripture is said to be "God-breathed" (2 Timothy 3:16, New International Version). Jesus "upholds all things by the *word* of His power" (Hebrews 1:3).

Since God is transcendent, His law is high above all creatures. But God's will for mankind is not out of reach; God's Holy Spirit is immanent (present), and so is the Bible. God came to meet with Moses on the mountain, to give him the commandments: "Thus you shall say to the house of Jacob. . . . Now then, if you will indeed obey My voice and keep My covenant, then you shall be My own possession among all the peoples of all the earth" (Exodus 19:3, 5).

The rejection of this first principle substitutes the supposed-transcendence of the State for the transcendence of God. The State demands obedience by denying God or acting in a neutral way toward Him. This is called "statism." The State is a substitute deity. It seeks to be close to the people, immanent, by creating a governmental system that controls through burdensome laws, bureaucratic forms, and centralization.

God is all-seeing (omniscient) and present everywhere (omnipresent). He knows everything. These are incommunicable attributes of God. He does not share them. No creature possesses them. Because Satan does not possess these attributes of God, he must make up for this lack by strengthening his demonic and human hierarchy (or as C. S. Lewis calls it in *The Screwtape Letters*, the "lowerarchy"). Others must see for him, report everything they have seen and remember to him, and carry out his orders. There is always a lot of information lost in the process. Thus, throughout history those who have relied on bureaucracy have failed in their struggles with those who rely on self-government under a perfect, sovereign God.

Authority/Hierarchy

God delegates sovereignty to men. He does this directly, for all men are created in His image. He also does this through government: some men become God's *representatives* in His ordained hierarchies. God establishes plural hierarchies.

The State is not synonymous with society. Society is much broader: associations, churches, schools, families, etc. In effect, "we" are not "the government." The government is simply an agency of force that has the power of the sword. It receives this power from God, but also through lawfully constituted transfers of power from the people. If people refuse to submit, no king can rule.

The Tenth Amendment of the U.S. Constitution makes a dis-

tinction between the "State" and "Society": "The powers not delegated to the *United States* by the Constitution, nor prohibited by it
to the States, are reserved to the States respectively, or *to the
people*." The State is not the depository of unbridled power. Individuals in their respective callings retain power. This diffuses the
potential for tyranny since such a system of government decen-
tralizes power by placing it in the hands of the many.

The concluding phrase of the First Amendment indicates that
the people are separate from the National government: "Congress
shall make no law respecting the establishment of religion, or prohibiting the free exercise thereof; or abridging the freedom of
speech, or of the press; or the right of the *people* peaceably to as-
semble, and to petition the *government* for a redress of grievances."
The people can petition the government, changing the direction
of the nation through all the constitutional means at their
disposal. Of course, the vote is a very powerful tool in the hands
of self-governed citizens.

A question that every human institution faces is this one:
"Who's in charge here?" Someone or some group must lay down
the law, meaning that someone has the authority to tell others
what to do. There must be some sort of system of accountability.
The Bible tells us that God establishes kings on their thrones. He
elevates leaders, and He pulls them down (Daniel 2:21). He is the
ruler of the nations, not men. The civil governments of men
merely reflect His power and rule; man's governments are not
creative and autonomous (*auto* = self, *nomos* = law).

For the messianic State, the basis of civil government develops
out of the will of man. Essentially, all men do what is right in their
own eyes, and those running for political office appeal to the self-
willed character of the people by promising them favors from the
State in exchange for their votes. In time, however, authority is
transferred to a powerful group of men who claim absolute power
for themselves, or other men abdicate responsible decentralized
judgment and thus forfeit jurisdiction. Man's court becomes the
final court of appeal. "The Constitution," in the words of U.S.
Supreme Court Justice (and evolutionist) Oliver Wendell

Holmes, "is what the Courts say it is." Man willingly submits to the State.

Ethically rebellious men choose a certain kind of hierarchy, a top-down hierarchy. This is Satan's model. God does not need such a bureaucracy, for He is absolutely sovereign. He can deal with men directly. They can pray to Him directly. Not so with Satan and his followers. Satan is a creature; he can be in only one place at a time. Thus, those who believe in the messianic State place all their hopes in a top-down hierarchy of *command* rather than in God's bottom-up hierarchy of *appeal.*

The State, however, has a single characteristic not given to the individual or society at large, that is, the legitimacy of its use of power and force: The State does not "bear the sword for nothing" (Romans 13:4). While we see the State usurping the power of individuals, families, and churches by the use of its own power, we should not deny the State its power in its Biblically designated jurisdictions. The Christian's dominion task is to call the State back to its proper Biblical role. This will mean Christian involvement in the seats of power.

Ethics/Law/Dominion

All governments require a reference point. If God is to be pleased by men, the Bible must become the foundation of all their governments, including civil government. This means that *Biblical law must be made the foundation of all righteous judgment in every government:* personal (self-government), ecclesiastical, familial, and civil.

There are those who do not want Biblical law to rule over them. Even some Christians place the State in a special category where it is obligated to follow something other that Biblical law: natural law, conscience, common sense, or the will of the people. Such anti-Biblical choices are sure roads to tyranny.

Neutral or objective law has brought on some of the greatest holocausts the world ever has seen — the pre-meditated murder of nearly 20 million unborn babies in the United States since 1973, and 35 to 50 million per *year* worldwide. Remember, these are

State-sanctioned holocausts. These are holocausts based on the "will of the people" and a natural law ethic. This system of ethics as it is related to economics, for example, has plunged much of the world into poverty, and the ravages of recession and inflation, while socialistic welfare programs are threatening the once-prosperous Christian West.

What Legal System Produces Tyranny?

But, the skeptic asks, can't Biblical law sometimes be used in a tyrannical way? The answer clearly is *no*. It was not Israel that God called tyrannical when its kings obeyed His law; it was those nations around Israel that were tyrannical. When Israel worshipped the false gods of the nations around them, God delivered them into foreign tyranny. Biblical law, *when enforced as a comprehensive system*, does not allow for the creation of tyranny. No doubt *parts of* Biblical law can be *misused* to impose tyranny, but not Biblical law as a unit. For instance, the Bible says that a State that taxes men at 10 percent of their income is tyrannical (1 Samuel 8). This means *all* levels of civil government *combined* are not allowed by God to extract as much as His tithe. How could modern tyrants operate their tyrannical regimes with so little tax money as a "mere" ten percent? Christians today live under tax burdens that are four to five times heavier than the system designated by God as tyrannical, yet they worry about Biblical law being tyrannical. They call Biblical freedom tyrannical, but democratically imposed tax tyranny they call freedom.

Doesn't Biblical law require people to become Christians? The answer to this questions is also *no*. The Bible calls on men everywhere to repent and to submit to the Lord Jesus Christ. But that same Bible does not give the State the power, authority, or jurisdiction to force people to become Christians. Christians, therefore, should not petition the State to *impose* Christianity upon the citizenry. Christianity is an inside-out religion. Only the Holy Spirit can regenerate the heart of a man or woman "dead in trespasses and sins" (Ephesians 2:1). No State has the jurisdiction or power to force someone to be a Christian. Still, those Biblical laws which directly address the civil magistrate should be enacted into law: protecting the unborn; the orphan, widow and stranger; maintaining just weights and measures (no fiat paper money); enforcing judicial laws regarding restitution and capital punishment; protecting the nation's borders; and establishing a tax rate that does not exceed 10 per cent for any citizen.

The purpose of Biblical civil government is not to create a perfect society but rather to create legal conditions for the voluntary establishment of a marketplace, free of tyranny. This is one of the reasons Paul urges us to pray "for kings and all who are in authority, in order that we may lead a tranquil and quiet life in all godliness and dignity" (1 Timothy 2:1, 2).

What is left if we cannot go to the Bible for our laws? By what *other* standard should governments be ruled? Will we be ruled by God or men? This is always the choice facing men. As Elijah said on Mt. Carmel to the people, choose this day whom you will serve, Baal or God. As usual, the people answered not a word (1 Kings 18:21) until *after* they saw whose God was more powerful, Elijah's God or the god of the false prophets.

God or Man?

The NBC television network in 1986 presented a drama about the gripping and courageous story of Raoul Wallenberg and his attempts to save European Jews from their Nazi tormentor, Colonel Adolf Eichmann. Wallenberg's efforts may have made the difference between life and death for nearly 120,000 Hungarian Jews.

During the course of the story, when the viewer is confronted by a scene of Jews being loaded into trucks for shipment to a concentration camp, a Jewish teenager turns to a rabbi and confronts him with what he perceives to be an unanswerable question: "How can you still believe in God after all of this?" The rabbi does not take long to respond: *"How can you still believe in man?"*

This is our dilemma today. If we do not believe in God for our laws, then man is all that is left. Such a foundation leads either to anarchy (as in Beirut, Lebanon) or totalitarianism (the Soviet

Union). Listen to Joshua's response: "And if it is disagreeable in your sight to serve the Lord, choose for yourselves today who you will serve: whether the gods which your fathers served which were beyond the River, or the gods of the Amorites in whose land you are living; but as for me and my house, we will serve the Lord" (Joshua 24:15).

Judgment/Sanctions

Joshua was *testifying* to his faith in God. He was therefore testifying to his opposition to all rival gods. The test of his faith was his *service*. Under which god will a person serve? In other words, which god's *law* will a person obey? Joshua was serving as a *witness for God*. He would serve God, he testified.

God tells His people to be witnesses for Him throughout the world. But to what are Christians to witness? The answer is simple: they are to witness to the faithfulness of God's holy Word, the Bible. When a Christian presents the gospel of salvation through faith in Christ to someone, he is *witnessing* for Christ. He presents the testimony of the Biblical account of sin and redemption. But what does this account involve? The Christian is to witness to the truth of the whole Bible. He does this when he testifies to the rule of God over His creation, the responsibilities that men have to God and other men, and the law of God as the proper blueprint of such personal and governmental responsibility.

What Christians seldom understand is that *all of life is essentially a law court*. We are undergoing a trial. We even speak of the "trials and tribulations" of life. The sin of man in the garden of Eden was a courtroom drama. Adam and Eve were supposed to judge Satan when he spoke words against God. Instead, they believed Satan and therefore did what he recommended. By doing what God's enemy said to do, *they testified publicly against the truth of God's Word*. Therefore, when God returned, He conducted a trial. He cross-examined the witnesses, Adam and Eve. God then pronounced judgment against the serpent, then Eve, and finally Adam. But there had to be witnesses. Adam and Eve had no choice: they had to testify against God or Satan, once the temptation came.

Every system of government has to have a court. There has to be a judge in the system who can settle disputes. His word is never absolutely final; only God's Word is absolutely final. But there must be a judge. This is why the Bible sometimes refers to men as gods (Psalm 82:6). Men are not divine in the sense of having some mythical "spark of divinity" within them. Only Jesus Christ was both God and man, and His two natures were without intermixture. But men are *judges*. They hold an office analogous to God's office as final judge.

All law structures are delegated by God. There is no single earthly law court that can command absolute obedience without violating the prohibition against bowing down to "any likeness of what is in heaven" that is a final earthly court of appeal that would substitute for God (Exodus 20:4; Acts 5:33-42). God has created a decentralized system of civil government (Exodus 18:17-27), and this is reflected in our constitutional system of "checks and balances." The fact that elections are held every two years speaks well of the decentralized character of civil government in the United States.

Rendering Judgment

There must be judgment, that is, evaluation of all our works. The Biblical pattern is self-government (self-control), family government, ecclesiastical government, and civil government. The Bible is the ethical standard for the individual in self-government, for parents and children in family government, for church members and elders in ecclesiastical, and for representatives and judges in civil government. Our pattern of evaluation is analogous to God's pattern of judgment. The words of Jesus in Matthew 7:1 are best understood in this context.

Humanist law sees no analogous judgment. Judgment is autonomous. "Every man does what is right in his own eyes" (Judges 17:6). In time, anarchy sets in. The people, the once-autonomous and "free" independent governors, turn to the State for definitive judgment (Judges 9:1-21). The State is chosen over God (1 Samuel 8:1-8). Where God gave an inscripturated and visible law, the

State's law becomes arbitrary, capricious,[1] and hidden (bureaucratic). All competitive governments are dismantled in principle.

God's judgment is sure. He judges in history to establish His judgment:

> It is He who sits above the vault of the earth, and its inhabitants are like grasshoppers, Who stretches out the heavens like a curtain and spreads them out like a tent to dwell in. He it is who reduces judges to nothing, who makes the judges of the earth meaningless (Isaiah 40:22-23).

There are many who believe it is the State's duty, through its judicial process, to right every wrong. This concept carries human courts beyond the Biblical system of justice. While some might desire such a State function, history shows us that it is impossible and dangerous. Only God can right every wrong, and His chosen means was by Christ's atoning sacrifice for those who believe in Him, and eternal punishment in Hell for those who do not turn to Jesus in repentance and faith. *The State is not God.* It is not given authority or power over eternity, but only the authority, power, and duty, in specified kinds of cases, to send convicted criminals to their judgment in time. Rulers in the State have neither the omniscience (all-knowledge) nor the omnipotence (all-power)—much less the perfect righteousness—required to right all wrongs. The State, therefore, must remain within divinely ordained limits of its authority when dealing with criminals.

Obviously, certain sins often may escape detection. Homosexuals who practice behind closed doors are out-of-bounds for the courts, of course, unless others witness their criminal behavior. Such behavior may not be dealt with by courts in history, but will be dealt with by God, either in history (e.g., AIDS) or eternity. The law that requires the death penalty for homosexual acts effectually drives the perversion of homosexuality underground, back to the closet, to the dark realm of shameful activity.

---

1. The constant changes in the tax code are ample evidence of the capricious nature of Statist law today.

Inheritance/Legitimacy/Continuity

Obedience to the law brings with it the future dominion of the faithful. "A good man leaves an inheritance to his children's children, and the wealth of the sinner is stored up for the righteous" (Proverbs 13:22). Predicting the future is easy if there is a set standard of ethical behavior with listed blessings and curses. There is an extension of kingdom blessings if people are faithful to the stipulations of the covenant.

For the rebel, who believes in the ultimate State, continuity is based on planning and bureaucratic control of all aspects of society. The past is denied, therefore, there are no fixed laws to guarantee a certain type of future. The people trust "experts" to tell them what the future will be like. Evil men seek to inherit the future by covetousness, theft, and envy. The theft of Naboth's vineyard is a perfect example (1 Kings 21): coveting led to the corrupting of justice through the hiring of false witnesses and then the murder of the righteous man.

We must substitute the God-ordained family for the pseudo-family of the modern messianic State. We must see continuity not in terms of statism but in terms of the Biblical covenant structure. The almighty State must be cut back to size—the size approved by the Bible.

Where to Begin

The loss of dominion by Christians did not just happen. A study of our nation's history will show that there was a time when the majority of the people were self-consciously Christian in their outlook. Even those who did not acknowledge Jesus Christ as Savior and Lord still looked upon Christianity as the cornerstone of a Christian civilization. Over time, the idea of a Christian civilization waned. What was gained was soon lost, not by a military coup, but simply by the passivity of Christians.

Dominion will not return through magic or even through a barrage of miracles. We cannot wait on dominion. It will not drop in our laps from heaven. There must be a starting point. Faithfulness is the word. First, we must believe that something can be done. We must cast off the shackles of pessimism and defeat. Second, we must deny that the State is our Savior. The State is the God of humanism. While the State has its proper role to play in society, we must be careful not to elevate it to the position of the humanists. The kingdom of God does not advance through the agency of the State. Remember, the State is just *one* of God's jurisdictional governments.

Modern-day humanism is dominant in our nation and has set the Church of Jesus Christ on the run. We can see the expression of a man-centered philosophy entrenched in the courts, schools, colleges, medical schools, the media, and in Congress. Even the Church has been overrun by pagan ideologies. Too often Christians believe that the world is evil and owned by the devil. The world belongs to Jesus, and as "fellow heirs" with Christ, we share in His possessions. The devil possesses what we fail to possess.

One reason for humanism's dominance is the Christian's preoccupation with retreatism. We have bought the bill of goods humanists have sold us — *that Christians have no business preaching and teaching about topics pertaining to this world.* "Preach about heaven and the return of Jesus Christ, but do not meddle in the areas of economics, law, politics, and education. These are strictly *secular* matters." As long as churches followed this prescription, Christian individuals, families, and churches were not opposed. *An ineffective church is a tolerated church.*

Transcendence/Presence

The State is not God. It therefore cannot save mankind. We must abandon any doctrine of salvation by law, especially statist law.

Since the State is a limited jurisdiction, we should not view it as "God walking on earth," ready, willing, and able to meet all our needs. I'm afraid, however, that this is too often the case, even for Christians.

One of the ways the State positions itself to a place of power is by using the inherent sinful desire of men and women to get something for nothing. They want their false god to make stones into bread. This is promised politically by plundering one segment of society, using the prosperous minority to gain the votes of the envy-motivated majority. Those seeking political power then "buy" the votes of the majority with the wealth of the minority. Of course, this is all done in the name of "fairness," "equality," and "justice." In the end, the entire nation suffers. Under such a system, the risk-taking entrepreneurs see no advantage in creating wealth because the benefits are minimal for the amount of risk involved. In time, the envy-motivated have no one to plunder.

What does this mean for the Christian? All of us should seek to minimize involvement in State welfare, wealth transfer, programs. Many Christians are demanding a "tax revolt" when they ought to demand a "benefits revolt." If you are receiving food stamps or small business loans or school loans, work yourself out of the trap of depending on the State for support! Remember, that's someone else's money.

Beware of political solutions to problems. It seems that every time Christians see a problem, they run off to Washington shouting "Do something!" They would be wise to shout "Do Nothing!"

Most of our problems can be dealt with either in the home, church, or school. Civil issues that seem to be national in scope can be taken care of at the local level where greater citizen involvement can take place. Many of our concerns are the result of Washington doing something. Instead of running to Washington, get things done at the local level where there is more accountability. The less we use Washington the sooner it will shrink in size, power, and influence.

Become aware of the political issues. The Bible informs us that the "sons of Issachar [were] men who understood the times, with knowledge of what Israel should do" (1 Chronicles 12:32). We have to understand the times so we'll be ready to offer the right solutions.

We've been told that we're not able to understand the complex issues of the day. There are "experts" in Washington who "know what to do." In fact, they are so "expert" that they even know how to spend our money better than we do. Of course, they also know what is best for our children's education. More money is taken to fund an educational system steeped in the man-centered religion of humanism. And what do we get for our money? Mediocrity, falling SAT (Scholastic Aptitude Test) scores, the proliferation of drugs, illiteracy, crime, violence, and teenage pregnancies in epidemic proportions. Then there is the prescribed remedy for all of this: more money.

We are made to believe that the issues of the day are complex. We are told that putting convicted murders to death is no solution. I guess locking them up, so they can be paroled after seven years to murder again is a better solution? It is quite apparent that capital punishment will stop at least one murderer from ever murdering again. But you better know what you're talking about if you hope to give answers. Being like the "sons of Issachar" is not easy.

Authority/Hierarchy

"If you take the Queen's shilling, you do the Queen's bidding." Alternatively, "He who pays the piper calls the tune." If men do not want to be under the control of the modern messianic State, they must cut off their dependence on this State. This means that the entire welfare system at every level — federal, state, and local — must be progressively dismantled. Every special-interest group must be willing to say, "We will get our hands out of your wallets, if you get your hands out of our wallets."

The Bible says that parents must educate their children in the law of God (Deuteronomy 6:6, 7). This means that Christian parents must pull their children out of the public school system. This means that Christians must vote no on all school bond issues.

The Bible says that children are to care for aged parents. This means that no Christian should become dependent on Social Security checks. The money from these checks should be given away each month to charities. (Turning back the money to the Social Security system only leads to an expansion of the federal government.)

Christians should run for office, in order to get power in the various government hierarchies. Then they should vote against every expansion of power and every tax hike and every bond issue. The State must be cut back.

This is the battle: the belief that the State is the only important government. As self-governed Christians, we must work to cut back the unbridled power and authority of the State. Dominion in the area of civil government does not mean that we desire the escalating power base available to those who seek and hold office. Rather, we should run for elected office to pull on the reins of power, to slow the growth of power run wild.

But Christians must also recognize that we need a peaceful transfer of power to a new Bible-based system of multiple authorities. They must recognize that God will drive out our enemies little by little, over many years (Exodus 23:29, 30). We are not to become revolutionaries. We are not to impose a top-down tyranny to ram the Bible down people's throats. The goal is to use every means available to *educate* voters, and only then to transform their increasingly Biblical outlook into legislation. Mostly, it will be legislation abolishing past legislation.

Ethics/Law/Dominion

The first step in overturning the messianic State is to place ourselves under God's law. We must meditate on the law. We must make the 119th psalm our hymn of obedience.

The second step is to teach our children the law (Deuteronomy 6:6, 7). We must demonstrate to them by our actions that we are self-governed by the law.

Third, we must proclaim the law to others. We must abandon the false theology that New Testament Christians are in no sense obligated to obey God's Old Testament law. We obey the sacrificial law by baptizing people and eating the Lord's Supper. We obey Biblical laws against murder, adultery, and many other capital crimes in the Bible.

Fourth, we must elect public officials who say they will vote for Biblical laws. First and foremost, this means voting to prohibit abortion. While few Christians are willing to go this far, the long-term goal should be the execution of abortionists and parents who hire them. If we argue that abortion is murder, then we must call for the death penalty. If abortionists are not supposed to be executed, then they are not murderers, and if they are not murderers, why do we want to abolish abortion? In short, *Christians must learn to think consistently.*

With respect to almost everything the modern State does to "help" people, Christians should vote "no." Such help is the first step to enslavement. "I'm from the government, and I'm here to help you" is the mythical creed of modern humanist religion. Christians should stop believing it.

Judgment/Sanctions

Christians must begin to serve on juries. They must not vote to convict people of crimes that the Bible says are not crimes, no matter what the corrupt civil law says. They must also convict evil doers, even if modern sociology says that they are merely "the victims of their environment." That is what Adam pleaded, too: Eve made him do it.

Juries must be instructed — as under Common Law and as denied under our current humanistic legal theory and practice — to look to the *justice or injustice of the law,* as well as to the *facts* of the case. This is absolutely essential if God's law is to be honored and the jury's verdict is not to be manipulated by judges who want people to be convicted under unjust laws. *The jury's declaration of "not guilty" is final.* In the jury room, the jury is sovereign — not the legislature, not the police, and surely not the judge.

The jury is the fundamental institutional safeguard of our liberties under the Common Law, the essence of the heritage of Magna Carta (1215). Nevertheless, judges frequently tell the jury that the jury has no right to decide the law, only the facts. This is a lie, and the judges know it. The U.S. Supreme Court declared that juries can decide the law of the case (*Sparf v. U.S.*, 1895). In some states, anyone who does not believe that the jury has a legal right to decide the law is told to identify himself before the jury is selected, and if he does, he is then excluded by the judge from serving on the jury. This is modern judicial tyranny in action.

Because those judges who tell juries this lie are immoral, the Christian should sit silently if any judge asks people to stand up if they believe that the jury has the right to decide the law as well as the facts. Then he should hang the jury if necessary, if the jury votes to convict the defendant of a bad law. This is the number-one check on bad politics today: the jury has the final say. Once in that jury room, the judge has no more authority to decide the outcome of the case than the defense attorney does.

In our day (and in most eras of human history), the administration of law is controlled by self-seeking men who desire power. The process of the courts are interfered with by lawyers and judges. For example, lawyers are allowed to exclude from a jury a certain number of people. They often exclude people of specific religious beliefs who might decide for or against a particular defendant. They also exclude people on the basis of sex, race, and suspected income level, and they are not required to say why they are excluding a particular candidate for the jury.

Witnesses are then called and testimony secured, but only *selected* witnesses and testimony are utilized. The jurors are not given access to the truth, the whole truth, and nothing but the truth.

There is a war on against the jury system. The jury must be defended in word and deed. Except for a major emergency, do not refuse a call to sit on a jury.

Find out who the judges are who are running for office, and get behind them. A political race for judge will have vastly more impact on your community than the race for any other political office. The judge has more authority in his courtroom than any single legislator is likely to have.

Another very important humanist modification of the judicial system in the United States has been the creation of a new system of law, called administrative law. These laws are written by the very bureaucrats who enforce them. The *Federal Register* publishes federal administrative laws each day, and this adds up to about

53,000 pages of fine print each year. Harvard legal scholar Harold Berman has written that the rapid escalation of administrative law in the West since 1900 threatens the West's whole tradition of law, and represents a major threat to liberty.[2]

The agencies have also created a new bureaucratic office called the "administrative law judge." It has the ring of authority about it. In fact, this officer is a paid employee of the particular federal agency involved in the dispute with citizens or organizations. This paid hireling of the agency renders his decision concerning the lawfulness of the bureaucracy's decision. This office should have its name changed. It should be made legal for any citizen to appeal administrative rulings directly to the civil courts, without having to take the case first through the time-consuming bureaucracy.

In effect, government bureaucracies have become legislators, judges, and executive enforcers. This violates the principle of federalism: checks and balances. Only one thing will roll back their power: a drastic reduction in their funding. An increase of agency funding is a form of judgment, a reward for good service. It is easier for politicians to increase spending if voters have forgotten how much government is costing them. Therefore, Gary North recommends two very simple administrative changes in government funding. *First*, require the taxes for any level of civil government to be due the day before elections. Today, due dates for taxes are deliberately scheduled seven months earlier than voting (April vs. November). The *second* simple administrative change would involve returning to the tax collection system that prevailed in the United States before World War II: no compulsory withholding of anyone's income during the year by the government. Each person must pay his taxes out of his own savings on tax day. He must learn to budget for himself.

The imposition of these two simple administrative changes would produce the greatest tax revolt since the American Revolu-

---

2. Harold J. Berman, *Law and Revolution: The Formation of the Western Legal Tradition* (Cambridge, Massachusetts: Harvard University Press, 1983), Introduction.

tion. Government would shrink overnight. (By the way, do you know what the level of taxation of the colonies by the British Parliament was in 1775? About one percent for the thirteen colonies as a whole, and under three percent for the most heavily taxed Virginia plantation region. Compare this with your local sales tax alone, or state income tax.)

Common law says that a person is innocent until proven guilty. This rule should control every government agency, including the Internal Revenue Service. At present, the IRS operates under the Napoleonic Code: guilty until proven innocent. Again, the citizen should be allowed to appeal an injustice directly to the civil courts, without having to pay the disputed tax before the *independent* court system renders verdict.

Every government agency that brings a case against a citizen or organization should pay all legal expenses of the defendant if he is declared "not guilty." This will restrain illegal harassment of innocent people. To be really effective, the agency that brought the suit should pay the defendant's expenses. Juries should *automatically* make this settlement part of any declaration of "not guilty."

What is the Christian's immediate responsibility? To pray. Prayer is our call to God to judge us and our society. Pray for the destruction of humanism and humanists. Pray for the President, the U.S. Supreme Court (either for changing their minds or changing the court through death or resignation), U.S. Senators from your state, U.S. Congressman in your district, the Cabinet, State Representative, State Governor, and City Council Members. Also, pray for the reduction in civil government in general, for the proliferation of Christian schools, for more solid Christian lawyers who know the score, for reformation in our churches, families, the media, the medical profession, and business. Pray also for our persecuted brothers and sisters in foreign lands.

Inheritance/Legitimacy/Continuity

As a symbol of the advent of a Christian civil government, all inheritance taxes should be abolished. All gift taxes should be abolished for the same reason. The State must not tax any person's family inheritance.

Because debt longer than seven years is prohibited by the Bible (Deuteronomy 15), Christians must on principle always vote against any bond issue that carries a debt repayment schedule longer than the Biblical limit of seven years. But all bond issues are long-term debt contracts. This means: *vote no on all bond issues*, no matter how "good" the purpose of the bonds. We must not rob our children's inheritance.

Register to vote. Voting is the way that Christians can affect the nature of the continuity of civil government. Your vote counts. As humanist voters' apathy increases, Christians have a better chance of capturing many political offices.

- In 1645, one vote gave Oliver Cromwell control of England.

- In 1776, one vote determined that English, not German, would be the American language.

- In 1845, one vote brought Texas into the Union.

- In 1923, one vote gave Hitler control of the Nazi Party.

- In 1948 in Texas, Lyndon B. Johnson was elected to the U.S. Senate by 87 votes out of 988,295 votes cast in 6,000 precincts. That figures out to be 1/69th of a vote per precinct.

- In 1958, six congressmen were re-elected to the U.S. House of Representatives by *less than one vote per precinct*.

- In 1960, John F. Kennedy defeated Richard Nixon by only 113,000 popular votes—one-half vote per precinct.

- In 1980, John East of North Carolina won the U.S. Senate seat by one vote per precinct.

The Christian community can make a difference if it will only vote: "According to Sacramento, California political consultant Wayne Johnson, 56 per cent of the evangelicals gave Jimmy Carter their votes in 1976, 56 percent gave their vote to Ronald Reagan in 1980, and 75 to 81 per cent gave their vote to President Reagan in 1984."[3]

---

3. *Candidates Biblical Scorecard*, 1986 Edition, p. 27.

Go to public meetings on current issues, especially if your representative is holding it. Most politicians hold no clear and consistent ideology. They vote according to the way they feel the winds are blowing. Let them feel the wind and some heat. Go prepared. Get their voting record. Study the issues and choose a spokesman to address the issues. If you don't know who your elected representative is, call the research department of your local public library.

Get involved in precinct politics. A precinct is "the smallest geographic or electoral unit used during an election." Precincts are "a way of dividing voters into manageable groups." The precinct is your neighborhood. Elections are won or lost in the precinct. Few people know the power of the precinct. With a little bit of leg work and some telephone calls, you can take over a precinct.

Influence your elected officials. If your representatives never hear from you, then they assume that they're doing a good job. I can guarantee you that other groups are bending the ear of your representatives on a daily basis. Write them letters, preferably not a copy of some other letter. They tend to ignore a flood of mail that looks the same.

If you are a leader of some group, then say so. Be friendly and courteous. Do not threaten or accuse. Keep your letter short, addressing a single issue. Type your letter if you can. Make sure you know what you're talking about. Speak in specifics, not generalities. Ask for a reply. You will probably get a form reply that does not address your specific questions. Write again, forcing your representative to show his or her colors. When your representative votes "right," send a note of thanks.

Address your letters in this fashion:

The Honorable_____
U.S. Senate
Washington, D.C. 20510
Dear Senator_____:

or

The Honorable_____
U.S. House of Representatives
Washington, D.C. 20515
Dear Congressman_____:

If you need to get a pending legislative Bill, you'll have to write to the appropriate office. You can obtain information on the status of particular legislation in the House or Senate by calling the Legislative Information Office at (202) 225-1772. Copies of pending legislation can be obtained for the Senate by writing Senate Documents Room, Senate Hart Building, Room B-04, Washington, D.C. 20510. Phone (202) 224-7860. For the House, write House Documents Room, U.S. House of Representatives, Washington, D.C. 20515. Phone (202) 225-3456.

Summary

It's difficult to swallow that change begins with you and me and something will come out of it if change really does occur. What difference can one person make? What difference does one rain drop make in a flood? What difference does one spark make in a forest fire. What difference did Joseph make in Egypt? What difference did Daniel make in Babylon?

God calls on us one by one to conform our lives to the image of His Son. There is no magical formula for change. The standard for righteousness is set forth in Scripture. Just think what would happen if Christians around the world would begin to affect their world where they live. There would be a tidal wave of change. Those without Christ would want what we have. Our works would be a testimony to our faith. What would your witness do to your neighborhood, your place of work, even your church? The transformation of our world is dependent on the transformation of the body of Christ. It begins with you. It begins with me.

Appendix

THE CHRISTIAN ORIGINS OF AMERICAN CIVIL GOVERNMENT

Our nation began as a Christian nation. Our earliest fore-fathers believed the Bible when it said "By Me kings reign, and rulers decree justice" (Proverbs 8:15). But it seems that the general public is being brainwashed to believe that our nation was founded on some neutral morality base. Secularism, we are told, has always ruled the day. Religion in general, and Christianity in particular, had little to do with the founding of these United States. Education, law, and politics were purposely "separated" from any religious affiliation. So the critics of an early Christian America want us to believe.

The present educational establishment, for example, wants to bury the past so our children have no way of comparing our Christian history with the secularists' vision of the future. A recent study of textbooks bears this out. Paul E. Vitz, professor of Psychology at New York University, spent months of careful analysis of 60 textbooks used in elementary schools across the country. The study was sponsored by the Department of Education.[1] The texts were examined in terms of their references to religion, either directly or indirectly. "The most striking thing," Vitz determined, "is the total absence of any primary religious text about typical contemporary American religious life. In particular, there is not one text reference to characteristic Protestant religious life in these books." When religious life is depicted, the references are so diluted as to be meaningless. For example, in a Spanish-speaking

---

1. Paul E. Vitz, *Censorship: Evidence of Bias in Our Children's Textbooks* (Ann Arbor, Michigan: *Servant Books, 1986*).

neighborhood, "churches have places for dances and sports events." Religion is trivialized. In another textbook, a "Puritan" church is not described as a center of religious life but rather as a center for a summer piano festival. For the secularists, religion is evolutionary. There was a time when people were religious. But now that we've come of age, we no longer need religion. Religion, in effect, is a projection of man's primitive past. Modern man can do without the superstitions of religious belief. What used to be places of worship are now nothing more than entertainment centers. The Enlightenment lives!

The depiction of religious life in America doesn't seem much different from that of religious life in the Soviet Union. Some of the churches in the Soviet Union are used as museums. For the most part, only the elderly are "religious" and go to church. The children are indoctrinated to believe that the State is the greatest good.

The report by Dr. Vitz is a frightening reality. George Orwell's "Ministry of Truth," where the past is discarded down the "memory hole," is no longer fiction. Orwell understood the importance of the past. He wrote the following in his prophetic novel *1984*: "Who controls the past, controls the future: who controls the present controls the past." Our job is to make Christianity the standard around the world. No discussion ought to take place unless the Biblical perspective is first discussed. This will mean gaining a better knowledge of the Bible and the development of skills to use the Bible. Further, it means gaining a knowledge of our rich Christian past, a past that is being cleverly and boldly written out of our history books.

The present educational establishment wants to bury the past so our children have no way of comparing the past with the secularists' version of history and their aspirations for the future. This tactic eliminates discussion and conflict. It's time that our nation is reintroduced to the past. As Christians, we must not remain silent as nearly every vestige of Christianity is being removed from public life: from the gospel being denied in Public (government) schools to the removal of signs that the Salvation Army put on buses in Fresno, California that read: "God bless you."

A Christian Commonwealth

Both religious and political persecution motivated our fore-fathers to leave the shores of England and to start a "Christian Commonwealth" in the New World. "The purpose of the New England colonies was, with respect to church and state, twofold: First, to establish the true and free church, free of the *control* of the state, free to be a co-worker in terms of the Kingdom of God, to establish God's Zion on earth, second, to establish godly magistrates, i.e., a Christian state, magistrates as ordained by God."[2]

The separation of Christianity from the workings of the State was never in the minds of these early settlers. The following evidence will show that Christianity was the motivating force behind this nation's advance.

The history of this nation began, not in 1776, but more than a century earlier. Since ideas have consequences, we should expect to see the beliefs of previous generations influencing subsequent generations. It's true that even today, the influence of our Christian forefathers is making an impact, albeit a small one.

William Bradford (1589?-1657), in his *History of Plymouth Plantation*, wrote,

> A great hope and inward zeal they had of laying some good foundation, or at least to make some way thereunto, for the propagating and advancing the Gospel of the Kingdom of Christ in those remote parts of the World; yea, though they should be but even as stepping stones unto others for the performing of so great a work.[3]

The Mayflower Compact, drafted prior to the Pilgrim's arrival off Cape Cod on November 11, 1620, was the first republican document of the New world, a forerunner to the United States Constitution. It reads in part:

---

2. R. J. Rushdoony, *This Independent Republic: Studies in the Nature and Meaning of American History* (Fairfax, Virginia: Thoburn Press, [1964] 1978), pp. 97-98.

3. William Bradford, *History of Plymouth Plantation: 1606-1646*, ed. William T. Davis (New York: Charles Scribner's Sons, 1908), p. 46.

In the name of God, Amen. We, whose names are underwritten, the loyal subjects of our dread sovereign lord King James, by the grace of God, . . . having undertaken for the glory of God and advancement of the Christian faith, and the honor of our king and country, a voyage to plant the first colony in the northern parts of Virginia; do by these presents, solemnly and mutually in the presence of God and one another, covenant and combine ourselves together into a civil body politic, for our better ordering and preservation and furtherance of other ends aforesaid . . . .[4]

The First Charter of Virginia emphasizes the Christian character of the infant nation:

We, greatly commending and graciously accepting of their desires for the furtherance of so noble a work, which may, by the providence of Almighty God, hereafter tend to the glory of His Divine Majesty, in propagating of the Christian religion to such people, as yet live in darkness and miserable ignorance of the true knowledge and worship of God . . . .[5]

The Fundamental Orders of Connecticut, drafted in January 14, 1639 at Hartford, was the first written constitution that created a civil government. It reads in part:

Forasmuch as it has pleased Almighty God by the wise disposition of His divine providence so to order and dispose [these] . . . lands . . . ; and well knowing where a people are gathered together the Word of God requires that to maintain the peace and union of such a people there should be an orderly and decent government established according to God, to order and dispose of the affairs of all the people at all seasons as occasions shall require; do therefore associate and conjoin ourselves to be as one public State or Commonwealth, and do, for ourselves and our successors and such as shall be adjoined to us at any time hereafter, enter into combination and confederation together, to

---

4. William Bradford, "Mayflower Compact," *History of Plymouth Plantation*, pp. 106-107.

5. "First Charter of Virginia," April 10, 1606, *Documents of American History*, 6th edition, ed. Henry Steel Commager (New York: Appleton-Century-Crofts, Inc., 1958), p. 8.

maintain and preserve the liberty and purity of the Gospel of our Lord Jesus which we now profess, as also the discipline of the churches, which according to the truth of the said Gospel is now practiced among us . . .[6]

The New England Confederation, put into effect on May 19, 1643, established a union of like-minded civil bodies:

Whereas we all came into these parts of America with one and the same end and aim, namely, to advance the Kingdom of our Lord Jesus Christ and to enjoy the liberties of the Gospel in purity with peace; and whereas in our settling (by a wise providence of God) we are further dispersed upon the sea coasts and rivers than was a first intended . . . .[7]

These early governmental documents have several things in common: First, they are not revolutionary documents, calling on men to overthrow the existing order through armed conflict. Second, God is acknowledged as the King and Sovereign, and earthly kings must bow in submission to His revealed will. Third, the adherents of these documents came to the New World to "advance the kingdom of the Lord Jesus Christ" and not some utopian, State-sponsored political order. Fourth, the Bible was accepted as the standard for an "orderly and decent government" as well as "for the discipline of churches." Fifth, the gospel preceded the advance of civilization. Sixth, the people covenanted with God before they "combined and confederated together." Seventh, their future depended upon faithfulness to God's commands. Eighth, liberty was the fruit of a Christian world order.

What About the Constitution?

On adoption of the U.S. Constitution in 1789, there was fear that the new national government would either interfere with the various states that had established religions (nine of the thirteen colonies) or institute a national church, making each state con-

---

6. "Fundamental Orders of Connecticut," January 14, 1639, *Documents*, p. 23.
7. "The New England Confederation," May 19, 1643, *Documents*, p. 26.

form to the decree of Congress. Because of these fears, many states petitioned the First Congress to include a Constitutional Amendment prohibiting the national government from funding a single Christian denomination and favoring it with legal action. This is why, historically, "the real object of the [F]irst Amendment was not to countenance, much less to advance Mohammedanism [Islam], or Judaism, or infidelity, by prostrating Christianity, but to exclude all rivalry among Christian sects [denominations] and to prevent any national ecclesiastical establishment which would give to an hierarchy the exclusive patronage of the national government." Such was the opinion of Chief Justice Joseph Story in the mid-19th century.

When the First Amendment was drafted, nine of the thirteen states had established churches. The First Amendment was a guarantee to the states that the states would be able to continue whatever church-State relationship existed in 1791, the year the Bill of Rights was ratified and made part of the Constitution. Maryland, Virginia, North Carolina, South Carolina, and Georgia all shared Anglicanism as the established religion. Congregational-· ism was the established religion in Massachusetts, New Hampshire, and Connecticut. New York, while not having an established church, allowed for the establishment of Protestant religions. Only in Rhode Island and Virginia were all religious sects disestablished. But the Christian religion was the foundation of all of the states. Their social, civil, and political institutions were based on the Bible. Not even Rhode Island and Virginia renounced Christianity, and both states continued to respect and acknowledge the Christian religion in their systems of law.

Congressman James Madison, the chief author of the First Amendment, informed his Congressional colleagues that he was responding to the desires of the various state Conventions to prohibit establishment of a national religion where one religious "sect might obtain a pre-eminence" over others.

As legal scholars point out, the critical word in the First Amendment's religion clauses is "respecting." "Congress shall make no law *respecting* an establishment . . . ." "Respecting" is synonymous with "concerning," "regarding," and "about." Professor Robert Cord writes that the provision does not "prohibit an establishment of religion; rather it prohibits *Congress* from making laws about, concerning or regarding an establishment of religion [i.e., the establishment of one denomination (sect) over all others]."

National Prayers

After passage of the First Amendment, the first congress petitioned the President to proclaim a *national* day of prayer and thanksgiving. The issue was raised by Rep. Tucker that prayer "is a religious matter and, as such is proscribed to us. If a day of thanksgiving must take place, let it be done by the authority of the several states. . . ." The prayer resolution passed in spite of the objections of Rep. Tucker and others. On September 24, 1789, the same day that it approved the First Amendment, Congress called on President Washington to proclaim a national day of prayer and thanksgiving. The First Congress resolved:

> That a joint committee of both Houses be directed to wait upon the President of the United States to request that he would recommend to the people of the United States a day of public thanksgiving and prayer, to be observed by acknowledging, with grateful hearts, the many signal favors of Almighty God, especially by affording them an opportunity peaceably to establish a Constitution of government for their safety and happiness.

The first congress also established the Congressional chaplain system by which official daily prayers to God are still offered. In the entire debate on the First Amendment, not one word was said by any Congressman about a "wall of separation between church and State" that would outlaw such a practice.

Government Buildings and Inscriptions

If men refuse to glorify God, He is able from stones to raise up children to praise Him (Matthew 3:9). The courts, through the legal maneuverings of the ACLU, are working to remove every vestige of Christianity from our land. Our Christian heritage is still etched in stone, in coins, on walls, on canvas, and in glass.

First, the Ten Commandments hang over the head of the Chief Justice of the Supreme Court.

Second, in the House and Senate chambers appear the words, "In God We Trust."

Third, in the Rotunda is the figure of the crucified Christ.

Fourth, on the walls of the Capitol dome, these words appear: "The New Testament according to the Lord and Savior Jesus Christ."

Fifth, on the Great Seal of the United States is inscribed the phrase *Annuit Coeptis*, "God has smiled on our undertaking."

Sixth, under the Seal is the phrase from Lincoln's Gettysburg address: "This nation under God."

Seventh, President Eliot of Harvard chose Micah 6:8 for the walls of the nation's library: "He hath showed thee, O man, what is good; and what doth God require of thee, but to do justly, and to love mercy, and to walk humbly with thy God."

Eighth, the lawmaker's library quotes the Psalmist's acknowledgment of the beauty and order of creation: "The heavens declare the glory of God, and the firmament showeth His handiwork" (Psalm 19:1).

Ninth, engraved on the metal cap on the top of the Washington Monument are the words: "Praise be to God." Lining the walls of the stairwell are numerous Bible verses: "Search the Scriptures," "Holiness to the Lord," and "Train up a child in the way he should go, and when he is old he will not depart from it."

Tenth, the crier who opens each session of the Supreme Court closes with the words, "God save the United States and the Honorable Court."

Eleventh, at the opposite end of the Lincoln memorial, words and phrases to Lincoln's Second Inaugural Address allude to "God," the "Bible," "providence," the "Almighty," and "divine attributes."

Twelfth, the plaque in the Dirksen Office Building has the words "IN GOD WE TRUST" in bronze relief.

Thirteenth, in the Capitol Building a room was set aside by the Eighty-third Congress to be used exclusively for the private prayer and meditation of Members of Congress. In this specially designated room there is a stained-glass window showing George Washington kneeling in prayer. Behind Washington a prayer is etched: "Preserve me, O God, for in Thee do I put my trust" (Psalm 16:1). The two lower corners of the window each show the Holy Scriptures and an open book and a candle, signifying the light from God's law: "Thy Word is a lamp unto my feet and a light unto my path" (Psalm 119:105).

The question then arises: If so much of American political history is Christian, where did we get the idea of the separation of church and State? The answer is: from infidel politicians and minority churches that did not want to be taxed for the benefit of other churches, so they gave up the idea of ruling in the civil sphere.[8] This development is illustrated nicely by the story of Thomas Jefferson and the Baptists.

Jefferson's Humanist Legacy

Ask almost any American if he believes in the separation of church and State, and he will tell you he does. Ask him why, and he may say that "it's in the Constitution." It *isn't* in the Constitution. It never was. It was in a letter from Thomas Jefferson to a group of Baptists.

Jefferson responded on January 1, 1802 to a group of Danbury Connecticut Baptists who called him an "infidel." There is no question that those Baptists had him dead to rights. He was indeed an infidel. He did not believe in the divinity of Christ, nor did he believe in the Bible as the Word of God. He even put together a special version of the Bible, one without any miracles in it. But he did believe in one thing: getting re-elected. He knew that he was dead politically if Christians ever found out what his true beliefs were, for Christians were the overwhelming majority

---

8. See the book by Sidney Mead, *The Lively Experiment: The Shaping of Christianity in America* (New York: Harper & Row, 1963), chaps. 3-5.

politically. So he covered his tracks. He hid behind a smoke screen of false concern over religious integrity and a free conscience.

This was a smart tactic. Baptists were not part of any State religious establishment. They resented the fact that they had to pay taxes that went to support State churches — a reasonable resentment in retrospect, but not a commonly shared opinion in 1802, anywhere on earth. So he appealed to their sense of injustice. He understood their fears. He wrote:

> Believing with you that religion is a matter which lies solely between man and his God, that he owes account to none other for faith or his worship, that the legislative powers of government reach actions only, and not opinions, I contemplate with sovereign reverence that act of the whole American people which declared that their legislature should "make no law respecting an establishment of religion, or prohibiting the free exercise thereof," thus building a wall of separation between church and state.

That "wall of separation" language appealed to what was then a small religious sect that was discriminated against, the Baptists. Fifty years later, they had become the dominant Protestant group numerically, as they remain today. Jefferson, the theological infidel, wanted nothing more than to get Christians out of his hair politically. So, in effect, he offered them a political deal: you get out of my hair politically, and I will get out of your hair ecclesiastically.

This deal was repeated again and again in U.S. history. It rested on a myth, the myth of neutrality. It rested on another myth, the myth of natural law. It rested on the greatest political myth in modern history: the separation of God and State. The infidels spoke of the separation of *church* and State, but what they were after was the separation of God and State, the separation of God's law and State, and (if they could achieve it), the separation of Christians and State. They wanted the Christians to *disenfranchise* themselves voluntarily, and to achieve this, they invented a new slogan, the separation of church and State. It worked, too, especially after 1925 (in the media reaction to the famous Scopes "monkey trial" over the teaching of evolution in government-funded high schools) until about 1975 (the candidacy of Jimmy Carter).

Jefferson had no hand in the drafting of the Constitution or the Bill of Rights. He was in France at the time. Since when do phrases in letters of presidents substitute for Constitutional language?

Jefferson Backs Off in Public

When he gave his Second Inaugural Address in 1805, Jefferson modified his private 1802 position to conform publicly to the Constitution. He did not want to kill his political machine unnecessarily. He publicly admitted that the states did possess lawful jurisdiction over many religious matters.

> In matters of religion I have considered that its free exercise is placed by the Constitution independent of the powers of the General [Federal or national] government. I have therefore undertaken on no occasion to prescribe the religious exercises suited to it, but have left them, as the Constitution found them, under the direction and discipline of the church or state authorities acknowledged by the several religious societies.

In a letter to Samuel Miller, Thomas Jefferson further clarified his position:

> I consider the government of the United States as interdicted [prohibited] by the Constitution from intermeddling with religious institutions, their doctrines, discipline, or exercises. This results not only from the provision that no law shall be made respecting an establishment or free exercise of religion, but from that also which reserves to the states the powers not delegated to the general government. It must rest with the states, as far as it can be in any human authority. . . .

Which God, Which Spokesman?

The legal language of church/State relations is not found in our Constitution, but it *is* found in the *Soviet* Constitution: "In order to ensure to citizens freedom of conscience, the church in the USSR is separated from the State, and the school from the Church. Freedom of religious worship and freedom of anti-religious propaganda is recognized for all citizens." But in the Soviet Union, there is nothing but the State. Thus, the separation of church and State means the separation of church and *everything*. This has been the goal of satanists and humanists from the beginning, and they struck a deal with fearful Christians who conceded in principle their goal: the retreat of Christianity from every area of public responsibility and authority.

What has happened since Jefferson's day is the steady intrusion of the State into every area of life. That is what false gods do, after all: *intrude*. At the same time, the humanists ("infidels") steadily preached the separation of church and State, meaning Biblical morality and State. Thus, as the State was getting bigger, it was also getting less and less restrained by Biblical law and Christian fears about unwarranted political power. The myth of separation of Christianity and State led inevitably to the secularization of every area of life and the centralization of power in the national government. There can be no freedom without Christ. Take Christ and the Bible out of any institution of government, and you thereby lose freedom.

The confusion of Christians over the question of lawful jurisdiction—"Who speaks for God in any given area?"—has led steadily to the monopoly of jurisdiction by the State, which speaks only for itself, the new god of the ages.

Judicial Schizophrenia

At the time of the drafting of the Constitution, the prevailing worldview, although waning in its effect on the nation, was Biblical Christianity. Justice was based on "the laws of nature and of Nature's God." Law was revealed to man in the Bible. Our Founders believed also in the "Law of Nature," or "natural rights," which were most clearly revealed to man in Scripture.

Their view of the law of nature was influenced heavily by the English jurist William Blackstone. His *Commentaries on the Laws of*

England, published in the decade before the American Revolution, was read by most lawyers in the colonies. Perhaps more than anyone else, Blackstone established the "terms of debate" for the Revolution. (Amazingly, his books are seldom read today, even by historians who specialize in the American Revolution.) In his *Commentaries*, Blackstone had argued that the Fall of man has made his mind untrustworthy, so it is necessary to use the Bible to rightly understand the universal laws that God has established.

In time, however, the "Law of Nature" degenerated into "Natural Law," a law devoid of Biblical content. In 1892, the United States Supreme Court determined, in the case *The Church of the Holy Trinity vs. United States*, that America was a Christian nation from its earliest days. The court opinion, delivered by Justice Josiah Brewer, was an exhaustive study of the historical and legal evidence for America's Christian heritage. After examining hundreds of court cases, state constitutions, and other historical documents, the court came to the following conclusion:

> Our laws and our institutions must necessarily be based upon and embody the teachings of the Redeemer of mankind. It is impossible that it should be otherwise; and in this sense and to this extent our civilization and our institutions are emphatically Christian. . . . This is a religious people. This is historically true. From the discovery of this continent to the present hour, there is a single voice making this affirmation . . . .We find everywhere a clear recognition of the same truth . . . .These, and many other matters which might be noticed, add a volume of unofficial declarations to the mass of organic utterances that this is a Christian nation.

Incorporation

In the *Everson* case of 1948, the court held that the First Amendment's Establishment Clause had been "incorporated" into and made a part of the "due process" clause of the Fourteenth Amendment (adopted in 1868), and was thus a restriction on the *states* as well as *Congress*. Yet, the "due process" clause of the Fourteenth Amendment makes no reference to religion, but simply provides that no state shall "deprive any person of life, liberty, or property, without due process of law."

"Incorporation" had been rejected by the Court for nearly three-quarters of a century after the Fourteenth Amendment. The Court in 1948 gave no explanation for its judicial move of incorporation. Since the *Everson* decision of 1948, eminent legal scholars have rejected "incorporation."

The Blaine Amendment was introduced in Congress seven years after adoption of the Fourteenth Amendment. It substituted the word "state" for "Congress": "No *state* shall make any law respecting an establishment of religion or prohibiting the free exercise thereof." The Blaine Amendment was considered twenty times by Congress between 1876 and 1929 but always failed. Even Blaine himself never suggested that the First Amendment was "incorporated" into the Fourteenth.

If the Fourteenth Amendment did incorporate the First Amendment as the Supreme Court now says, why did its authors think the Blaine Amendment was necessary to restrict the power of the states as to religion?

What the Supreme Court Says Isn't Necessarily Law

The U.S. Constitution recognized this from the beginning, although for the past century, few legal scholars and virtually no politicians have acknowledged what the Founders wrote into the Constitution. If Congress is convinced that the Court is usurping jurisdiction that belongs to Congress, they can remove appelate jurisdiction from the Supreme Court (Art. III, Sec. 2, Clause 2). This was done in a case in 1869, *Ex parte McCardle*.[9]

It is interesting that law professors in prestigious law schools teach their students that what the Supreme Court says is not "the law," that it is not final, and they encourage their students to try to get cases overturned that appear to be settled by Supreme Court

---

9. *The Constitution of the United States of America: Analysis and Interpretation*, prepared by the Congressional Research Service, Library of Congress (Washington, D.C.: Government Printing Office, 1972), pp. 751-52.

precedent. But in public, they seldom admit this. "Yes, what the Court says is the law of the land," they tell television interviewers. Then they return to their classrooms and tell their students that the Supreme Court has only decided one case at one point in time, but it has not decided the law of the land.

Summary

Jefferson's legacy had its origins in the Enlightenment where Reason was crowned as god, natural law substituted for Biblical law, and neutrality became the new legal fiction. The Christian community was sucked into the vortex of this emerging mythical world view. But institutions built on myths are collapsing. The world views based on reason over revelation, natural law over Biblical law, and neutrality over the religious presuppositions of Thomas Jefferson in politics, Horace Mann and John Dewey in education, and Oliver Wendell Holmes in law are disintegrating.

So, the goal is to steadily recover our religious-historical roots, but without such medieval mistakes as State-financed churches and State-financed schools. We need to get back to the tradition that Jefferson fought, but without restoring what the Baptists fought.

The First Amendment was added to the Constitution to protect the Church from a national establishment of religion. There is an abundant amount of evidence supporting the claim that America's early history was based on Biblical principles. The phrase "the separation of church and State" comes from a letter written by Thomas Jefferson. Jefferson had nothing to do with the drafting of the First Amendment.

Recent courts and humanist politicians have illegitimately substituted Jefferson's anti-Constitutional phrase in place of the First Amendment. The Communists followed their lead. The Soviet Constitution maintains that the "Church is . . . separated from the State." What the Constitution was clearly designed to prevent—the intrusion by Congress into state and local ecclesiastical affairs—recent interpreters of the Constitution have mandated in the name of the Constitution. Christians who have never learned the Christian history of the United States have ignorantly and complacently gone along with this deliberate rewriting of American judicial history. They still think the words "the separation of church and state" are in the Constitution. They are: in the *Soviet* Constitution.

The humanists in the United States are no more neutral religiously than the humanists in the Soviet Union. In both cases, the national State is assumed to have divine rights: immunity from judicial appeal. Religiously "neutral" natural law theory cannot protect Christians in the United States from the inevitable loss of liberty that every non-Christian system of government inevitably produces. There is only one appeal that can assure men of liberty: an appeal to God and His Bible.

BIBLIOGRAPHY

Bahnsen, Greg L. *By This Standard: The Authority of God's Law Today.* Tyler, TX: Institute for Christian Economics, 1985

DeMar, Gary. *God and Government: A Biblical and Historical Study.* Atlanta, GA: American Vision, 1982.

_____. *Issues in Biblical Perspective.* Atlanta, GA: American Vision, 1984.

_____. *The Restoration of the Republic.* Atlanta, GA: American Vision, 1986.

Eidsmoe, John. *God and Caesar: Christian Faith and Political Action.* Westchester, IL: Crossway Books, 1984.

Foster, Marshall and Mary-Elaine Swanson. *The American Covenant: The Untold Story.* Thousand Oaks, CA: Foundation for Christian Self-Government, 1981.

Grant, George. *The Changing of the Guard: Biblical Blueprints for Political Action.* Ft Worth, TX: Dominion Press, 1987.

North, Gary, ed. *The Journal of Christian Reconstruction*: 1) Symposium on Politics, 2) Symposium on Christianity and the American Revolution; 3) Symposium on Puritanism and Society; and 4) Symposium on Biblical Law (Chalcedon, P.O. Box 158, Vallecito, CA 95251). These journals are not going to be reprinted, according to the publisher, so order them immediately: $7.50 each.

Rushdoony, Rousas John. *Christianity and the State.* Vallecito, CA: Ross House Books, 1986.

_____. *The Institutes of Biblical Law.* Nutley, NJ: Craig Press, 1973.

241

_____. *Law and Liberty*. Fairfax, VA: Thoburn Press, 1977.

_____. *Law and Society*. Vallecito, CA: Ross House Books, 1982.

_____. *The Nature of the American System*. Nutley, NJ: The Craig Press, 1965. Reprinted by Thoburn Press, Tyler, TX.

_____. *This Independent Republic: Studies in the Nature and Meaning of American History*. Nutley, NJ: The Craig Press, 1964. Reprinted by Thoburn Press, Tyler, TX.

_____. *Politics of Guilt and Pity*. Nutley, NJ: The Craig Press, 1970. Reprinted by Thoburn Press, Tyler, TX.

Singer, C. Gregg. *A Theological Interpretation of American History* (Nutley, NJ: The Craig Press, 1981 (Revised Edition).

Sutton, Ray R. *That You May Prosper: Dominion By Covenant*. Tyler, TX: Institute for Christian Economics, 1987.

_____. *Who Owns the Family? God or the State?* Ft. Worth, TX: Dominion Press, 1986.

Thoburn, Robert L. *The Christian and Politics*. Tyler, TX: Thoburn Press, 1984.

Whitehead, John W. *The Second American Revolution*. Westchester, IL: Crossway Books, 1985.

_____. *The Separation Illusion*. Milford, MI: Mott Media, 1977.

SCRIPTURE INDEX

OLD TESTAMENT

NEW TESTAMENT

SUBJECT INDEX

253

The Myth of Overpopulation, 194

natural law, 207
New Age Humanism, 151
Nineteen Eighty-Four, 13
North, Gary, 40, 50, 62, 122, 151, 158, 187, 188, 190-91, 220

occultism, 151
O Come, Let Us Worship, 170-71
oligarchy, 22
Orwell, George, 13

pantheism, 170
Paradise Restored: A Biblical Theology of Dominion, 171
Parents' Rights, 201-202
Penn, William, 7
Plato, 48
political involvement, 149-151, 223
politics, 128
pornography, 64
Pride, Mary, 202
prostitution, 64

Rayburn, Robert, 170
reconstruction
in church, 169
civil, 203
process, 9
reformation, 42
Republican Party, 148
Robertson, Pat, 148, 149
Roman Catholic Church, 180
Rousseau, Jean Jacques, 47
Rushdoony, R. J., 172, 177, 181, 186, 194
Rutherford, Samuel, 21, 93

salvation in Old Testament, 120-21
sanctification, 150-51
collective, 63-64
definitive, 62

final, 62
individual, 61
progressive, 62-63
The Screwtape Letters, 205
self-government, xvi, 7, 192
The Separation Illusion, 23
separation of church and State, 227-231, 133-36
Seventy-Five Bible Questions Your Professors Pray You Won't Ask, 122
Shaw, George Bernard, 24
The Sinai Strategy, xiii, 188
slavery
defined, 72
to the State, 73
socialism, 24
sovereignty of God, 11
Sowell, Thomas, 194
Stalin, Joseph, 48, 50
State, jurisdiction of, 76
Statism, 205
Stone, Justice, 22
Supreme Court, 22, 238-39
Sutton, Ray, xii

taxes, 75, 109-111, 208, 222
Tell It to the Church: Reconciling Out of Court, 182
Tenth Amendment, 205
That You May Prosper: Dominion by Covenant, xiii
theocracy
biblical, xiv, xvi
humanist, xvi
The Third Wave, 185
This Independent Republic, 2
Thoburn, Robert L., 202
Toffler, Alvin, 185
Tolstoy, 18
totalitarianism, 209
Tower of Babel, 29, 30, 185
Trinity, 17
The Treasury of David, 155-56

WHAT ARE BIBLICAL BLUEPRINTS?
by Gary North

How many times have you heard this one?

"The Bible isn't a textbook of . . ."

You've heard it about as many times as you've heard this one:

"The Bible doesn't provide blueprints for . . ."

The odd fact is that some of the people who assure you of this are Christians. Nevertheless, if you ask them, "Does the Bible have answers for the problems of life?" you'll get an unqualified "yes" for an answer.

Question: If the Bible isn't a textbook, and if it doesn't provide blueprints, then just how, specifically and concretely, does it provide answers for life's problems? Either it answers real-life problems, or it doesn't.

In short: *Does the Bible make a difference?*

Let's put it another way. If a mass revival at last hits this nation, and if millions of people are regenerated by God's grace through faith in the saving work of Jesus Christ at Calvary, will this change be visible in the way the new converts run their lives? Will their politics change, their business dealings change, their families change, their family budgets change, and their church membership change?

In short: Will conversion make a visible difference in our personal lives? If not, why not?

Second, two or three years later, will Congress be voting for a different kind of defense policy, foreign relations policy, environmental policy, immigration policy, monetary policy, and so forth?

Will the Federal budget change? If not, why not?

In short: Will conversion to Christ make a visible difference in our civilization? If not, why not?

The Great Commission

What the Biblical Blueprints Series is attempting to do is to outline what some of that visible difference in our culture ought to be. The authors are attempting to set forth, in clear language, *fundamental Biblical principles* in numerous specific areas of life. The authors are not content to speak in vague generalities. These books not only set forth explicit principles that are found in the Bible and derived from the Bible, they also offer specific practical suggestions about what things need to be changed, and how Christians can begin programs that will produce these many changes.

The authors see the task of American Christians just as the Puritans who came to North America in the 1630's saw their task: *to establish a city on a hill* (Matthew 5:14). The authors want to see a Biblical reconstruction of the United States, so that it can serve as an example to be followed all over the world. They believe that God's principles are tools of evangelism, to bring the nations to Christ. The Bible promises us that these principles will produce such good fruit that the whole world will marvel (Deuteronomy 4:5-8). When nations begin to marvel, they will begin to soften to the message of the gospel. What the authors are calling for is *comprehensive revival*—a revival that will transform everything on earth.

In other words, the authors are calling Christians to obey God and take up the Great Commission: to *disciple* (discipline) all the nations of the earth (Matthew 28:19).

What each author argues is that there are God-required principles of thought and practice in areas that some people today believe to be outside the area of "religion." What Christians should know by now is that *nothing* lies outside religion. God is judging all of our thoughts and acts, judging our institutions, and working through human history to bring this world to a final judgment.

We present the case that God offers *comprehensive salvation* — regeneration, healing, restoration, and the obligation of total social reconstruction — because the world is in *comprehensive sin.*

To judge the world it is obvious that God has to have standards. If there were no absolute standards, there could be no earthly judgment, and no final judgment because men could not be held accountable.

(Warning: these next few paragraphs are very important. They are the base of the entire Blueprints series. It is important that you understand my reasoning. I really believe that if you understand it, you will agree with it.)

To argue that God's standards don't apply to everything is to argue that sin hasn't affected and infected everything. To argue that God's Word doesn't give us a revelation of God's requirements for us is to argue that we are flying blind as Christians. It is to argue that there are *zones of moral neutrality* that God will not judge, either today or at the day of judgment, because these zones somehow are *outside His jurisdiction.* In short, "no law-no jurisdiction."

But if God *does* have jurisdiction over the whole universe, which is what every Christian believes, then there must be universal standards by which God executes judgment. The authors of this series argue for God's *comprehensive judgment,* and we declare His *comprehensive salvation.* We therefore are presenting a few of His *comprehensive blueprints.*

The Concept of Blueprints

An architectural blueprint gives us the structural requirements of a building. A blueprint isn't intended to tell the owner where to put the furniture or what color to paint the rooms. A blueprint does place limits on where the furniture and appliances should be put — laundry here, kitchen there, etc. — but it doesn't take away our personal options based on personal taste. A blueprint just specifies what must be done during construction for the building to do its job and to survive the test of time. It gives direction to the contractor. Nobody wants to be on the twelfth floor of a building that collapses.

Today, we are unquestionably on the twelfth floor, and maybe even the fiftieth. Most of today's "buildings" (institutions) were designed by humanists, for use by humanists, but paid for mostly by Christians (investments, donations, and taxes). These "buildings" aren't safe. Christians (and a lot of non-Christians) now are hearing the creaking and groaning of these tottering buildings. Millions of people have now concluded that it's time to: (1) call in a totally new team of foundation and structural specialists to begin a complete renovation, or (2) hire the original contractors to make at least temporary structural modifications until we can all move to safer quarters, or (3) call for an emergency helicopter team because time has just about run out, and the elevators aren't safe either.

The writers of this series believe that the first option is the wise one: Christians need to rebuild the foundations, using the Bible as their guide. This view is ignored by those who still hope and pray for the third approach: God's helicopter escape. Finally, those who have faith in minor structural repairs don't tell us what or where these hoped-for safe quarters are, or how humanist contractors are going to build them any safer next time.

Why is it that some Christians say that God hasn't drawn up any blueprints? If God doesn't give us blueprints, then who does? If God doesn't set the permanent standards, then who does? If God hasn't any standards to judge men by, then who judges man?

The humanists' answer is inescapable: *man* does—autonomous, design-it-yourself, do-it-yourself man. Christians call this man-glorifying religion the religion of humanism. It is amazing how many Christians until quite recently have believed humanism's first doctrinal point, namely, that God has not established permanent blueprints for man and man's institutions. Christians who hold such a view of God's law serve as *humanism's chaplains*.

Men are God's appointed "contractors." We were never supposed to draw up the blueprints, but we *are* supposed to execute them, in history and then after the resurrection. Men have been given dominion on the earth to subdue it for God's glory. "So God created man in His own image; in the image of God He created him; male and female He created them. Then God blessed them, and God said to them, 'Be fruitful and multiply; fill the earth and subdue it; have dominion over the fish of the sea, over the birds of the air, and over every living thing that moves on the earth'" (Genesis 1:27-28).

Christians about a century ago decided that God never gave them the responsibility to do any building (except for churches). That was just what the humanists had been waiting for. They immediately stepped in, took over the job of contractor ("Someone has to do it!"), and then announced that they would also be in charge of drawing up the blueprints. We can see the results of a similar assertion in Genesis, chapter 11: the tower of Babel. Do you remember God's response to that particular humanistic public works project?

Never Be Embarrassed By the Bible

This sounds simple enough. Why should Christians be embarrassed by the Bible? But they *are* embarrassed . . . millions of them. The humanists have probably done more to slow down the spread of the gospel by convincing Christians to be embarrassed by the Bible than by any other strategy they have adopted.

Test your own thinking. Answer this question: "Is God mostly a God of love or mostly a God of wrath?" Think about it before you answer.

It's a trick question. The Biblical answer is: "God is equally a God of love and a God of wrath." But Christians these days will generally answer almost automatically, "God is mostly a God of love, not wrath."

Now in their hearts, they know this answer can't be true. God sent His Son to the cross to die. His own Son! That's how much God hates sin. That's wrath with a capital "W."

But why did He do it? Because He loves His Son, and those who follow His Son. So, you just can't talk about the wrath of God without talking about the love of God, and vice versa. The cross is the best proof we have: God is both wrathful and loving. Without the fires of hell as the reason for the cross, the agony of Jesus Christ on the cross was a mistake, a case of drastic overkill.

What about heaven and hell? We know from John's vision of the day of judgment, "Death and Hades [hell] were cast into the lake of fire. This is the second death. And anyone not found written in the Book of Life was cast into the lake of fire" (Revelation 20:14-15).

Those whose names are in the Book of Life spend eternity with God in their perfect, sin-free, resurrected bodies. The Bible calls this the New Heaven and the New Earth.

Now, which is more eternal, the lake of fire, or the New Heaven and the New Earth? Obviously, they are both eternal. So, God's wrath is equally ultimate with His love throughout eternity. *Christians all admit this*, but sometimes only under extreme pressure. And that is precisely the problem.

For over a hundred years, theological liberals have blathered on and on about the love of God. But when you ask them, "What about hell?" they start dancing verbally. If you press them, they eventually deny the existence of eternal judgment. We *must* understand: they have no doctrine of the total love of God because they have no doctrine of the total wrath of God. They can't really understand what it is that God in His grace offers us in Christ because they refuse to admit what eternal judgment tells us about the character of God.

The doctrine of eternal fiery judgment is by far the most unacceptable doctrine in the Bible, as far as hell-bound humanists are concerned. They can't believe that Christians can believe in such a horror. But we do. We must. This belief is the foundation of Christian evangelism. It is the motivation for Christian foreign missions. We shouldn't be surprised that the God-haters would like us to drop this doctrine. When Christians believe it, they make too much trouble for God's enemies.

So if we believe in this doctrine, the doctrine above all others that ought to embarrass us before humanists, then why do we start to squirm when God-hating people ask us: "Well, what kind of God would require the death penalty? What kind of God would send a plague (or other physical judgment) on people, the way He sent one on the Israelites, killing 70,000 of them, even though they had done nothing wrong, just because David had conducted a military census in peacetime (2 Samuel 24:10-16)? What kind of God sends AIDS?" The proper answer: "The God of the Bible, *my* God."

Compared to the doctrine of eternal punishment, what is some two-bit judgment like a plague? Compared to eternal screaming agony in the lake of fire, without hope of escape, what is the death penalty? The liberals try to embarrass us about these earthly "down payments" on God's final judgment because they want to rid the world of the idea of final judgment. So they insult the character of God, and also the character of Christians, by sneering at the Bible's account of who God is, what He has done in history, and what He requires from men.

Are you tired of their sneering? I know I am.

Nothing in the Bible should be an embarrassment to any Christian. We may not know for certain precisely how some Biblical truth or historic event should be properly applied in our day, but every historic record, law, announcement, prophecy, judgment, and warning in the Bible is the very Word of God, and is not to be flinched at by anyone who calls himself by Christ's name.

We must never doubt that whatever God did in the Old Testament era, the Second Person of the Trinity also did. God's counsel and judgments are not divided. We must be careful not to regard Jesus Christ as a sort of "unindicted co-conspirator" when we read the Old Testament. "For whoever is ashamed of Me and My words in this adulterous and sinful generation, of him the Son of Man also will be ashamed when He comes in the glory of His Father with the holy angels" (Mark 8:38).

My point here is simple. If we as Christians can accept what is a very hard principle of the Bible, that Christ was a blood sacrifice for our individual sins, then we shouldn't flinch at accepting any of the rest of God's principles. As we joyfully accepted His salvation, so we must joyfully embrace all of His principles that affect any and every area of our lives.

264 Ruler of the Nations

The Whole Bible

When, in a court of law, the witness puts his hand on the Bible and swears to tell the truth, the whole truth, and nothing but the truth, so help him God, he thereby swears on the Word of God — the *whole* Word of God, and *nothing but* the Word of God. The Bible is a unit. It's a "package deal." The New Testament doesn't overturn the Old Testament; it's a *commentary* on the Old Testament. It tells us how to use the Old Testament properly in the period after the death and resurrection of Israel's messiah, God's Son.

Jesus said: "Do not think that I came to destroy the Law or the Prophets. I did not come to destroy but to fulfill. For assuredly, I say to you, till heaven and earth pass away, one jot or one tittle will by no means pass from the law till all is fulfilled. Whoever therefore breaks one of the least of these commandments, and teaches men to do so, shall be called least in the kingdom of heaven; but whoever does and teaches them, he shall be called great in the kingdom of heaven" (Matthew 5:17-19). The Old Testament isn't a discarded first draft of God's Word. It isn't "God's Word emeritus."

Dominion Christianity teaches that there are four covenants under God, meaning four kinds of *vows* under God: personal (individual), and the three institutional covenants: ecclesiastical (the church), civil (governments), and family. All other human institutions (business, educational, charitable, etc.) are to one degree or other under the jurisdiction of these four covenants. No single covenant is absolute; therefore, no single institution is all-powerful. Thus, Christian liberty is *liberty under God and God's law.*

Christianity therefore teaches pluralism, but a very special kind of pluralism: plural institutions under God's comprehensive law. It does not teach a pluralism of law structures, or a pluralism of moralities, for as we will see shortly, this sort of ultimate pluralism (as distinguished from *institutional* pluralism) is always either polytheistic or humanistic. Christian people are required to take dominion over the earth by means of all these God-ordained institutions, not just the church, or just the state, or just the family.

The kingdom of God includes every human institution, and every aspect of life, for all of life is under God and is governed by His unchanging principles. All of life is under God and God's principles because God intends to *judge* all of life *in terms of* His principles.

In this structure of *plural governments*, the institutional churches serve as *advisors* to the other institutions (the Levitical function), but the churches can only pressure individual leaders through the threat of excommunication. As a restraining factor on unwarranted church authority, an unlawful excommunication by one local church or denomination is always subject to review by the others if and when the excommunicated person seeks membership elsewhere. Thus, each of the three covenantal institutions is to be run under God, as interpreted by its lawfully elected or ordained leaders, with the advice of the churches, not the compulsion

Majority Rule

Just for the record, the authors aren't in favor of imposing some sort of top-down bureaucratic tyranny in the name of Christ. The kingdom of God requires a bottom-up society. The bottom-up Christian society rests ultimately on the doctrine of *self*-government under God. It's the humanist view of society that promotes top-down bureaucratic power.

The authors are in favor of evangelism and missions leading to a widespread Christian revival, so that the great mass of earth's inhabitants will place themselves under Christ's protection, and voluntarily use His covenantal principles for self-government. Christian reconstruction begins with personal conversion to Christ and self-government under God's principles, then spreads to others through revival, and only later brings comprehensive changes in civil law, when the vast majority of voters voluntarily agree to live under Biblical blueprints.

Let's get this straight: Christian reconstruction depends on majority rule. Of course, the leaders of the Christian reconstructionist movement expect a majority eventually to accept Christ as savior. If this doesn't happen, then Christians must be content with only partial reconstruction, and only partial blessings from

God. It isn't possible to ramrod God's blessings from the top down, unless you're God. Only humanists think that man is God. All we're trying to do is get the ramrod away from them, and melt it down. The melted ramrod could then be used to make a great grave marker for humanism: "The God That Failed."

The Continuing Heresy of Dualism

Many (of course, not all!) of the objections to the material in this book series will come from people who have a worldview that is very close to an ancient church problem: dualism. A lot of well-meaning Christian people are dualists, although they don't even know what it is.

Dualism teaches that the world is inherently divided: spirit vs. matter, or law vs. mercy, or mind vs. matter, or nature vs. grace. What the Bible teaches is that this world is divided *ethically* and *personally*: Satan vs. God, right vs. wrong. The conflict between God and Satan will end at the final judgment. Whenever Christians substitute some other form of dualism for ethical dualism, they fall into heresy and suffer the consequences. That's what has happened today. We are suffering from revived versions of ancient heresies.

Marcion's Dualism

The Old Testament was written by the same God who wrote the New Testament. There were not two Gods in history, meaning there was no dualism or radical split between the two testamental periods. There is only one God, in time and eternity.

This idea has had opposition throughout church history. An ancient two-Gods heresy was first promoted in the church about a century after Christ's crucifixion, and the church has always regarded it as just that, a heresy. It was proposed by a man named Marcion. Basically, this heresy teaches that there are two completely different law systems in the Bible: Old Testament law and New Testament law (or non-law). But Marcion took the logic of his position all the way. He argued that two law systems means two Gods. The God of wrath wrote the Old Testament, and the God of mercy wrote the New Testament. In short: "two laws-two Gods."

Many Christians still believe something dangerously close to Marcionism: not a two-Gods view, exactly, but a God-who-changed-all-His-rules sort of view. They begin with the accurate teaching that the ceremonial laws of the Old Testament were fulfilled by Christ, and therefore that the *unchanging principles* of Biblical worship are *applied differently* in the New Testament. But then they erroneously conclude that the whole Old Testament system of civil law was dropped by God, and *nothing Biblical was put in its place*. In other words, God created a sort of vacuum for state law.

This idea turns civil law-making over to Satan. In our day, this means that civil law-making is turned over to humanists. *Christians have unwittingly become the philosophical allies of the humanists with respect to civil law.* With respect to their doctrine of the state, therefore, most Christians hold what is in effect a two-Gods view of the Bible.

Gnosticism's Dualism

Another ancient heresy that is still with us is gnosticism. It became a major threat to the early church almost from the beginning. It was also a form of dualism, a theory of a radical split. The gnostics taught that the split is between evil matter and good spirit. Thus, their goal was to escape this material world through other-worldly exercises that punish the body. They believed in *retreat from the world of human conflicts and responsibility.* Some of these ideas got into the church, and people started doing ridiculous things. One "saint" sat on a platform on top of a pole for several decades. This was considered very spiritual. (Who fed him? Who cleaned up after him?)

Thus, many Christians came to view "the world" as something permanently outside the kingdom of God. They believed that this hostile, forever-evil world cannot be redeemed, reformed, and reconstructed. Jesus didn't really die for it, and it can't be healed. At best, it can be subdued by power (maybe). This dualistic view of the world vs. God's kingdom narrowly restricted any earthly manifestation of God's kingdom. Christians who were influenced by gnosticism concluded that God's kingdom refers only to the insti-

tutional church. They argued that the institutional church is the
only manifestation of God's kingdom.

This led to two opposite and equally evil conclusions. *First*,
power religionists ("salvation through political power") who accepted this definition of God's kingdom tried to put the institutional church in charge of everything, since it is supposedly "the
only manifestation of God's kingdom on earth." To subdue the
supposedly unredeemable world, which is forever outside the
kingdom, the institutional church has to rule with the sword. A
single, monolithic institutional church then gives orders to the
state, and the state must without question enforce these orders
with the sword. The hierarchy of the institutional church concen-
trates political and economic power. *What then becomes of liberty?*

Second, escape religionists ("salvation is exclusively internal")
who also accepted this narrow definition of the kingdom sought
refuge from the evil world of matter and politics by fleeing to hide
inside the institutional church, an exclusively "spiritual kingdom,"
now narrowly defined. They abandoned the world to evil tyrants.
What then becomes of liberty? What becomes of the idea of God's progressive restoration of all things under Jesus Christ? What,
finally, becomes of the idea of Biblical dominion?

When Christians improperly narrow their definition of the
kingdom of God, the visible influence of this comprehensive kingdom (both spiritual and institutional at the same time) begins to
shrivel up. The first heresy leads to tyranny *by* the church, and the
second heresy leads to tyranny *over* the church. Both of these narrow definitions of God's kingdom destroy the liberty of the responsible Christian man, self-governed under God and God's law.

Zoroaster's Dualism

The last ancient pagan idea that still lives on is also a variant
of dualism: matter vs. spirit. It teaches that God and Satan, good
and evil, are forever locked in combat, and that good never trium-
phs over evil. The Persian religion of Zoroastrianism has held
such a view for over 2,500 years. The incredibly popular "Star
Wars" movies were based on this view of the world: the "dark" side
of "the force" against its "light" side. In modern versions of this an-

cient dualism, the "force" is usually seen as itself impersonal: individuals personalize either the dark side or the light side by "plugging into" its power.

There are millions of Christians who have adopted a very pessimistic version of this dualism, though not in an impersonal form. God's kingdom is battling Satan's, and God's is losing. History isn't going to get better. In fact, things are going to get a lot worse externally. Evil will visibly push good into the shadows. The church is like a band of soldiers who are surrounded by a huge army of Indians. "We can't win boys, so hold the fort until Jesus comes to rescue us!"

That doesn't sound like Abraham, Moses, Joshua, Gideon, and David, does it? Christians read to their children one of the children's favorite stories, David and Goliath, yet in their own lives, millions of Christian parents really think that the Goliaths of this world are the unbeatable earthly winners. Christians haven't even picked up a stone.

Until very recently.

An Agenda for Victory

The change has come since 1980. Many Christians' thinking has shifted. Dualism, gnosticism, and "God changed His program midstream" ideas have begun to be challenged. The politicians have already begun to reckon with the consequences. Politicians are the people we pay to raise their wet index fingers in the wind to sense a shift, and they have sensed it. It scares them, too. It should.

A new vision has captured the imaginations of a growing army of registered voters. This new vision is simple: it's the old vision of Genesis 1:27-28 and Matthew 28:19-20. It's called *dominion*.

Four distinct ideas must be present in any ideology that expects to overturn the existing view of the world and the existing social order:

A doctrine of ultimate truth (permanence)
A doctrine of providence (confidence)
Optimism toward the future (motivation)
Binding comprehensive law (reconstruction)

The Marxists have had such a vision, or at least those Marxists who don't live inside the bureaucratic giants called the Soviet Union and Red China. The radical (please, not "fundamentalist") Muslims of Iran also have such a view.

Now, for the first time in over 300 years, Bible-believing Christians have rediscovered these four points in the theology of Christianity. For the first time in over 300 years, a growing number of Christians are starting to view themselves as an army on the move. This army will grow. This series is designed to help it grow. And grow tougher.

The authors of this series are determined to set the agenda in world affairs for the next few centuries. We know where the permanent answers are found: in the Bible, and *only* in the Bible. We believe that we have begun to discover at least preliminary answers to the key questions. There may be better answers, clearer answers, and more orthodox answers, but they must be found in the Bible, not at Harvard University or on the CBS Evening News.

We are self-consciously firing the opening shot. We are calling the whole Christian community to join with us in a very serious debate, just as Luther called them to debate him when he nailed the 95 theses to the church door, over four and a half centuries ago.

It is through such an exchange of ideas by those who take the Bible seriously that a nation and a civilization can be saved. There are now 5 billion people in the world. If we are to win our world (and these billions of souls) for Christ we must lift up the message of Christ by becoming the city on the hill. When the world sees the blessings by God upon a nation run by His principles, the mass conversion of whole nations to the Kingdom of our Lord will be the most incredible in of all history.

If we're correct about the God-required nature of our agenda, it will attract a dedicated following. It will produce a social transformation that could dwarf the Reformation. This time, we're not limiting our call for reformation to the institutional church.

This time, we mean business.

American Vision
P.O. Box 720515
Atlanta, GA 30328
(404) 988-0555

Gentlemen:

I just finished reading Gary DeMar's *Ruler of the Nations*. I understand that you carry his three volume *God and Government* series as well as his tape series on *God and Government* and *A Theology of Christian Activism*. Also, please put me on your mailing list so I can begin to receive your monthly newsletter, *The Biblical Worldview*.

_____
name

_____
address

_____
city, state, zip

_____
area code and phone number

☐ I understand that American Vision presents seminars on "Biblical World View Issues," addressing such topics as Christian Activism, Economics, ethical issues such as abortion, homosexuality, and pornography, the Christian foundation of America, Church and State, education, and many more. Please send me more information.

Jesus said to "Occupy till I come." But if Christians don't control the territory, they can't occupy it. They get tossed out into cultural "outer darkness," which is just exactly what the secular humanists have done to Christians in the 20th century: in education, in the arts, in entertainment, in politics, and certainly in the mainline churches and seminaries. Today, the humanists are "occupying." But they won't be for long. *Backward, Christian Soldiers?* shows you why. This is must reading for all Christians as a supplement to the *Biblical Blueprints Series*. You can obtain a copy by sending $1.00 (a $5.95 value) to:

> Institute for Christian Economics
> P.O. Box 8000
> Tyler, TX 75703

---

name

---

address

---

city, state, zip

---

area code and phone number

Dr. Gary North
Institute for Christian Economics
P.O. Box 8000
Tyler, TX 75711

Dear Dr. North:

I read about your organization in Gary DeMar's book, *Ruler of the Nations*. I understand that you publish several newsletters that are sent out for six months free of charge. I would be interested in receiving them:

☐ *Biblical Economics Today*
  Christian Reconstruction
  and Covenant Renewal

Please send any other information you have concerning your program.

_____
name

_____
address

_____
city, state, zip

_____
area code and phone number

☐ Enclosed is a tax-deductible donation to help meet expenses.

The *Biblical Blueprints Series* is a multi-volume book series that gives Biblical solutions for the problems facing our culture today. Each book deals with a specific topic in a simple, easy to read style such as economics, government, law, crime and punishment, welfare and poverty, taxes, money and banking, politics, the environment, retirement, and much more.

Each book can be read in one evening and will give you the basic Biblical principles on each topic. Each book concludes with three chapters on how to apply the principles in your life, the church and the nation. Every chapter is summarized so that the entire book can be absorbed in just a few minutes.

As you read these books, you will discover hundreds of new ways to serve God. Each book will show you ways that you can start to implement God's plan in your own life. As hundreds of thousands join you, and millions more begin to follow the example set, a civilization can be changed.

Why will people change their lives? Because they will see God's blessings on those who live by His Word (Deuteronomy 4:6-8).

Each title in the *Biblical Blueprints Series* is available in a deluxe paperback edition for $7.95, or a classic leatherbound edition for $15.95.

The following titles are scheduled for publication:

- Liberating Planet Earth: An Introduction to Biblical Blueprints
- Ruler of the Nations: Biblical Blueprints for Governments
- Who Owns the Family?: Biblical Blueprints for Family/State Relations
- In the Shadow of Plenty: Biblical Blueprints for Welfare and Poverty
- Honest Money: Biblical Blueprints for Money and Banking
- The Children Trap: Biblical Blueprints for Education
- Inherit the Earth: Biblical Blueprints for Economics
- The Changing of the Guard: Biblical Blueprints for Political Action
- No Entangling Alliances: Biblical Blueprints for Foreign Relations
- Life Light: Biblical Blueprints for Life and Death
- Chariots of God: Biblical Blueprints for National Defense
- Second Chance: Biblical Blueprints for Divorce and Remarriage

Please send more information concerning this program.

_____
name

_____
address

_____
city, state, zip

Dominion Press • P.O. Box 8204 • Ft. Worth, TX 76124